The Flemish Architecture Institute (VAi) is a centre for contemporary architecture whose aim is to increase awareness of high-quality architecture among both the public at large and professionals, researchers, the media and the authorities.
The VAi organises a range of activities including talks, debates, guided tours and educational work for children and adolescents, and develops publications, studies, websites, etc.
In this way the VAi stimulates critical reflection on topical subjects currently exercising minds in the architectural world. In this activity the VAi cooperates with a variety of partners.
The Centre for Flemish Architectural Archives (CVAa) has also been inserted into the operations of the VAi. This organisation coordinates the advancement of architectural archives and cooperation between the archive institutions, and organises research and public activities related to the architectural heritage.

vai
FLEMISHARCHITECTUREINSTITUTE

THE FLEMISH ARCHITECTURE INSTITUTE
IS SUBSIDISED BY THE FLEMISH COMMUNITY.

Flanders Architectural Yearbook 02 I 03 I edition 04 I Flemish Architecture Institute

Colophon

Publisher
Flemish Architecture Institute (VAi)

Registered Publisher
Katrien Vandermarliere
Flemish Architecture Institute
Jan Van Rijswijcklaan 155, 2018 Antwerp

Editorial Board
Katrien Vandermarliere, editor-in-chief
Tom Avermaete
Lieven De Boeck
William Mann
Bruno Notteboom
Edith Wouters

Guest editors
Adam Caruso
Ákos Moravánszky

Coordination and secretariat
Siska Claessens
Edith Wouters

Text editing
Marieke Van Giersbergen
Edith Wouters

Authors
Tom Avermaete
Adam Caruso
Wouter Davidts
Caroline Goossens
William Mann
Ákos Moravánszky
Raf Snoeckx
Sven Sterken
Pieter T'Jonck
Katrien Vandermarliere
Hera Van Sande
Koen Van Synghel
Els Vervloesem

Publications, exhibitions, architectural prizes, subsidies
Bregje Provo, Edith Wouters

Translators
Gregory Ball (DU-EN)
Vandevelde-Michielsen (EN-DU)

Photographers
Commissioned photography:
Karin Borghouts
Paul d'Haese
André Nullens
Stefan Vandermeulen

Others:
Sarah Blee, Kristien Daem, Luc Deleu, Jan De Vylder, Koen de Waal
Huiswerk architecten, Jan Kempenaers, Reiner Lautwein,
Peter Lorré, Ondersteunend Centrum GIS Vlaanderen,
Wouter Rawoens, Christian Richter, Wim Ruigrok,
Steven Van Den Bergh, Hans Werleman,
Xaveer De Geyter architecten

Design
koen bruyñeel
gd | mark graham dunn

Pre-press and printing
Die Keure

Distribution
Exhibitions International

Identification number
ISBN 9080778745 (DU)
ISBN 9080778753 (EN)
D/2004/10.202/2 (DU)
D/2004/10.202/4 (EN)
NUGI 923

FLEMISHARCHITECTUREINSTITUTE

THE FLEMISH ARCHITECTURE INSTITUTE IS SUBSIDISED BY THE FLEMISH COMMUNITY.

Flanders Architectural Yearbook 02 | 03

edition 04

Flemish Architecture Institute

Contents

FLANDERS ARCHITECTURAL YEARBOOK 2002-2003

Foreword

Architecture has been subject to the attention of the cultural authorities for the last ten years. The Flanders Architectural Yearbook, an initiative that arose in the Department of Culture, has reached its sixth edition and is for the first time published by the Flemish Architecture Institute. As a consequence of the Heritage Act, attention has been devoted to architectural archives since 2003 and a four-year plan, implemented by the Centre for Flemish Architectural Archives, will make possible more specific traceability, better access, historical research, broader public activities and better cooperation between the existing architectural archives. In addition, the cultural authorities, having been advised by the Commission for Architecture and Design, is subsidising public initiatives in and research into architecture and design.

The appointment of the Flemish Government Architect changed the architectural climate in Flanders. His most important task, to enable the Flemish Government to perform an exemplary role in commissioning architecture, has already got off to a good start. As Minister of Culture and the Civil Service I am delighted to have been able to contribute to the development of these government initiatives. Their effect proves that they are steps in the right direction and that the support for architecture is growing.

As a result of my personal and now closer acquaintance with architecture I am convinced that the quality of the built environment extends far beyond the authority of a Minister of Culture. Architecture is the responsibility of all governments and departments, of all private individuals and architects. All buildings are, after all, the materialisation of our view of society. It is through architecture that we shape our society. The way we live together is formulated on the basis of a cultural perspective. The homes we live in, the schools in which we educate our youngsters, where we care for our elderly, the surroundings we spend our leisure time in... each building, each environment is the result of the formation of values and of cultural reflection. For this reason every area of policy must be challenged and responded to by architecture.

One last thought: now, at the beginning of this third millennium, building means building with respect. Good architecture is born in an historic perspective with respect for what went before. Even today, good architecture means sustainable building and respect for nature, our weary supplier of raw materials. The third pillar of architecture is a social component. Every private individual, every company or official body should be more than aware that the building is also a social act. Habitation means cohabitation because living means living together. Good architecture is created when quality is paid as much attention as quantity.

Paul Van Grembergen
Flemish Minister of Home Affairs, Culture, Youth and the Civil Service

Introduction

Katrien Vandermarliere

The Flemish Architecture Institute

When the Flemish Architecture Institute (VAi) was set up in 2001, one of the tasks the minister gave it was the publication of the Flanders Architectural Yearbook. In the very first exploratory discussions it became clear that handing over publication of the Yearbook to the VAi offered the opportunity to invent a new concept for the book. The new Yearbook is after all part of the broader work of the Institute in general and its publication strategy in particular. Projects by young architects, current topics, exemplary projects, ranging from housing through public space to industrial buildings, are all given a forum in a wide range of initiatives including Architecture Day, guided tours and such publications as the Young Architects in Flanders series and the Background series of monographs.

The publication

As has been customary, the contents of the book resulted from a positive selection of exemplary projects. The concept of the book was not a framework laid down in advance, against which the various projects were measured, but rather an agreement among equals which developed into editorial debates about the entries submitted and the repeated site visits. It reflects the editors' views on what they consider to be a high-quality showing by contemporary architectural practice.

This Yearbook illustrates the editors' goal of creating a book that tries to point out the intrinsic qualities of the selected buildings to both professionals and interested laymen. To achieve this a number of important editorial decisions were taken. First of all it was decided not so much to offer an exhaustive report or survey of the last two years, but much more a book about buildings. The descriptions of the projects were intended to combine accessibility and thoroughness, without lapsing into superficiality or hermeticism. The focus was to be not on an overall view, but on insight. The editors considered that a detailed description and documentation of projects from several practice-based angles was probably the best way of meeting this ambition. They opted for elaborate project descriptions and extensive documentation using plans and photos. In this way each project was analysed in detail on several scales: from the building detail to the urban planning location. The authors were asked to assess the projects not only in the cultural context but also in the urban planning framework and to consider the whole field of building regulations. This meant that not only the programme, concept, construction, materials and architectural details, but also functionality, budget and sustainability were to be subjected to criticism. In this way the emphasis would be placed on the craft and the building process itself and the particular points of focus that ensue from them. This approach illustrates the intention of stimulating a subtle form of architectural criticism which takes the built project as its basis. This is a form of architectural criticism which should once again become inherent in architectural practice itself.

It was on the basis of the same idea that a three-part photographic assignment was also launched. Stefaan Vandermeulen portrayed each project in its spatial context. Its use and the life that goes on in and around it was captured in the pictures by Karin Borghouts and André Nullens. In his turn, Paul d'Haese mainly photographed architectural details. This last series is supplemented with outstanding existing pictures by Kristien Daem, Jan Kempenaers, Hans Werleman, Wouter Rawoens, Sarah Blee and Peter Lorré.
The buildings in this Yearbook display great architectural qualities that certainly match international standards. In addition to this it is striking what a variety of briefs and of scales Flanders' architectural firms have to deal with. For the first time we see the construction of a number of larger public buildings, ranging from office buildings through schools to cultural buildings resulting from competitions (limited and otherwise). The 'exemplary clientship' shown by various authorities has been taken more seriously, in, among other things, the Flemish Government Architect's 'Open Call' for designs, and this is leading to a new 'civic architecture'. In the housing construction sector what is most striking are the innovative inner city housing types by several young architectural firms and others.

The selection of the buildings crystallised into a number of themes which the editors experienced as topical and significant. Some provided the basis for the articles in the book, while others fuelled the discussions with authors and have been incorporated into the articles or project descriptions.

Sustainability is one such theme. This subject has for several years turned out to be too wide-ranging to devote an article to it in the context of a Yearbook. All the projects selected integrate intrinsic aspects of sustainability; in the form of their chosen site or the suitability to their purpose, the reuse of existing buildings, and the choice and economic use of materials. In Flanders, the debate on sustainability is still in its infancy. Taking the latest developments in sustainable techniques into account, what is the actual influence of office building on the outskirts of a town? How sustainable is the introduction of a new function into an existing building that is impossible to insulate fully? How can one estimate a building's suitability to its purpose or its significance, in future generations? There are more questions than answers. The VAi will in any case remain alert to new developments in this debate.

Identity

In an architectural Yearbook one focuses on the characteristics of the architecture of a certain region at a particular time. The ambition is always to advance certain statements about this same region more generally. What is the cultural identity of a place and how does it relate to building and the production of architecture? Does this still count, or are we in Europe building in an increasingly similar way? Is Flanders one of the few places where the architect still concerns himself with building practice from urban planning down to constructional detail? After all, architects are very closely involved with the design and conceptual aspects of architecture. At the same time, in Flanders they are as builders in contact with contractors and with building practice. The question is whether this traditional architectural practice will for much longer be able to retain its close links with the building industry, which is making advances in Flanders too. This discussion, which we held with our two guest writers from abroad, Ákos Moravánszky and Adam Caruso, led to a personal account in Moravánszky's article. On the basis of a balanced analysis of Robbrecht and Daem's Concert Hall in Bruges and an historical evocation of Bruges, he leads us into an interesting exposition on identity and tectonics. He states that identity is the result of a multifaceted and complex historical construction. As a designer one can ignore this, ironically deconstruct it, or anticipate it in an 'idyllic way' as Robbrecht and Daem did. Moravánszky unravels the design to gain an insight into the way the architects materialise this using structure, skin, volumetrics, void and solid.

Cultural infrastructure in the nebular city

In the second article, entitled 'Flanders the cultural nebular city', Wouter Davidts presents a confrontational examination of cultural infrastructure over the last 10 years. Building policy could play a crucial part in cultural policy. It is architecture's move, but it is also 'at stake'. The essential question is whether, as a small region, Flanders should with all our strength try to jump on the boat of prestigious international architectural projects. It can certainly carry weight in terms of city branding. But does it yield the most suitable architectural solutions or sustainable leverage for a city and its artistic life? Some architects are aware of this tension and in their designs attempt to anticipate it. In addition, one might wonder whether faint-hearted subsidies for culture and the arts can cope with the investment for such exceptional operations. In fact we noted that it is only such events as Brugge 2002 that create sufficient basis for the realisation of a building and the financing of a proper artistic programme. Once the bunting has been taken down, its viability appears limited and commercial operations are needed to keep the business going. According to Davidts, architecture can play a different and more sustainable role in culture in general and urban culture in particular.

If we assume that all the cultural actors side with the choice of Flanders' position and identity as a cultural nebular city, this has consequences for architectural practice and production. In the long term this means the appearance both of more small-scale and new sorts of places to work on and show arts and of architecture. A future Minister of Culture will in any case have to say something about this position and development.

Urban living with a rural quality or the relativeness of density

Of all the projects submitted, one particular sort of design brief leapt to the eye: those for high-quality contemporary living in the inner city. In 2003, even Flemish architects were somewhat hesitant about putting forward the rural villa as an 'exemplary project'. As a consequence of the RSV and the resultant regulations, the home in the inner city has become a common building assignment. Architects in Flanders appear to have an exceptionally good command of these building and conversion briefs.

But the question is whether they have all the instruments needed to fulfil the challenging task of new urbanisation and the role the home plays in it. Urban design and strategic initiatives depend on politics and policy. Even now, architects are still being involved in these processes at too late a stage.[1] In addition, other factors also play an undeniable part: the investors, the market and the mentality of the public. William Mann advances an interesting critique on the practical applicability of greater urban density for housing in the inner city. In so doing he analyses four exceptional urban dwellings. He concludes that certain types of house allow for greater density and argues for combining housing with other functions. Quality and quantity can only be successfully ensured when architecture and urban planning are designed together in an overall concept (possibly by the same designer). The morphology of the old inner areas and the typology of the dwelling form an inseparable whole. Mann also examines whether these exceptionally successful examples could be used as prototypes and how designers experiment with them in competition designs for collective housing. He also argues for more and exploratory design at an intermediate level between the abstraction of the streetmap and the micro-design of the home.

Design-based research

The subject of the fourth article is the architectural design as a form of research (into the city). Following the development of this phenomenon internationally, design-based research has also acquired a place in Flanders. By way of Le Corbusier, Christopher Alexander and Lévi-Strauss, Tom Avermaete questions the specific nature of design and any similarity it has to scientific research. The author asserts that the architectural design represents a knowledge of its own and can generate its own insights. He verifies whether design can be a way of knowing reality and whether it can occupy a full position alongside other scientific forms of knowledge regarding the built environment. Avermaete illustrates this strategic deployability of the design on the basis of projects by Luc Deleu, Christian Kieckens & Peter Downsborough, Xaveer De Geyter Architects, 51N4E and Bruno De Meulder. Unlike the design-based research that is the subject of international architectural debate, which is striking for its appealing analysis and methods of representation, it seems that in Flanders the strategic principle is above all a linkage to a concrete place and a concrete problem. It appears, though often only after a decade, that the plans were no noncommittal exercises in possible urban design. As a result of its concrete spatial dimension and its integrating capacities (and architectural design has the ability to bring together miscellaneous elements from the built environment to form a spatial figure), design-based research may provide an answer to complex and contradictory problems.

What is more, the role of design-based research need not remain limited to the analysis of the city. In the years to come, there will in Flanders be a need for new solutions to collective housing and the school infrastructure is in very urgent need of renewal. The development of new housing programmes in villages and towns and the legacy of the architecture of the nineteen-sixties and seventies will also present new challenges. Here too, design-based research is able to put pertinent questions and produce new concrete spatial proposals. In all these contexts we would like to summon the clients to challenge architects and urban planners to achieve this. The editorial board would like to call on architectural education to prepare architectural students for this and on the authorities to cherish design-based research as a breeding ground for creativity and evolution. Design-based research very definitely has a role to play in architectural practice, and that includes Flanders.

Social challenges and architectural policy

The editors' intention in this book is to send out a positive signal. The climate for interesting architecture continues to improve: sound client behaviour, inventive architects, a series of established architects who are able to develop in major assignments, and the young architectural firms that present us with new promise. We are also very gradually seeing an increase in international communication between European design firms and between the participants in the architectural debate.

This Yearbook is an optimistic report on the progressive evolution towards a more mature architectural culture in Flanders. This is the result of growing expertise on the part of policy-makers, clients and architects, to which previous Yearbooks have contributed. But the challenges remain immense. Architects must understand and guide the constant transformation of existing buildings and landscapes. Architects have to organise an ever-greater diversity of people and social forms. New technology for communication and mobility, the need for energy-conscious and sustainable development, all play a decisive role in this. The crucial question is whether architecture and architects already have developed sufficient maturity to cope with these social challenges in their own discipline and whether their clients give them the opportunity and trust them to put forward alternatives.

The role played by the Yearbook in the past, as a spur to architectural policy, is no longer so explicit. After all, both the Flemish Government Architect's team and the Flemish Architecture Institute have in their practice, for five and two years respectively, already developed the Flemish Government's first policy options. In addition, a subsidy arrangement for public activities concerning architecture has also been established, which helps support all manner of initiatives. These subsidies are recommended by the Commission for Architecture and Design which also makes architectural policy proposals to the minister. But a sustainable architectural policy must remain assured in the future. So it is high time that the procedure was made clear for the succession of the new Flemish Government Architect, who should take up his post on 1st January 2005. The independent nature and specific profile of this post make it a complex task. It has also become apparent that the post is indispensable. It remains an open question whether the new Arts Act will succeed in giving the VAi and its still burgeoning local architectural network time to get started and grow. What is certain is that there will have to be substantial financial input if the policy-makers opt for professionalisation of the architecture and design sectors. Is it not so that subsidies based on four-year policy plans, which the Arts Act will introduce from 2006, will mean that it is mainly those organisations and institutions from other arts sectors which are already professionally organised that will attract the resources? A future Minister of Culture will here have the perfect opportunity to set a course and allow the cautious optimism of the architectural world either to blossom.

The Flemish Government Architect, the VAi and the Commission for Architecture and Design are happy to enter into discussions with the following government and with all Flemish administrative departments. Together they wish to argue for a more transverse Flemish architectural policy based on an overall vision of the built environment. The architecture and design policy document compiled this spring by the present office of the Minister of Culture, the administrative department, the VAi and the Commission for Architecture and Design is the first major step in this direction.

1. An initiative such as 'Thuis in de Stad', with its 13 strategic interventions in Flemish towns is proof of change after long-term preparatory action.

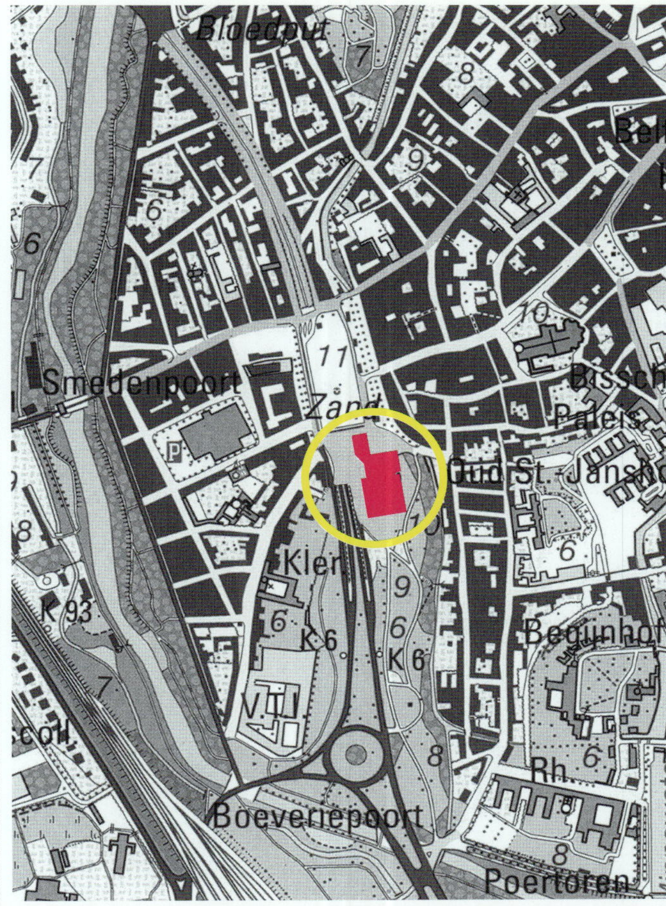

CONCERT HALL

architect **ROBBRECHT AND DAEM ARCHITECTS**

location 't Zand, Bruges

client	vzw Concertgebouw
design	1998-1999
building	1999-2003
project-workers	Piet Crevits I William Mann I Wim Walschap [project architects]
	Matthias Baeten I Sofie Delaere I Brigitte d'Hoore
	Freddy Maenhoudt I Gert Swolfs I Pieter Vandendries [assistant architects]
engineers	Advising architects: Eugène Van Assche & Michel Van Langenhove, Bruges
	Building coordinator: coordination agency R. De Brock, Bruges
	Acoustics: Arup Acoustics, Winchester
	Theatre installations: GCA Ingenieure ag, Ottobrunn-Munich
	Stability: Studium nv, Bruges
	Technical installations: Ingenium nv, Bruges
	Layout of surroundings: Engineer Lobelle, Bruges
	Landscape architect: Wirtz International, Schoten
	Control agency: Seco, Brussels
contracted work	Main contractor for structural work: De Nul, Aalst
area	17,251 sq. m
volume	111,827 cubic. m
building costs	35,000,000 EUR
building costs/sq. m	2,028.87 EUR/sq. m
project description	Sven Sterken
photography	Karin Borghouts p.21a I Kristien Daem p.17,18,19,21b,26,27
	Heynderickx [aerial photos] p.16b I Stefan Vandermeulen p.16a

 CONCERT HALL ▸ architect **ROBBRECHT AND DAEM ARCHITECTS**

When Bruges was granted the title of 'Cultural Capital of Europe' for 2002, the city council decided to mark this major cultural milestone permanently by building a large multifunctional concert hall on the square called the Zand. This is where the city's station used to be. When the railway was moved outside the city walls in the nineteen-thirties, an elongated park and urban motorway were built on its route. When a tunnel and big underground car park were dug in the nineteen-eighties, the Zand returned to its original state as an empty urban space. Before the station was built in 1838 it had been a military exercise ground where the cattle market was also held on Fridays. The new building was intended to form a transition between the long park, the busy urban motorway and the old city centre, and thereby give the Zand the quality of a square.

The selection of the design by Robbrecht and Daem Architects, after an international competition (1998) led to a heated debate in the local press and among the public; the winning design, a 'pastoral building' according to the architects, was not considered progressive and extravagant enough. However, the city council did not give in to the trend of using new architecture as a spectacular but soon dated urban attraction, and ultimately opted for this somewhat wilful design that does not immediately put its cards on the table. Robbrecht and Daem took as their basis the tower of the Church of Our Lady, in the immediate vicinity of

the site. With its huge mass of brickwork, this tower is a uniform volume which, despite its awe-inspiring monumentality, has no trouble taking its place in the city. It is this sort of effect that the architects had in mind. They integrated the sizeable programme into a gradated concrete monolith of more than a hundred metres long, clad entirely in terracotta tiles; their red-brown colour harmonises with the dominant range of colours of the roofs of Bruges city centre.

Each of the Concert Hall's facades has a different character; it thereby makes a completely different impression depending on whether one approaches it from the city or from outside. In the latter case the building appears like an imposing monochrome sculpture at the end of the long park. The facade facing the city centre, with its abundance of small windows, reminds one of a house of many rooms. These are the performers' dressing rooms; so while they are here they to a certain extent live in Bruges. Behind the other side wall, which faces the mouth of the tunnel and the bus station (also designed by Robbrecht and Daem), we find the logistical functions. Trucks have a spacious parking area here for loading and unloading. From the bus station, one has a surprising angled view, through the windows high in the facade, of the tower of the Church of Our Lady; at street level, however, this facade is almost entirely blank, with the result that it is regarded somewhat as the 'back' of the building. From the city side, one immediately sees the 28-metre high 'lantern tower'. This stands slightly apart from the main volume and is shifted forwards towards the Zand like an outpost. It contains a chamber music hall with 300 seats arranged in a single row along a balcony that spirals up over three floors. At the top is a café with an outdoor terrace enjoying a breathtaking view of the roofs of Bruges.

Although the ground floor of this tower might function as a sort of vestibule for the building as a whole, the architects opted to arrange the entrance hall around a new square in the 'axil' of their building, at the point where the Lantern Tower joins the main volume. The continuity between inside and outside that they achieved here is after all impossible on the Zand itself, because the Concert Hall is separated from it by a busy flow of incoming car and bus traffic.

The ceiling of the entrance hall and the cloakroom is kept deliberately low, which makes the explosion of space in the foyer, which one approaches up a ramp, almost dramatic. In fact it is only in this space, three storeys high and entirely in exposed concrete, that one really gets an impression of the scale of this building. The large window in the facade above the main entrance is not only a giant projection screen, but also a sort of camera obscura through which the city can during the daytime project itself into the building. Daylight flows in abundantly, whereby the immense windows frame the urban landscape at unexpected moments; some of them

are coloured and thereby form monochrome luminous planes. Apparently random touches of blue, green and brown have been applied to the uprights of the balustrades, and in fact these colours resonate throughout the building.

The surfeit of space in the foyer offers numerous possibilities and even encourages alternative ways of presenting concerts. For example, for Edgard Varèse's Poème Electronique, an electronic sound collage purchased by the Concert Hall, the foyer provides precisely the spatiality it needs. This piece comprises a succession of sound fragments which are not only very exactly placed in time, but also in space.

The sloping concrete surfaces in the ceiling of the foyer in fact remind one of the legendary Philips pavilion by Le Corbusier and Xenakis at the Brussels World Exhibition in 1958, specially designed to create the space for Varèse's piece. So it is no wonder that it now feels so much at home in Bruges.

The main concert hall, with 700 seats in the stalls and 600 on the two large projecting balconies, is conceived as an acoustic instrument and can be used both for concerts and for opera. This despite the fact that they have almost completely opposed architectural and acoustic requirements: whereas for opera the view is most important, for concerts it is the sound; the desired reverberation times are also different. The choice in this hall was for a cross between the 'shoebox' of the ideal concert hall and the 'horseshoe' of the typical opera theatre; the maximum distance between listener and performer is thirty metres, which implies very close contact. Mobile wooden screens and a suspended ceiling make it possible to close off the fly-tower for concerts and let the stage and the auditorium function as a single acoustic volume.

The floor of the orchestra pit is also adjustable, which enables the stage to be extended into the auditorium or extra rows of seats to be installed. In order to achieve the most homogeneous possible reflection of the sound in the auditorium, it was clad in white plaster panels with irregular grooves, some of which are coloured; this creates a visual counterpoint on the walls. Although the roof is made of a double concrete shell with a 3-metre air cavity, daylight is still able to penetrate right into the concert hall. This light, emerging from two recesses high in the ceiling, has an almost mystical appearance.

Compared to the architectural virtuosity the main concert hall displays, the chamber music hall is of an almost primitive simplicity. It thereby reduces the concert to its original meaning: a sort of collective ritual whose participants are both the performers and the audience. The sound here is

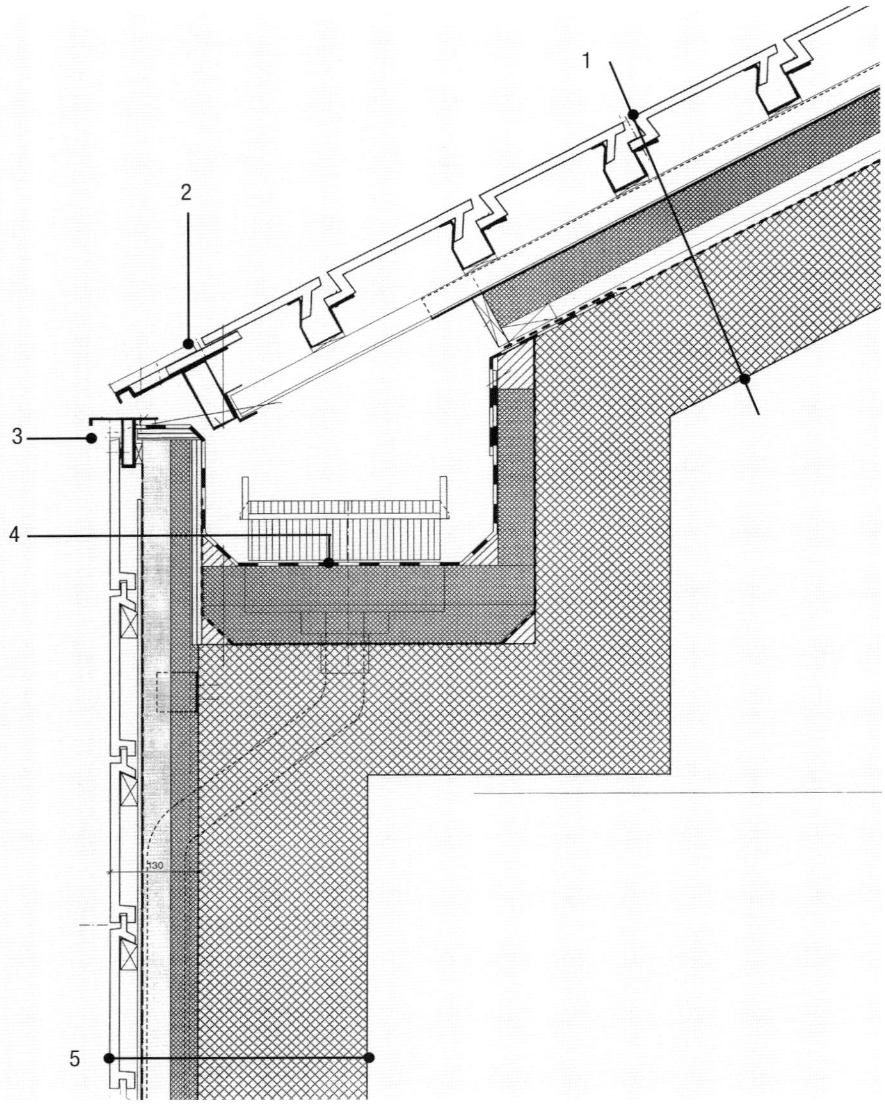

Detail diagram:
vertical section through built-in terracotta gutter with roof inclination of 25°

1 roof build-up:
- terracotta tiles, screw fixing to aluminium batten
- extruded aluminium batten with drainage opening
- composite panel: profiled steel sheet and polyurethane insulation
- surface levelled with wooden battens
- reinforced concrete, 200 mm

2 edge tiles assembled from 2 tiles, glued
3 redge profiles in extruded aluminium, 2 mm, black anodised
4 box gutter:
- EPDM,single-ply
- polyurethane insulation, 2 x 60 mm
- vapour barrier
- syphonic drainage system

5 wall build-up:
- terracotta tiles, screw fixing to wooden batten
- hardwood batten
- vertical timber elements + insulation
- reinforced concrete, 250 mm

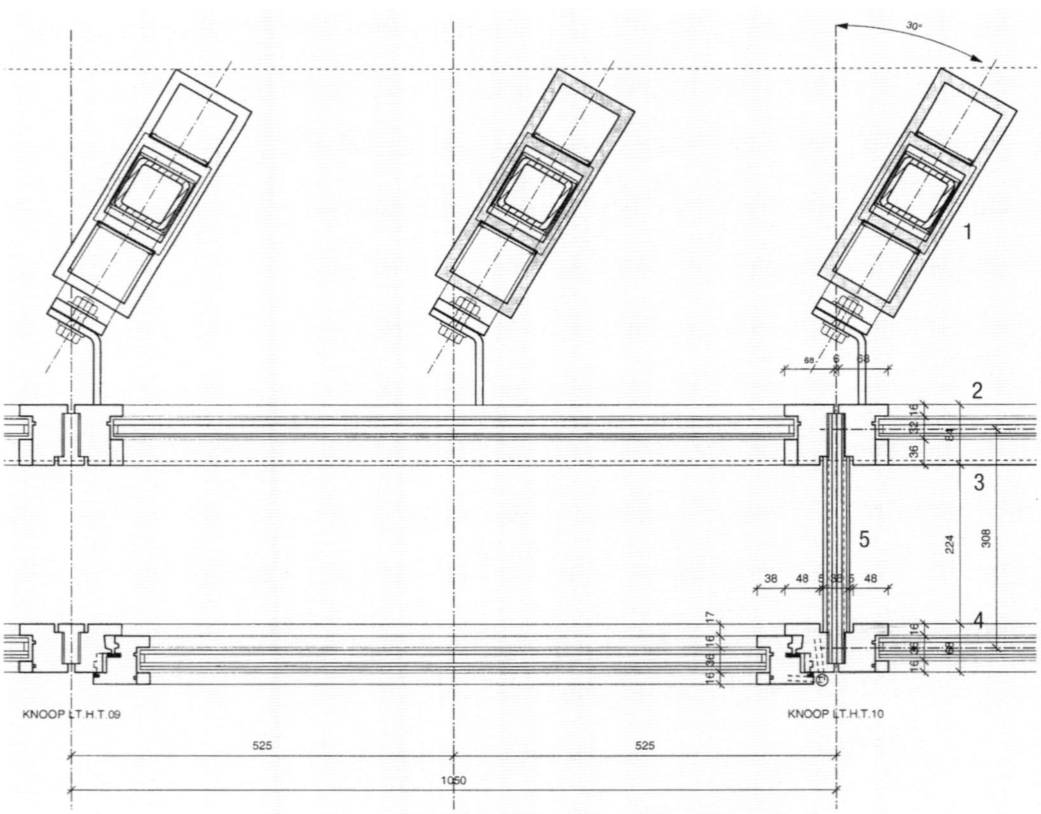

Detail diagram:
mullions and double glazing chamber music hall

1 terracotta mullions:
- extruded terracotta profiles 120 x 340 x 495 fixed via stainless steel plates to
- stainless steel RHS 80 x 80 bolt fixing to concrete slab via stainless steel brackets

2 hardwood windows (moabi), double glazing 8/12/4
3 edge of concrete slab
4 hardwood windows (moabi), double glazing 6/12/5+5
5 plywood stiffeners at steps in window profile

let loose in the space. Profiled wooden panels and cloths help soften the hard reflections off the concrete structure. Daylight floods in here, while one is also able to see the city through the solid, vertical ribs of the Lantern Tower. This transparency is a metaphor for the paradoxical nature of the building: it is a monolith, but only seemingly so; it is after all composed mainly of light.

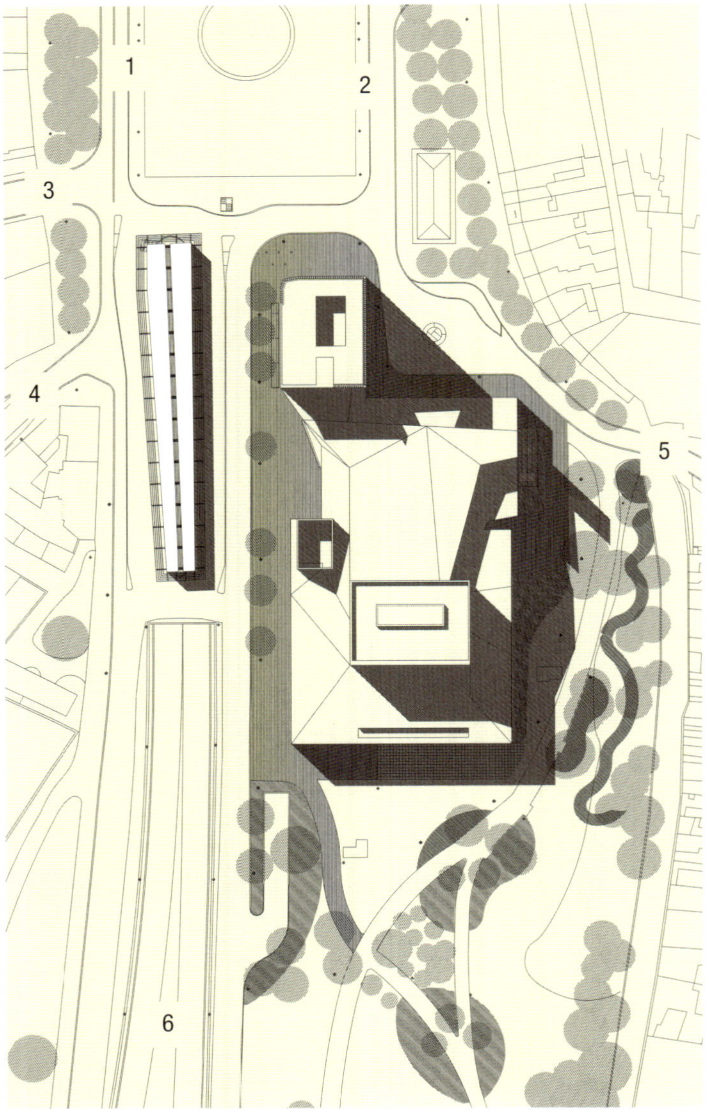

1 Vrijdagmarkt
2 't Zand
3 Hauwerstraat
4 Boeveriestraat
5 St Jan in de Meers
6 Koning Albert 1 laan

0 10 50 m

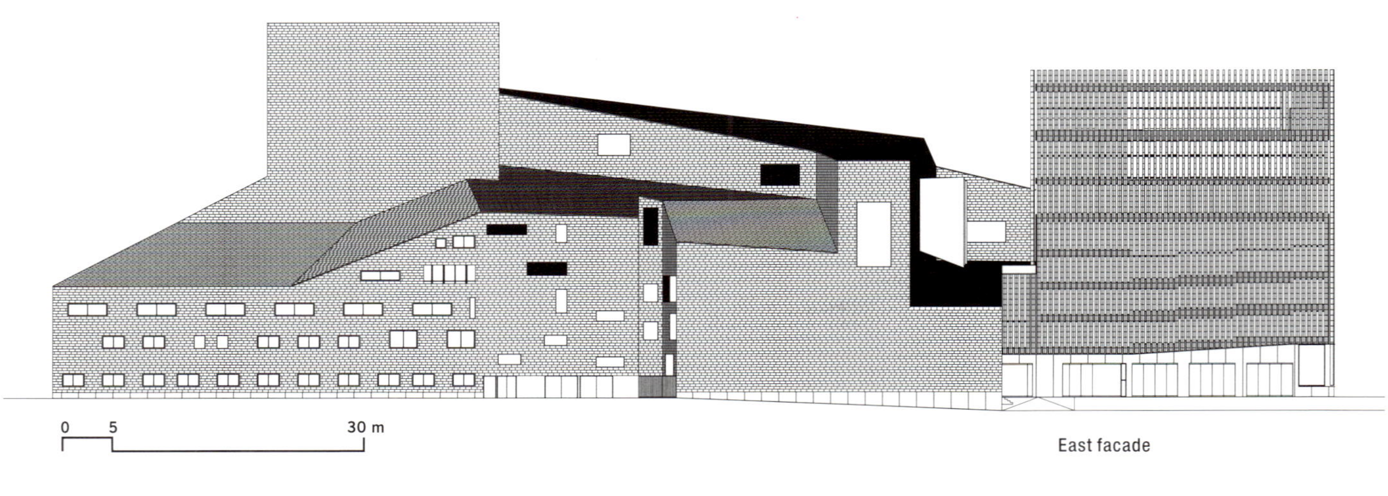

East facade

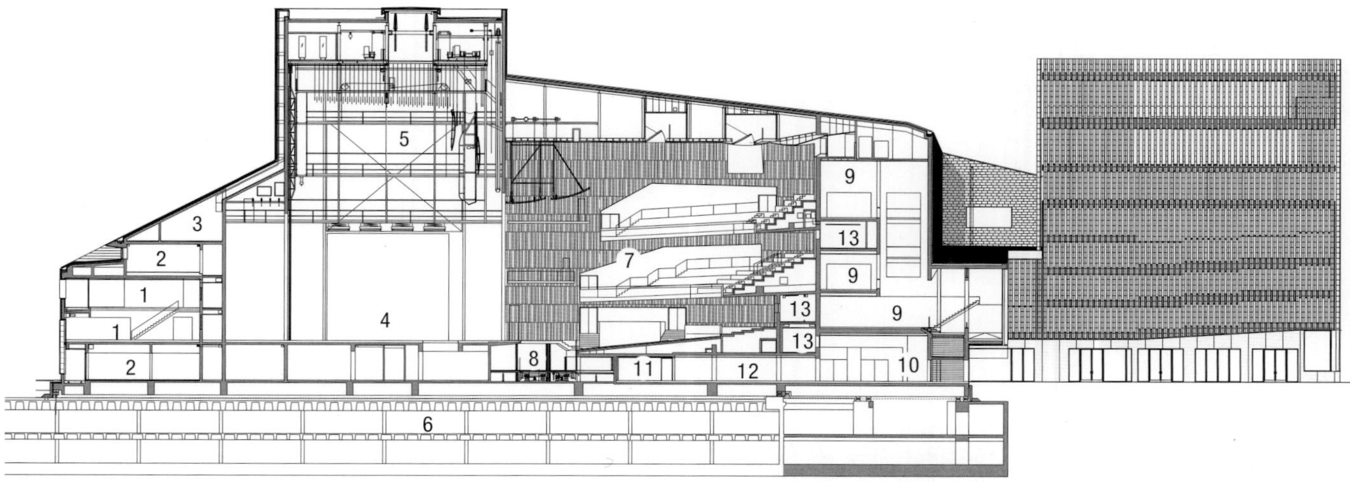

Section AA'

1 green room
2 office
3 technical area
4 stage
5 fly-tower
6 car park
7 auditorium
8 orchestra pit
9 foyer
10 entrance hall
11 toilets
12 cloakroom
13 control cabin

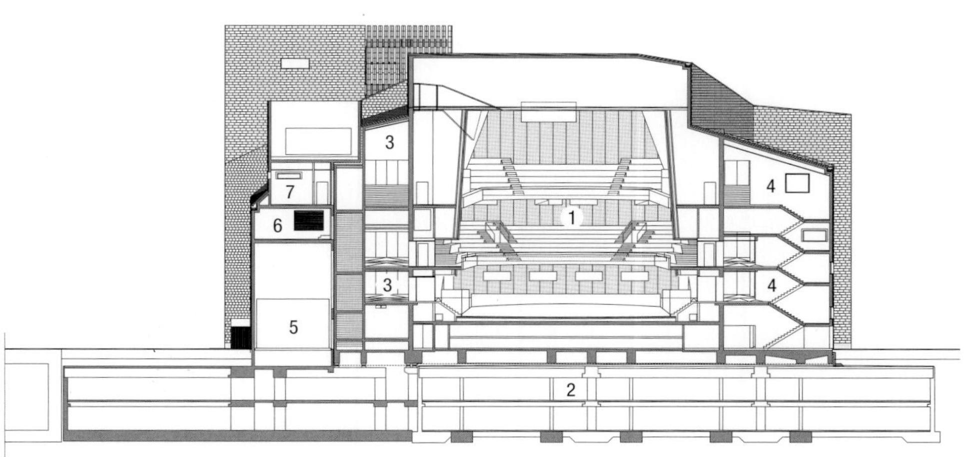

Section BB'

1 auditorium
2 car park
3 west side-foyer
4 east side-foyer
5 truck lift
6 technical area
7 toilets

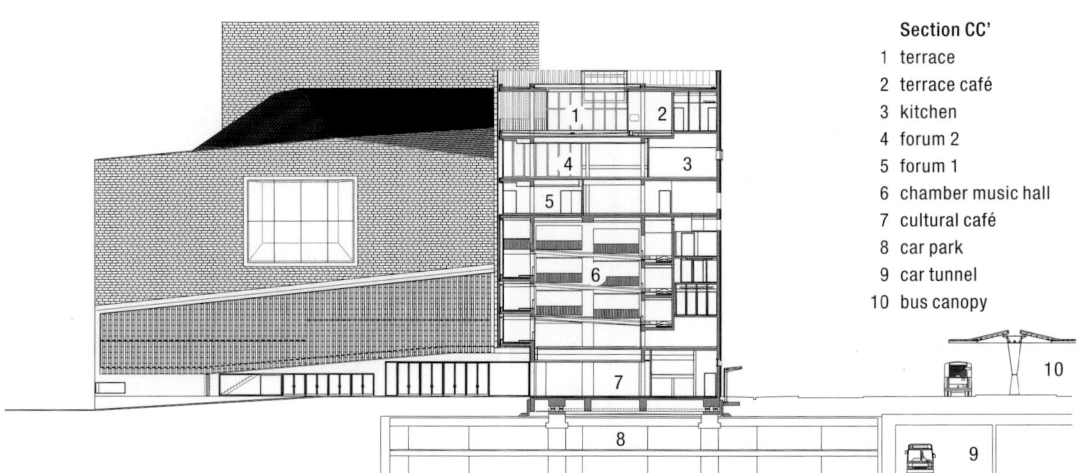

Section CC'

1 terrace
2 terrace café
3 kitchen
4 forum 2
5 forum 1
6 chamber music hall
7 cultural café
8 car park
9 car tunnel
10 bus canopy

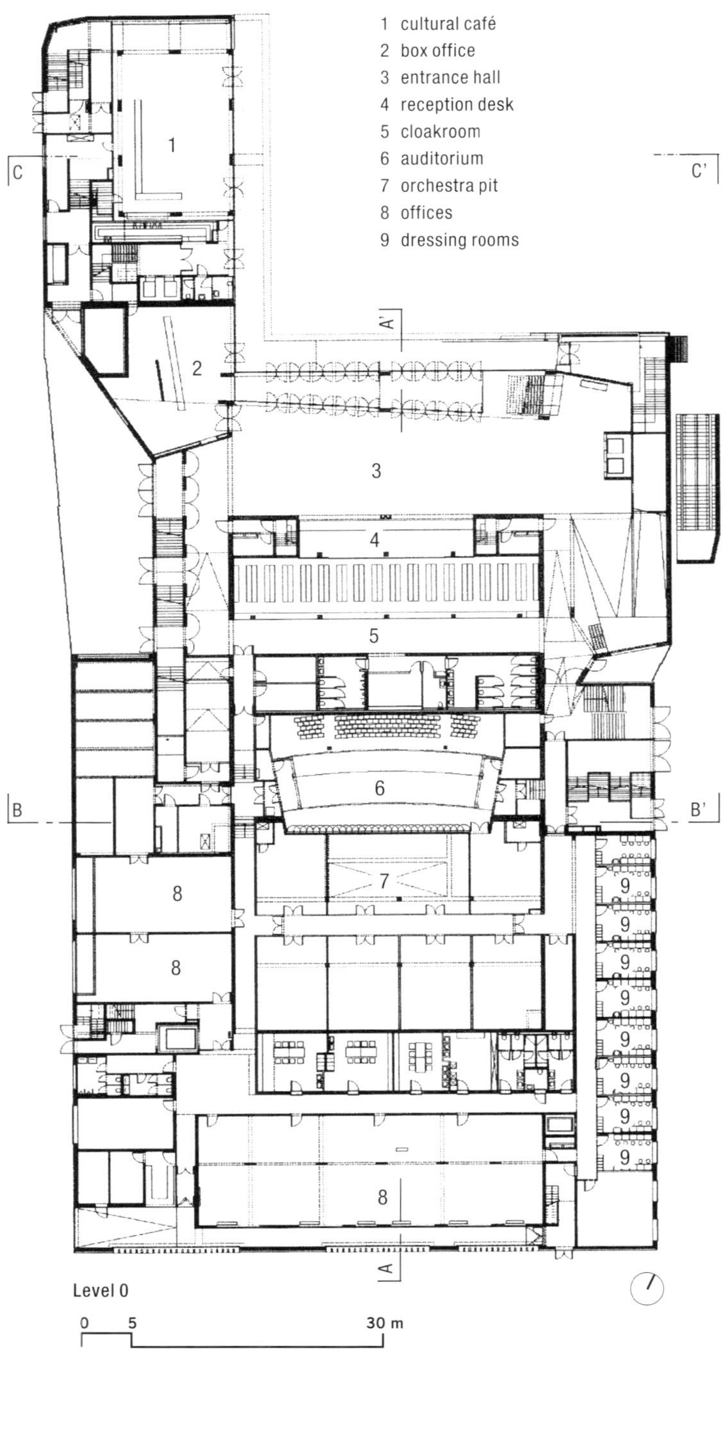

Level 0

1 cultural café
2 box office
3 entrance hall
4 reception desk
5 cloakroom
6 auditorium
7 orchestra pit
8 offices
9 dressing rooms

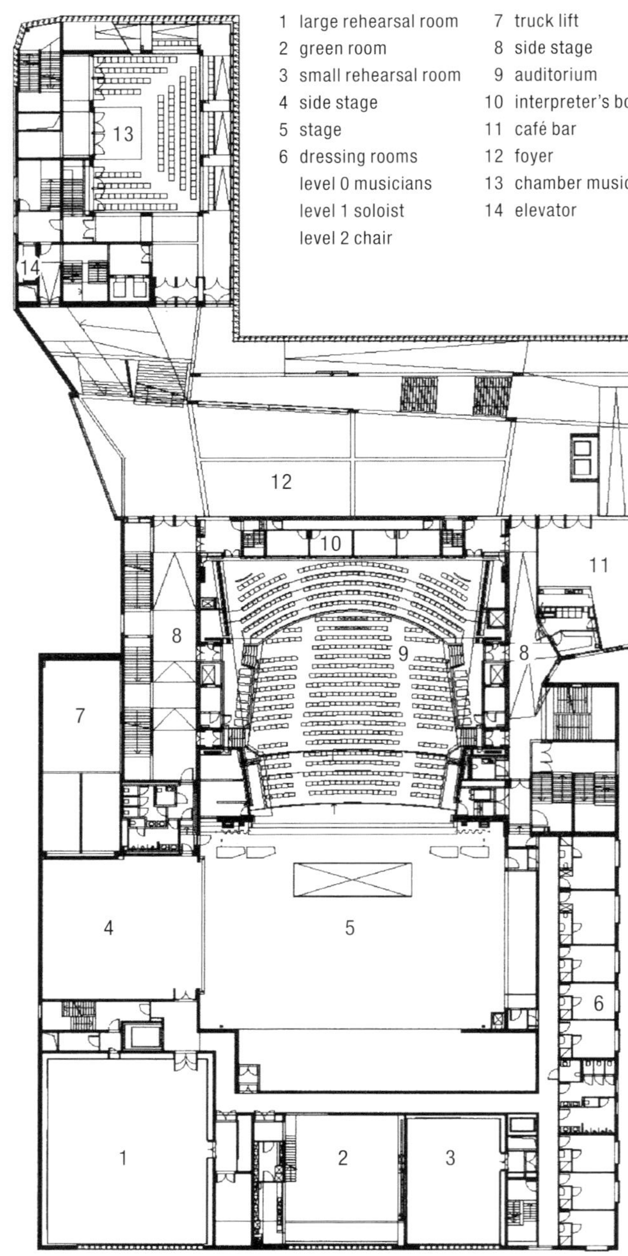

Level 1

1 large rehearsal room
2 green room
3 small rehearsal room
4 side stage
5 stage
6 dressing rooms
level 0 musicians
level 1 soloist
level 2 chair
7 truck lift
8 side stage
9 auditorium
10 interpreter's box
11 café bar
12 foyer
13 chamber music hall
14 elevator

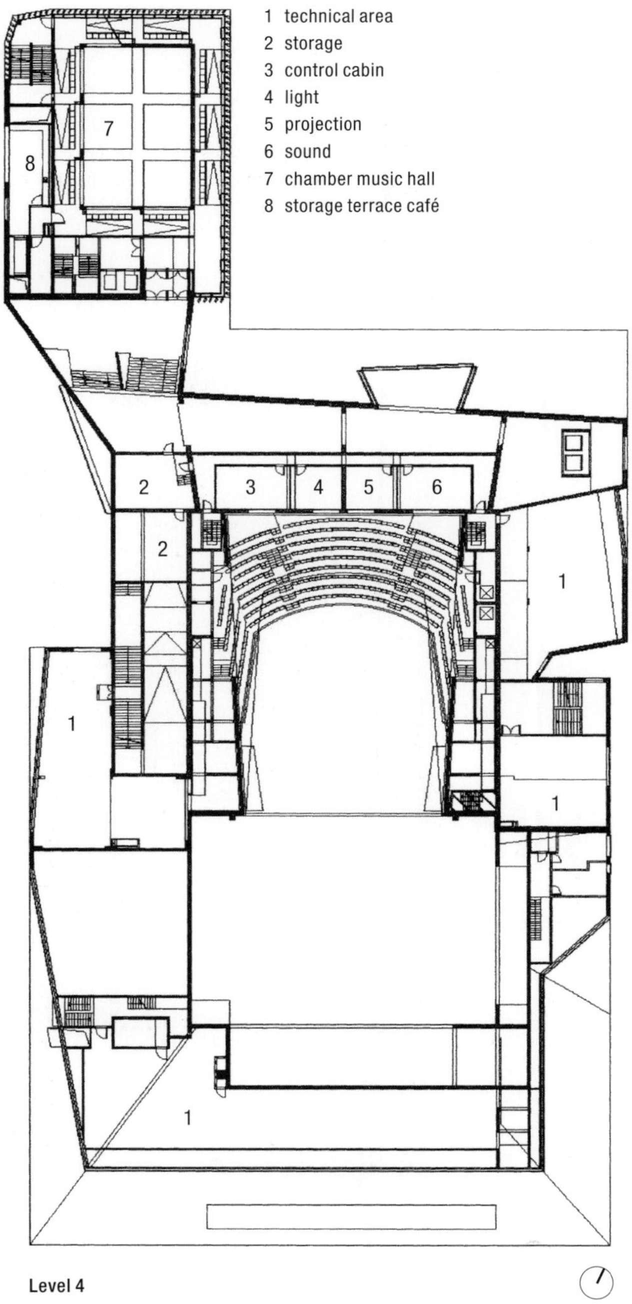

1 technical area
2 storage
3 control cabin
4 light
5 projection
6 sound
7 chamber music hall
8 storage terrace café

Level 4

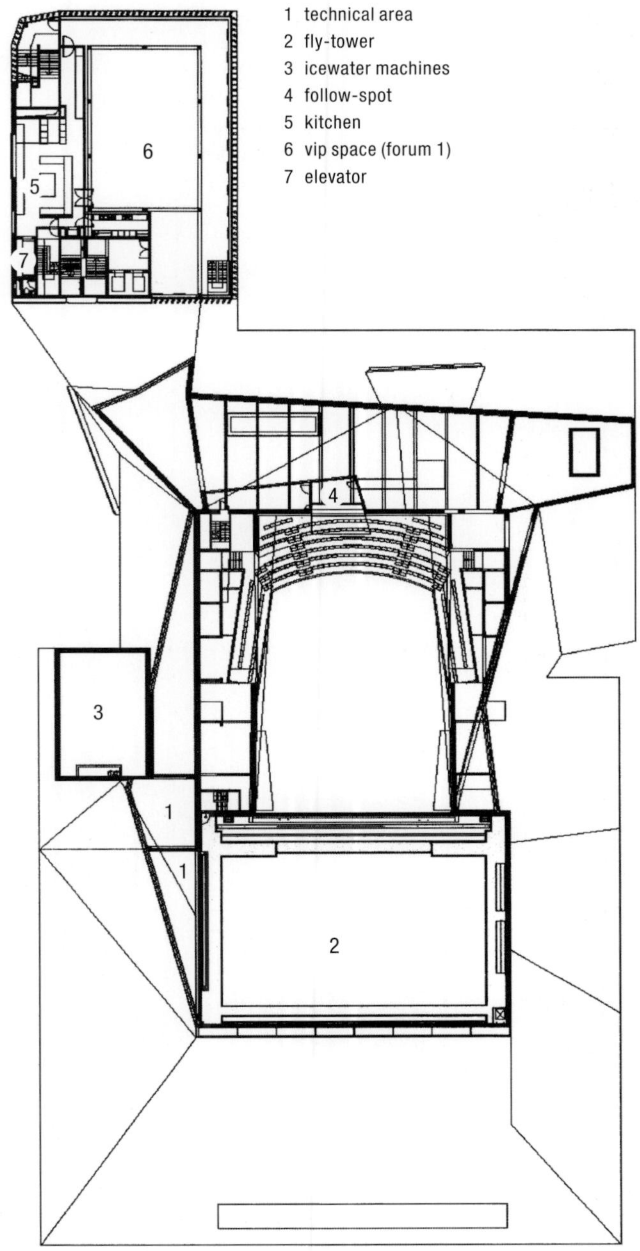

1 technical area
2 fly-tower
3 icewater machines
4 follow-spot
5 kitchen
6 vip space (forum 1)
7 elevator

Level 6

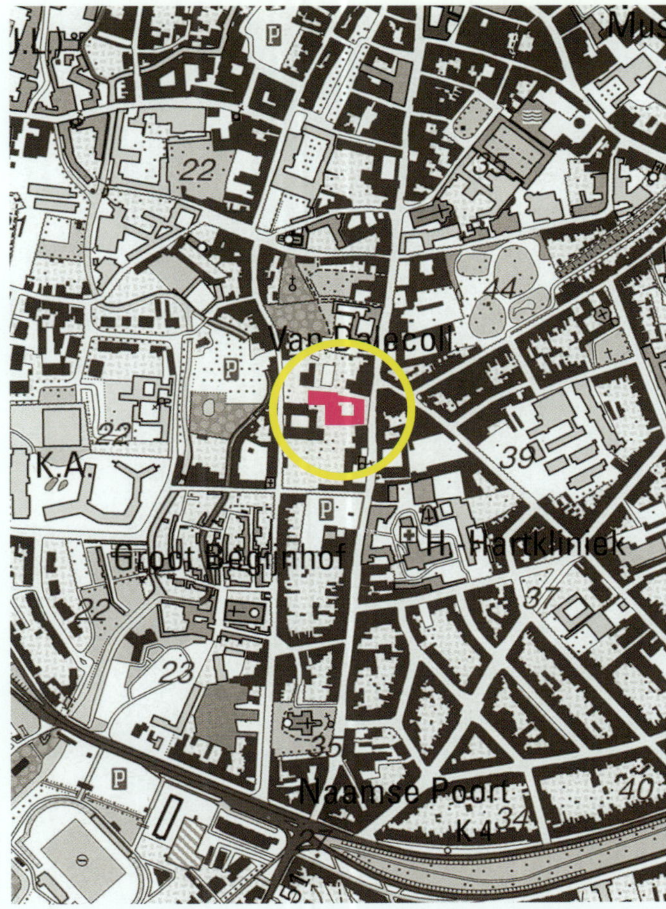

STUK ARTS CENTRE

architect **NEUTELINGS RIEDIJK ARCHITECTS** in association with Bureau Bouwtechniek

location Naamsestraat 96, Leuven

client	STUK Kunstencentrum vzw
design - building	1998-2002
project-workers	Willem Jan Neutelings I Michiel Riedijk I Jago van Bergen
	Dirk Hendriks I Dimitri Meessen I Ute Schnieder I Tania Ally
	Marc De Bruyne I Piet Crevits I Bas Suijkerbuijk
engineers	Bureau Bouwtechniek, Antwerp
	Jan Moens, Nadja van Houten [project support]
	Construction: engineer Dirk Jaspaert, Leuven
	Installations: Roelandts & Rys bvba, Herent
	Building physics: Daidalos Bouwfysisch Ingenieursbureau, Leuven
	Theatre installations: Theater Technieken Advies en Studie, Ghent
contracted work	Van Hout, Geel
area	10,000 sq. m.
building costs	6 miljoen EUR (excl. VAT)
building costs/sq. m	600 EUR/m2 (excl. VAT)
project description	Pieter T'Jonck
photography	Sarah Blee p.31a,32,34b,38,39 I André Nullens p.31b,34a
	Stefan Vandermeulen p.30

STUK ARTS CENTRE ▸ architect NEUTELINGS RIEDIJK ARCHITECTS

In the late seventies, STUK in Leuven was one of the new arts centres that took up the struggle against the fossilised theatre world of Flanders. Despite its shabby accommodation in a hall on a University of Leuven campus, the centre soon acquired an outstanding reputation. Extra performance space was found in, among other places, the abandoned 'laboratoires de chimie générale', in Naamsestraat. However, its scattered location hindered rational management and good public visibility. Its relationship with the university and the city itself were hardly warm, and this threatened even the certainty of its existence. The director Michel Uytterhoeven had tried as early as 1986 to get city council and university support for his plan for an arts centre in the gigantic 'laboratoires' in Naamsestraat. Ten years were to pass before the council and the university, now with the new province of Flemish Brabant and the Flemish Community at their side, gave the green light.

This policy turnaround by the council and the university is characteristic of the changed climate in which cultural institutions operated from the nineties on. With the diminishing importance of socio-political groupings, as far as the university was concerned the arts centre changed from a thorn in its side to a trump card in the struggle for student recruitment. The council expected the city centre to have greater appeal as the new provincial capital. As far as the Flemish Community was concerned, the investment was in line with its new policy: theatre as a remedy against the rapid souring of the major cities. However, for STUK itself the move was a risky business: would the arts centre, which, according to W.J. Neutelings, had built its reputation on 'an underground operation in small smoky halls', retain its identity in a 10,000 sq. m. complex?

The conversion by Neutelings-Riedijk Architects does justice to the complex sensitivities concerning this project by means of a convincing though modest gesture. In this respect, the existing building itself was both a gift and a hindrance. Years of neglect meant it was in a poor structural state. Its varied building history impeded simple 'routing' through the building. But its site on a 17-metre-high ridge did make it the perfect link between the upper and lower towns. The central courtyard, one storey lower than Naamsestraat, was the perfect halt in this walking route. And that is precisely what this plan does.

A staircase in Naamsestraat descends to the existing sunken courtyard. Two of the four wings around it have been replaced by new buildings. By raising the theatre wing, opposite the foyer, from the ground, a breathtaking perspective was opened up of the descent to Schapenstraat below. The central courtyard thereby becomes a patio on a new urban footpath. Striking changes in the street-fronts, like the silver-coloured sawtooth roof on the front building, the

secondary glazing at the back and the huge letters spelling STUK at the front and back tempt the passer-by to traverse the building. The varied nature of the new and existing wings around the courtyard give this walking route an urban diversity. This recurs in the internal cladding of the building, conceived as a city of many houses. The theatres, exhibition spaces, rehearsal rooms, offices, performers' accommodation and café are each given an 'address' on the courtyard plus an interior that is emphatically their own.

A clever acoustic design means that all these spaces can be used at the same time without hindering each other. In the wings that were retained, the design relies heavily on the original architecture, while in the new spaces every register is played. Many of the spaces also open onto the courtyard.

Everywhere you look you see small balconies over and views of the courtyard. They are all starting points for 'location theatre' within the complex. The stage of the large theatre even looks out onto the courtyard through a huge window of 6 by 10 metres. Although the building inside is a patchwork of heterogeneous fragments, the outer walls were deliberately treated as a unit. Everything was given the same colour as the existing brick walls, including the pigmented concrete for the stairs and the roofs, which can also be used. It is only volumetrically that the new wings on the courtyard contrast tensely with the existing ones. The overall image of the building thereby acquires the natural aspect of true urban walls. However, the purpose of this design is not only to present a new urban approach. The 'city of many houses' also embodies a distinct idea of new theatre architecture. In a lucid argument, W.J. Neutelings states that the link between urban life and medieval theatre on the market square became increasingly lost in later developments. From the Renaissance, the auditorium represented the market square only symbolically. With the introduction of the proscenium arch the theatre withdrew even further from the public space. The hubbub of the mediaeval market square was silenced in the later theatre, where the audience was urged to pay attention. The open space theatre, or black box, is the end result of this development.

Although the removal of the proscenium seems to take down the barrier between the actor and the audience, the audience is in reality 'dragged roughly through the proscenium'. '... the amphitheatre has become a school situation: one has to pay attention.' Neutelings here detects a complete break between the city and architecture. In a black box, architecture is only to be found in a negative sense, as the support for the technical installations and to screen off the disturbing exterior. Extreme neutrality and flexibility become the only ambition. This historical outline leads straight to the purpose of the design: is there any way back? This is the relevance of the theatre's 'idiosyncrasies'.

PAUZE
PAUZE

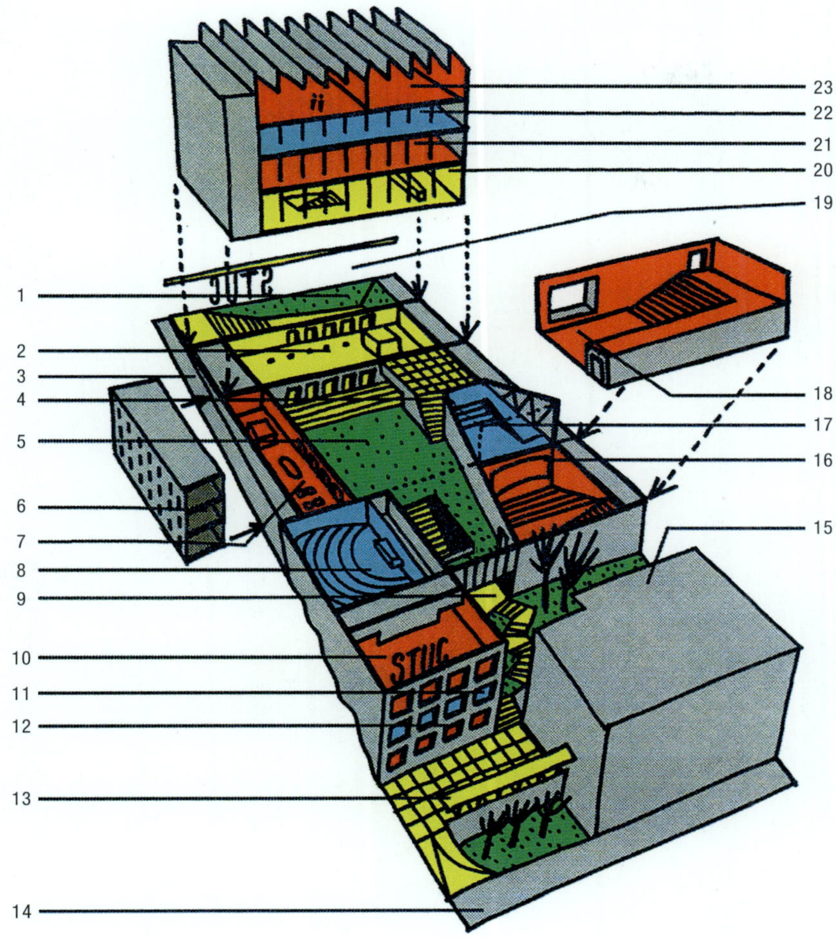

Axonometry

1 forecourt
2 foyer
3 alleyway
4 outdoor theatre
5 patio
6 offices
7 green room
8 auditorium
9 passage
10 lab theatre
11 pavilion theatre
12 rehearsal rooms
13 square at rear
14 Schapenstraat
15 Hollenberge
16 film theatre
17 ensemble theatre
18 main theatre
19 Naamsestraat
20 café
21 hall of pillars
22 cultural studies
23 dance and theatre studios

The openings to the outside world of the courtyard, and the striking interior decoration are arguments in a complex debate. The large theatre or Soetezaal has pride of place. This classical rectangular box is by no means a 'black box'. The fixed tiered seating immediately undermines the dogma of flexibility. The technical material has been rendered invisible by means of fixed concrete bridges above the auditorium and stage. As a homogeneous ceiling they considerably enhance the visual power of the room, despite the disadvantage of the substantial height of the space. The oiled concrete walls, with their emphatic zigzag motif, brightened with polished bronze discs, accentuate even more the unity of the stage and auditorium as a single space, just like the floor that runs from the stage to the seats. In short, the audience and performers share the same space. But they are also connected to the outside world.

After all, the stage and the auditorium open up on every side. Next to the stage, by means of the huge window looking onto the courtyard, and at the entrance steps with a glazed loggia that offers a view of the auditorium, the dressing rooms and the town. In this way the Soetezaal is reminiscent of an Elizabethan hall, a decorated box that unites the actors and audience under a single roof. Not all theatre people accept this choice. The window openings are often covered over. The bronze discs on the stage too. In other spaces the architects were more restrained. In the university's assembly room student music ensembles rehearse. Gold paint on brick walls, red parquet, a curved blue ceiling and light entering from high up evoke, not without irony, both the image of the cheaply adorned village hall and the sugary symbolism of churches and chapels. The film room with its cladding in black artificial leather coffering alludes to the somewhat clandestine atmosphere of the club (for cineastes or others). The 'Labozaal', an existing room, has even been decorated in an extremely neutral style.

However, the finest room in the building is the studio on the roof of the front building. This space is bathed in soft light that enters through the sawtooth roof. Here, that which is demonstrated so rhetorically in the Soetezaal succeeds quite naturally. The windows on both sides of the room offer unique panoramas of the town. In this way it alludes to the representation of the town, which once structured the iconography and form of the theatre. At the same time it allows in the town in a meticulously mediated way.

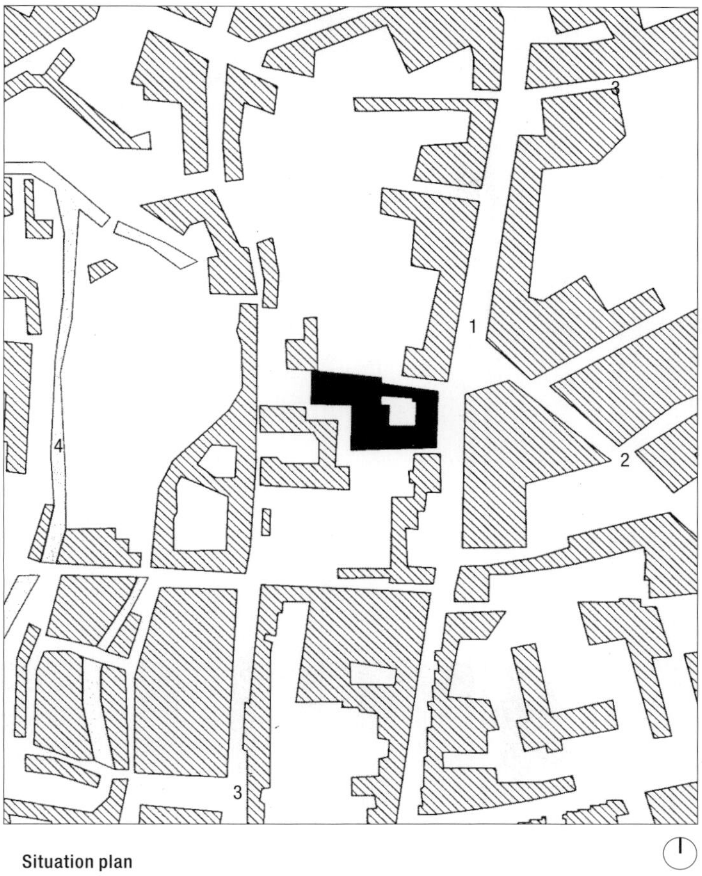

Situation plan

1 Naamsestraat
2 Parkstraat
3 Schapenstraat
4 Dijle

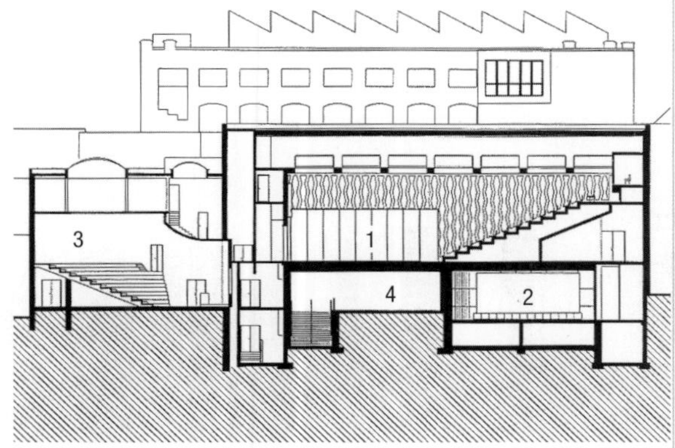

Section CC'

1 main theatre
2 film theatre
3 auditorium
4 passage

Section AA'

1 main theatre
2 café
3 foyer
4 exhibition hall
5 cultural studies
6 studios
7 forecourt
8 patio
9 square at rear
10 passage

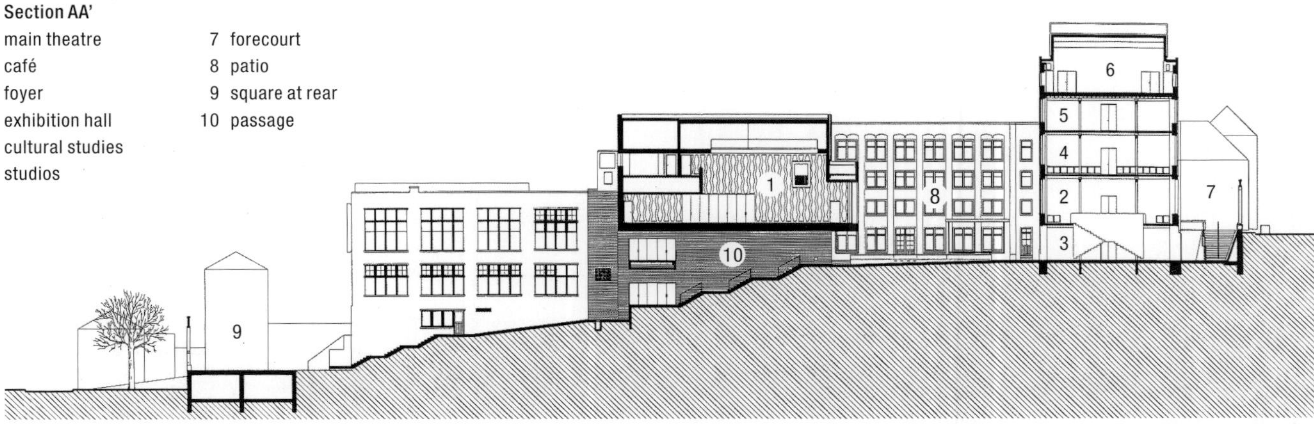

Section BB'

1 ensemble theatre
2 film theatre
3 outdoor theatre

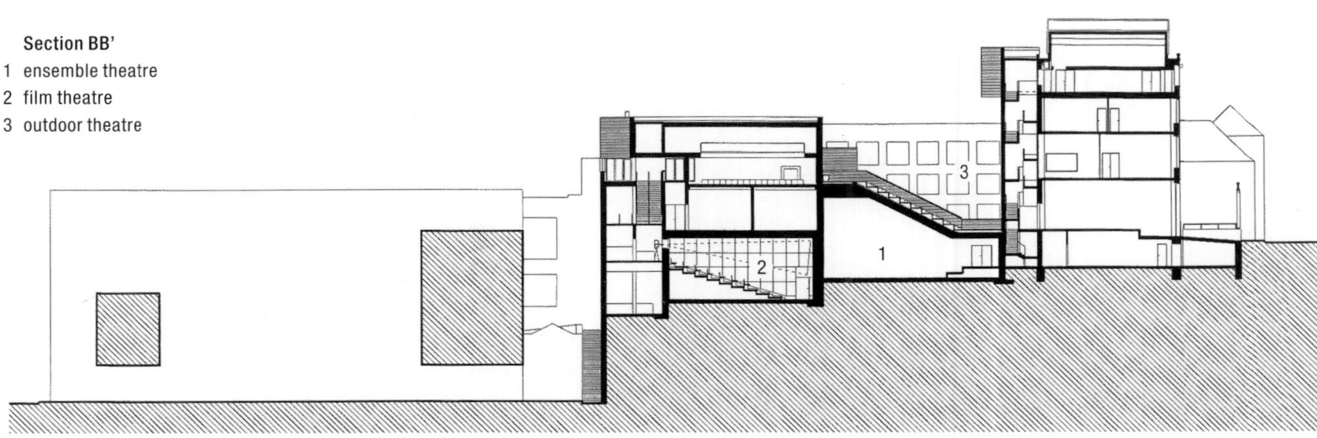

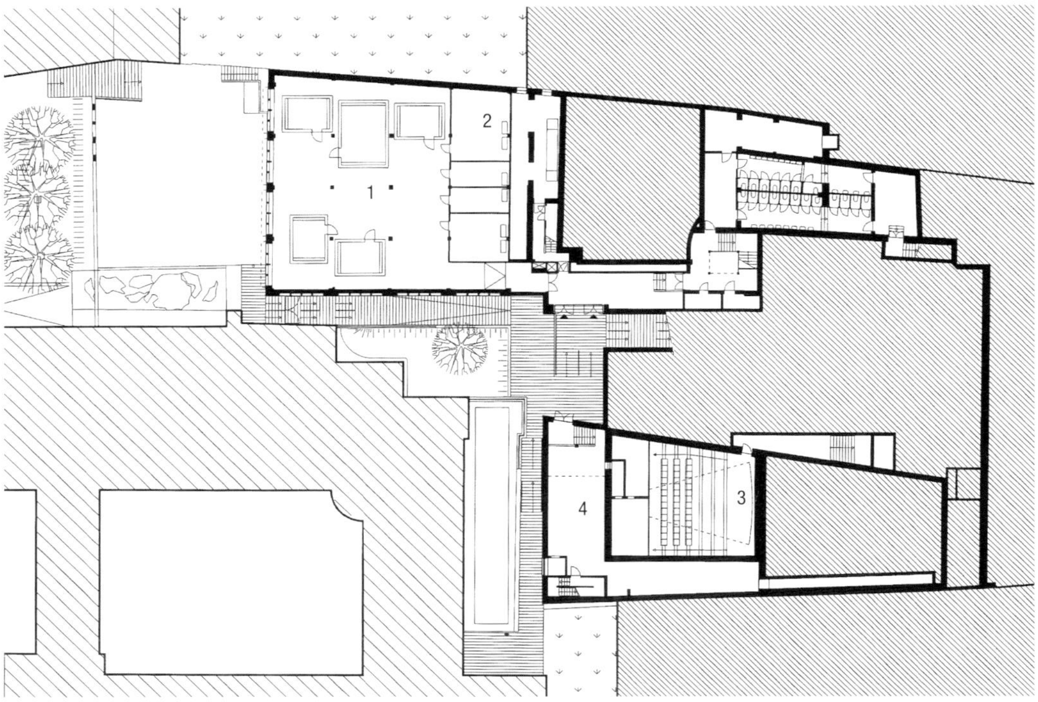

Level -2

1 rehearsal rooms
2 darkrooms
3 film theatre
4 technical area

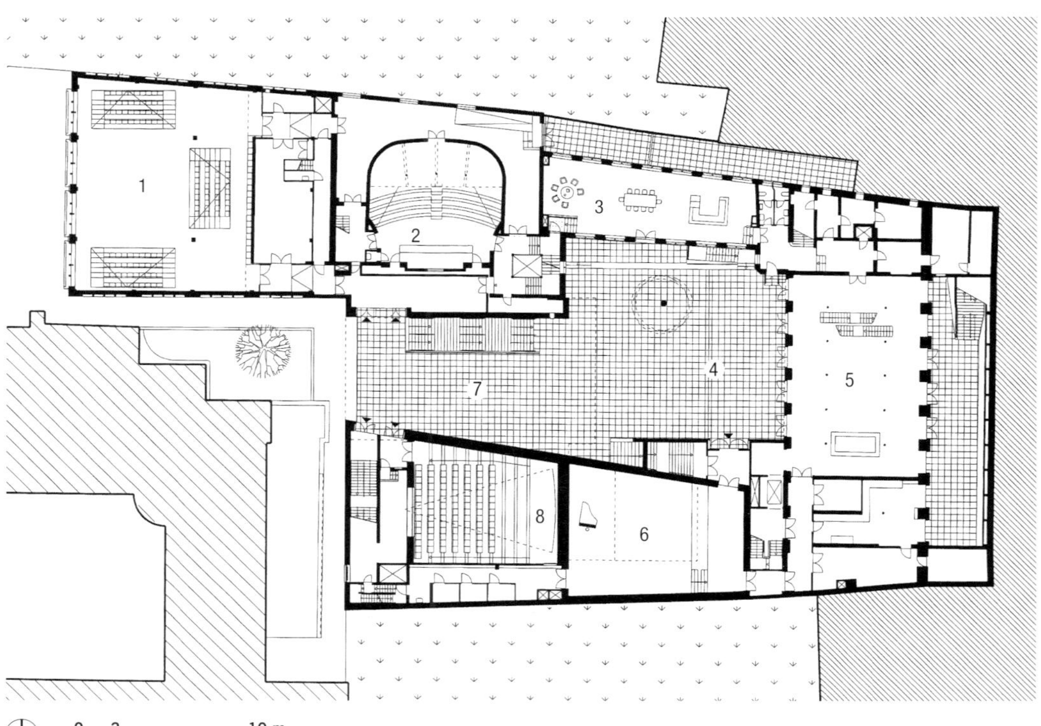

Level -1

1 small theatre
2 auditorium
3 green room
4 patio
5 foyer
6 ensemble theatre
7 passage
8 film theatre

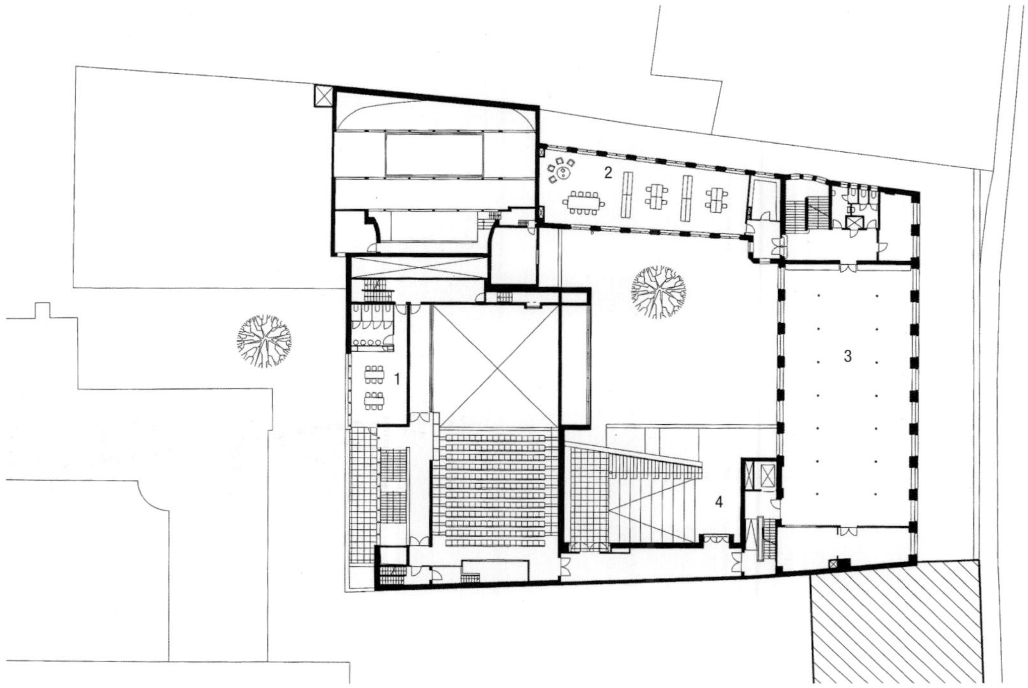

Level 2

1 dressing rooms
2 offices
3 exhibition hall
4 outdoor theatre

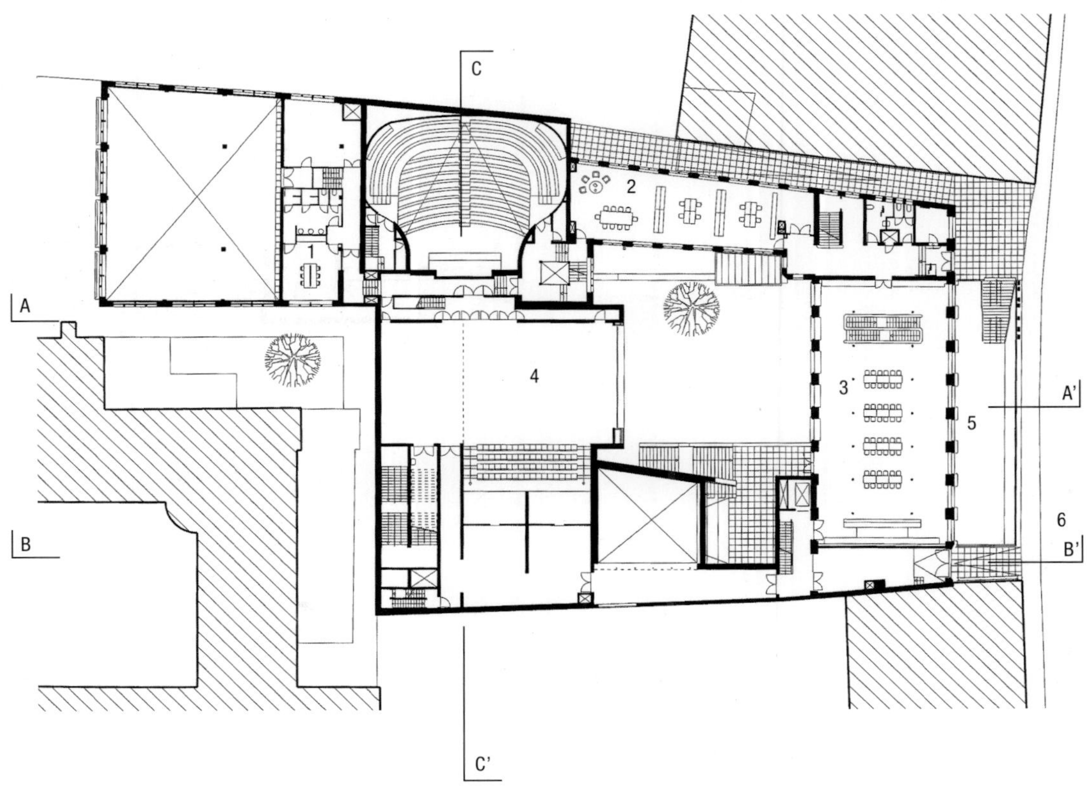

Level 0

1 dressing rooms
2 offices
3 café
4 main theatre
5 forecourt
6 Naamsestraat

MODENATIE

architect **MARIE-JOSÉ VAN HEE** in association with Bureau Bouwtechniek

location Nationalestraat 28, 2000 Antwerp

client	vzw Immode I nv Modenatie
design - building	2000-2002
project-workers	Leslie Burm I Dirk Goyens I Shin Hagiwara I Filip Reumers Johan Suykens I Tania Vandenbussche I Rolf Vansteenwegen Dietlinde Verhaeghe I Wim Voorspoels
engineers	Bureau Bouwtechniek Bureau voor Architectuur en Stabiliteit Dirk Jaspaert Jan D'hondt [techniques] Technum [sound and vibration department]
contracted work	Bouwondernemingen Frans Willems nv I nv Goedleven
area	9,773 sq. m.
volume	38,318 cubic. m.
building costs	7.92 miljoen EUR (incl. fittings, fees and VAT)
building costs/sq. m	811 EUR/sq. m. (incl. fittings, fees and VAT)
project description	Pieter T'Jonck
photography	Kristien Daem p.44,45,50 I André Nullens p.43,51 Stefan Vandermeulen p.42

 MODENATIE ▸ architect **MARIE-JOSÉ VAN HEE** in association with Bureau Bouwtechniek

The Modenatie houses the ModeMuseum, the Flanders Fashion Institute and the Mode-Academie, all institutions which have in recent decades established Antwerp's international reputation as a city of fashion. A brasserie and bookshop are also included in the building. The premises originally belonged to the Gas Company and were built in 1910. The site is in a prominent location but has an awkward shape: a narrow triangle created by the construction of Nationalestraat. This linking route to the new 'South' district cut through the old urban fabric around the Groenplaats. The architecture is appropriate to this Haussmann-like operation. The corner is affirmed by a drum with a dome. The wings of the building along Drukkerijstraat and Nationalestraat are distinguished from this end section by an intermediate bay topped with a tympanum. The austere wings with their neoclassical plastered facades on a stone plinth are subservient to the grand gesture at the apex.

From the outside, the building, with its distinguished anonymity, could just as easily pass for a hotel, a residential complex or offices. However, the composition of the construction inside shows that this building was in fact conceived as offices. The wings, which contain the majority of the floor area, were erected in structural steelwork around a triangular internal patio which introduced abundant light into the workrooms on two sides. The structure, with its rigid modulation, turned out to be suited to the reorganisation because it allows for free arrangement of the plan, tailor-made for the user, on every floor: stacking is here an organisational principle. These two simple observations: the 'appropriate' urban design gesture the building represents and the basic constructional intention, were decisive elements in Marie-José van Hee's design work.

This is in part focused on the external appearance of the building. Like a dignified and excellently-cut suit, the facade was retained almost intact. This 'suit' was only subtly, almost unnoticeably adjusted here and there to meet its new needs. Often using simple means. The showy, poorly-fitting concrete structure of a later addition in Drukkerijstraat, now the store for the museum and library, was as it were painted out using dark-grey paint. Joinery details play a leading part in the treatment of the facade. In the drum, the 'face' of the building, the original, richly-profiled woodwork on the upper floors was preserved, in recognition of the importance of the urban setting. However, in the wings the new woodwork reinforces the archetypical nature of the neoclassical urban street frontage: a purely tectonic play of planes and openings. For this reason the window frames on the ground and first floors were completely concealed. This neutrality also matches the alternating use of the forum and the exhibition rooms of the ModeMuseum, which are housed here. But even the slender window frames of the offices and studios higher up are made of painted wood with steel glazing bars.

The cornice completes the simplification of this wall. The brickwork piers between the windows of the old dormers are extended up to the new cornice, a narrow, dark-coloured metal canopy that replaces the old, lower moulding. This canopy also bears the parapet of the roof terrace. This emphatic delineation of the facade has yet another advantage: the sewing workshop, situated like a penthouse on top of the roof, is free to develop its own form of expression, with a floating metal canopy and steel windows.

The approach to the inside is as radical as that to the outside is cautious. The existing structure was taken right down to the skeleton. A monumental staircase and lift were located as an independent volume at a certain distance from the internal walls in the triangular atrium between the wings. This atrium has been covered by a new ceiling in which large rectangular openings have been left for light. They allow plenty of light onto the stair and the wings. This staircase plays a subtle game with the bisector of the triangular plan. The treads are not at right angles to this bisector, but to the wing along Drukkerijstraat. This means the first flight of stairs narrows from about 6.5 m to 2.5 m wide at the first landing, where the next flight leads to the entrance of the ModeMuseum. From the entrance landing of the museum the staircase, which spirals round the lift, becomes ever-narrower. On the second floor it leads to the offices of the Flanders Fashion Institute, ModeMuseum and the library. On the Nationalestraat side a narrow passage leads to the agora, which hangs like a canopy above the corridor and the entrance of the ModeMuseum. The final, narrow staircase leads to the top floor, the studios of the Mode-Academie.

This staircase is the building's fundamental gesture. Its sculpted wooden volume stands out against the white surfaces of the roof and the walls of the patio. With their regular grid of rectangular openings – small in the inner facades and large in the roof, they form a pleasant neutral background to the stairs. The stairs and the walls of the atrium fit together perfectly. The staircase is signalled in these facades by means of a pronounced modification – the only one. Up against the adjoining premises Van Hee created a passage through the building, from Nationalestraat to Drukkerijstraat. Steel gates with open bars close it off in the evening, but during the day they fold upwards like elegant canopies. Although this corridor naturally forms a passage, the two exits each have their own purpose. The 'real' entrance is on the Nationalestraat side. It is here that the atrium 'bulges' outwards. Video screens provide the visitor with a foretaste of what awaits inside. But the fact that the atrium turns through an angle means one only notices the staircase later. The eye is first seduced by the bookshop that here protrudes a little from behind the street facade with a set of invitingly broad entrance steps, and then the reception desk. On the right, behind reception, you see a glass

wall. It offers a view through to the patio of a small gallery in the inner area between the adjoining plots. The entrance in Drukkerijstraat lacks this display: this bare white vestibule offers no surprises. It passes alongside the storeroom and is a loading bay more than it is the start of a passageway.

Considering the way the stair volume first narrows in perspective, to then lose itself as it rises, it might have been stately, or even magnificent. One can quite easily imagine a fashion show taking place here. But the choice of material contradicts this: the walls and treads of the stairs and the lift-tower are in wide merbau planks, a coarse-grained tropical wood which suggests that the staircase consists of stacked beams. As if the interior were a warehouse. The glazed strips of lighting using fluorescent tube-lights, set into the walls and white-plastered ceilings of the volumes projecting overhead, emphasise this soberness even more. This building is indeed not only intended to show the world Antwerp's fashion expertise, but it is also a stack of workspaces. In the gentle contradiction between the shape and execution of the staircase, the architecture reflects a balance between these two facets. What is more, the staircase creates long sightlines and through-views in every direction in the atrium. It thereby symbolises the cohesion between the organisations housed here.

As distinct from these visual fireworks, there is the simple and businesslike decoration of the offices and workshops with their flexible connections between the various users: black linoleum floors, bare, white-painted walls. This simplicity never becomes demonstrative, but shows up the search for a receptive neutrality. The rooms radiate calmness by means of the meticulous orchestration of the joins between new walls and materials and the existing structure. For example, the wall of the outer facade is detailed like a false wall that conceals storage cabinets and technical installations (with ventilation grills as a rhythmical detail

rather than meaningless technical intrusions). The deep recesses thus formed around the windows soften the light that enters. The window recesses in the museum rooms are given an extra detail: small shutters concealed in the side walls can shut out the sun completely.

This subtle but persistent detailing shows the precise reflection Marie-José van Hee entered into regarding every aspect of this conversion. She thereby reveals the potential of an existing urban artefact and at the same time enriches the programme housed there.

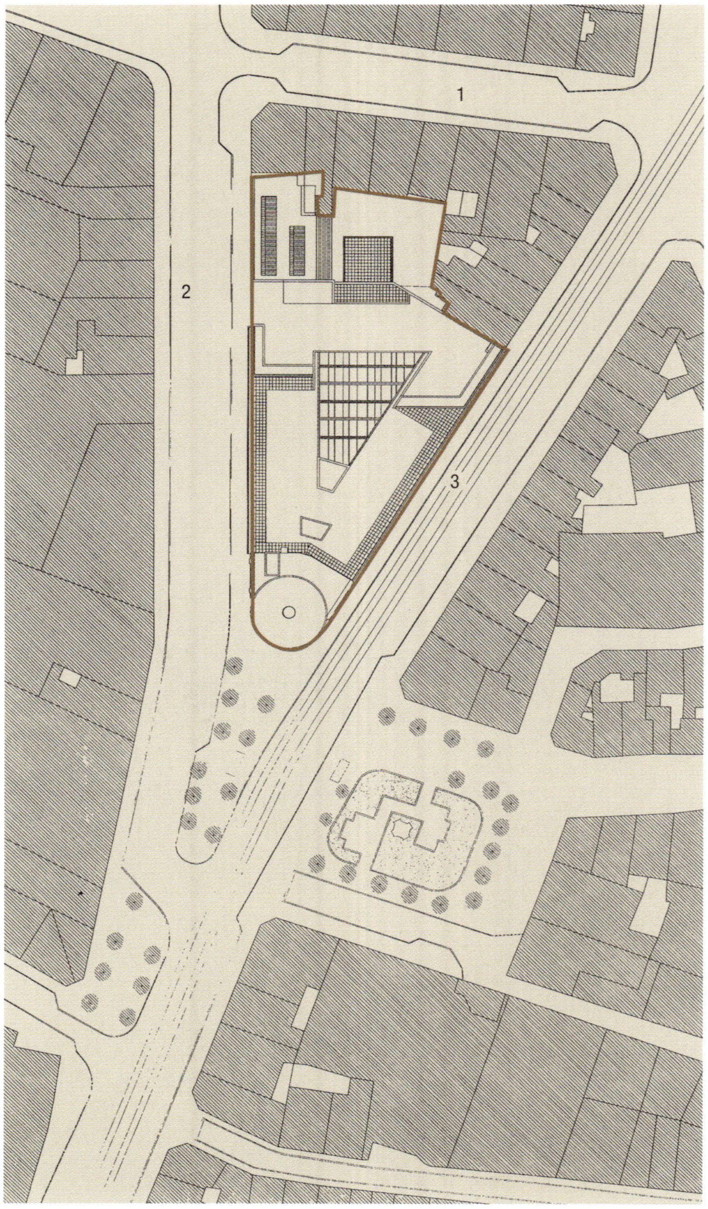

Situation plan

1 Steenhouwersvest
2 Drukkerijstraat
3 Nationalestraat

Drukkerijstraat facade

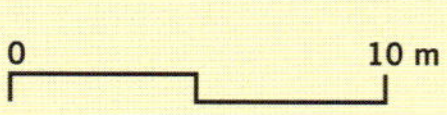

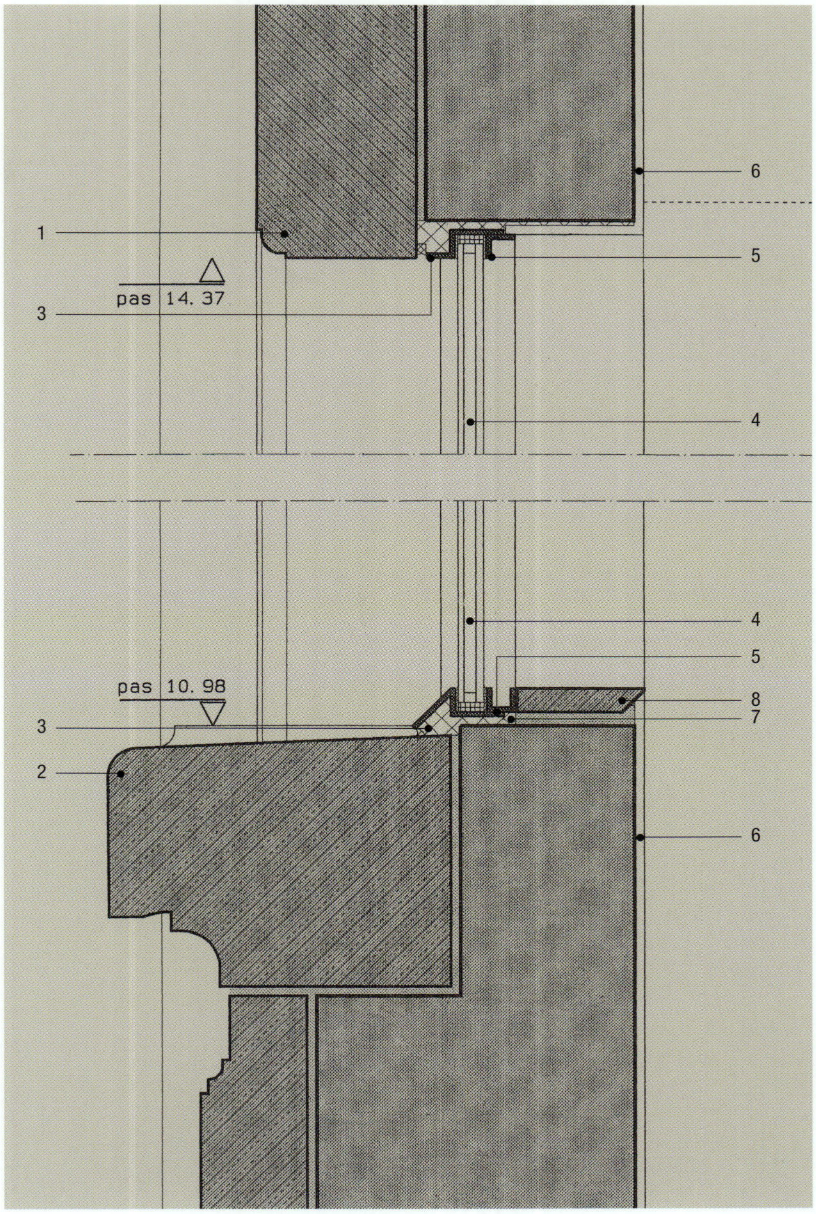

Vertical section through ground floor window
1 existing stone lintel
2 existing bluestone cill
3 cement joint
4 double acoustic glazing
5 frame in steel sections, enamelled in RAL colour
6 plastering
7 PU foam
8 stone window ledge

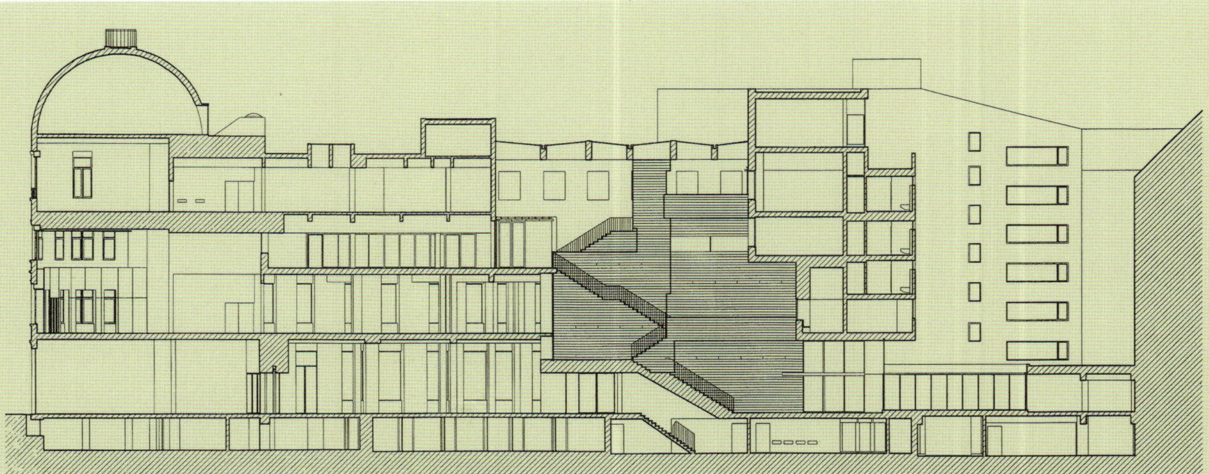

Longitudinal section

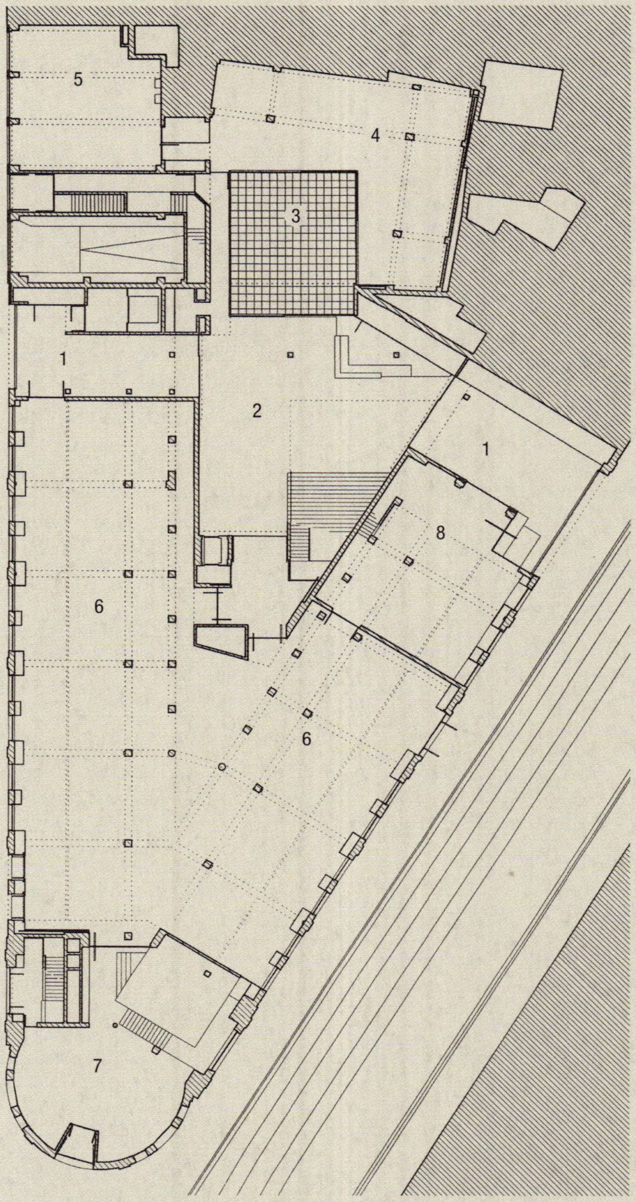

Level 0

1 entrance
2 atrium
3 patio
4 MoMu gallery
5 educational area
6 forum
7 brasserie
8 bookshop

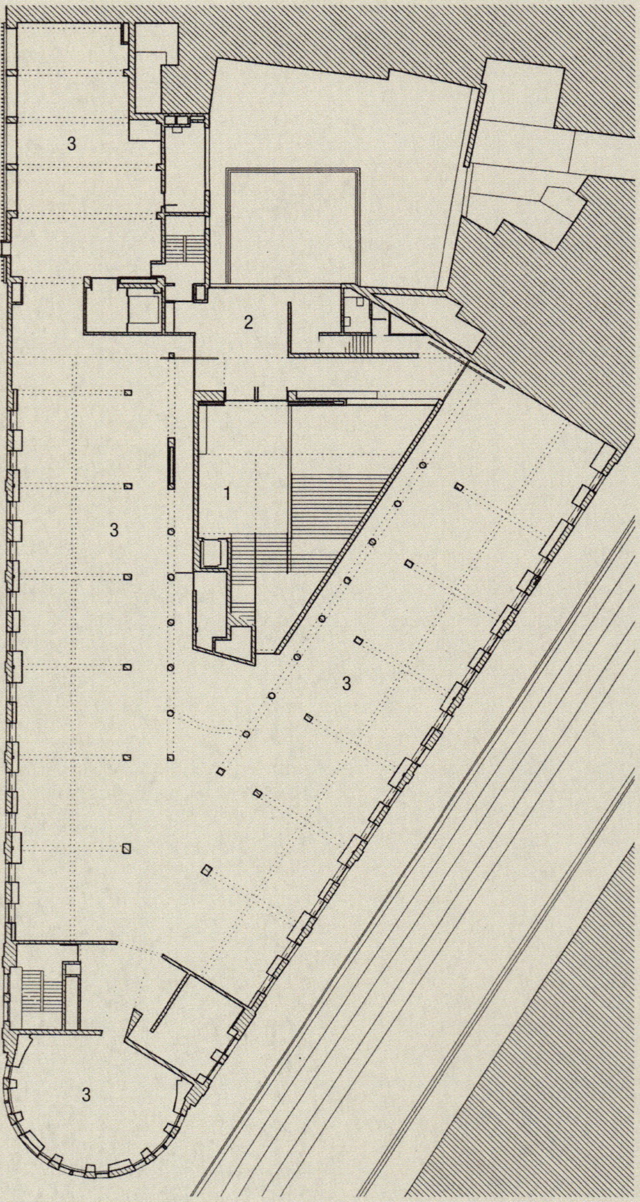

Level 1

1 atrium
2 MoMu museum hall
3 MoMu exhibition area

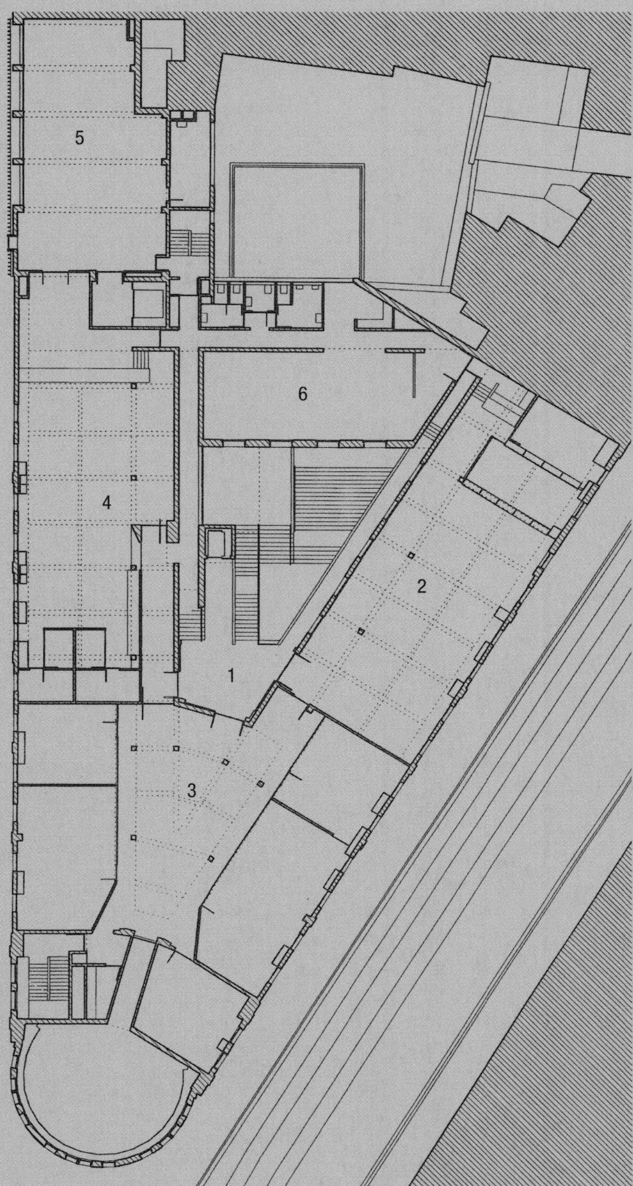

Level 2

1 atrium
2 FFI offices
3 MoMu offices
4 library and reading room
5 library archives
6 agora

Level 3

1 atrium
2 Mode Academy agora
3 Mode Academy studios
4 MoMu archives

0 10 m

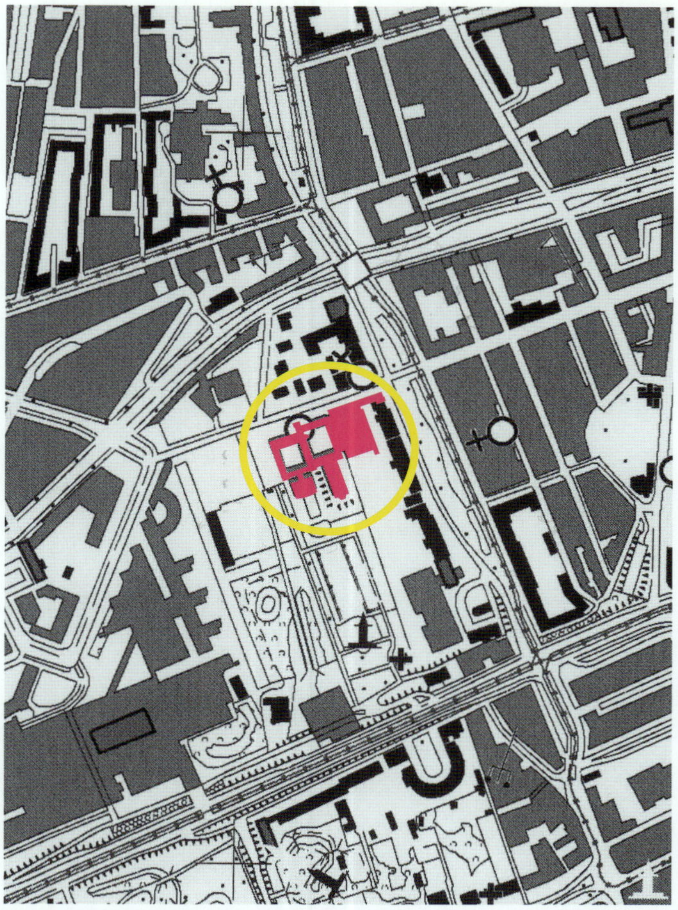

MUSEUM BOIJMANS VAN BEUNINGEN

architect **ROBBRECHT AND DAEM ARCHITECTS**

location Museumpark 18-20, Rotterdam (NL)

client	Museum Boijmans Van Beuningen [director at the time: Chris Dercon] Rotterdam city council [Hans Kombrink, former alderman for culture]
brief	Restructuring and refitting of the existing classified museum building and extension (5,000 sq. m.) in the form of a new wing containing exhibition rooms, library, offices and storage
design	1997-1998
building	1999-2003
project-workers	Kristoffel Boghaert [project architect] I Sofie Delaere I Brigitte D'hoore Catherine Fierens I Gilberte Claes I Fransesca de Fonseca Shin Hagiwara I Hugo Vanneste [assistant architects]
engineers	Project manager: PKB bouwadviseurs, Diemen – Amsterdam (NL) Architectural adviser: TUNS + HORSTING architecten, Rotterdam (NL) Stability engineer: CORSMIT advising engineers, Rijswijk [engineer Pim Peters] (NL) Technical installations engineer: Huisman & Van Muijen adviser for installations, 's-Hertogenbosch (NL) Building physics engineer: Dorsseblesgraaf advising engineers, The Hague (NL) Glass adviser: GTC-Nederland, Delft (NL)
contracted work	Bouwbedrijf Hulshof, Houten (NL) [general contractor for new building]
area	5,000 sq. m.
volume	17,500 cubic. m.
building costs	17,350,000 EUR
building costs/sq. m	3,470 EUR/sq. m.
project description	Koen Van Synghel
photography	Karin Borghouts p.55,60,61 I Kristien Daem p.54b,56 Stefan Vandermeulen p.54a

MUSEUM BOIJMANS VAN BEUNINGEN ▸ architect ROBBRECHT AND DAEM ARCHITECTS

The Boijmans van Beuningen Museum in Rotterdam is the result of several phases of building. Over the years, new wings have been added to the original 1935 brick building by Johan A.G. van der Steur, with its symmetrical frame of museum rooms around two courtyards. In 1972 Alexander Bodon, in response to performance and installation art and the consequent need for an extensive exhibition area, built a large top-lit exhibition hall.

It is a businesslike space whose dimensions mean it can easily be considered as a third – covered – courtyard. Later still, under pressure from a growing culture of entertainment, the museum was given a new entrance with a bookshop and restaurant, built in the full modernist glory of steel and glass architecture but now already demolished. In 1991 Hubert-Jan Henket built what is called the Van Beuningen-De Vriese pavilion in high-tech style on the garden side of the museum.

The extension carried out by the museum's former director and the architects Robbrecht and Daem goes beyond the addition of the umpteenth new wing or pavilion. A new exhibition circuit was developed throughout the existing buildings. To achieve this, not only was an enfilade of small museum rooms built round the Bodon room: subtle but vigorous modifications to the existing buildings also made for a thorough transformation of the museum. This transforma-

tion begins with the moving of the entrance. The construction of the Bodon wing had completely upset the original symmetry of the Van der Steur building with its entrance under the tower and on the axis of the two courtyards. This entrance also presented the museum with problems, since it was not suitable for the smooth running of public exhibitions. For this reason the entrance was moved to the courtyard where the original staff entrance was.

The restructuring of this courtyard meant that the entrance came very naturally to be at the centre of the museum. All at once a reassuring symmetry could be sensed once again. This courtyard, transformed into a forecourt, also plays an important urban design role. It is an intimate public space, made urban by its openness but related to the museum by the sculptures, and forms a counterpoint to the expanse of the city of Rotterdam and the museum park.

The ambition of integrating the museum into the city is also expressed in the new building along the street, a narrow wing that extends as far as the Westersingel. The fact that Rotterdam's Picasso sculpture has been moved to the Westersingel at the end of the new wing emphasises this intention even more.

The new wing also enters into dialogue with its surroundings by means of its form. The articulation and pattern of the windows, the concrete panels and the mouldings and cornices, and especially the shallowness of the building, enable the museum to link up effortlessly with the historical residences on the Westersingel. The flexible arrangement of the new wing is notable. For example, the offices on the second, third and fourth floors, above the library and exhibition rooms, can be put into use as exhibition rooms with only minor adjustments.

Robbrecht, who is very familiar with Italian Renaissance and Baroque architecture is here making reference to the Uffizi in Florence, an office building which, by displaying art, became a world-class museum. Another notable feature is the range of small exhibition rooms around the Bodon wing, similar to the apsidal chapels in a cathedral. It is as if they have given thickness to the wall, and that forgotten rooms have been rediscovered.

The transitions between old and new have been consistently articulated. For example, at the point where the Van der Steur building and the concrete architecture of the new wing join, a deep, black service passage has been installed. Not only can the works of art here be loaded in and out of a truck under shelter, but they can also be brought right into the heart of the building. Visually speaking, this dark service entrance comes across as an enigmatic 'black hole', which gives refined expression to the line of contact between the

old and the new. Robbrecht and Daem's architecture is characterised by the sublimation of practical problems into a pure, visual, almost sensual experience. They approach their materials, such as glass and concrete, in a way which one might call 'painterly'. It becomes clear precisely what this means in the interaction between the concrete architecture and the floating glass screens used in front of the facade of the new wing. The opaque cathedral glass of these screens makes the view to the outside blurred.

So the visitor does have contact with the outside world, but without its penetrating fully through to him and getting in the way of contact with the art. At the same time, this cathedral glass, at certain positions of the sun, is able to capture light and radiate it. This light effect is intended to make the museum building appear to dematerialise. Robbrecht actually considers glass and concrete to be related materials. And it has to be said that in the new wing the velvety grey etched concrete harmonises perfectly with the opaque illuminated glass.

And these pictorial concerns may make one forget that Robbrecht and Daem's modifications are subservient to the art. The fact that the museum rooms in the new wing are in bare concrete shows that Robbrecht and Daem are confident that this 'naked' building provides suitable accommodation for the art. They are not dogmatic in this however, since in the rooms upstairs they use classic white walls. When Robbrecht designed a floor and wall construction for the 'Floor for a sculpture, wall for a painting' exhibition in 1987, for the best possible presentation of a sculpture and a painting, he drew up all the guidelines for an autonomous but above all subservient architecture. With the discreet but defining presence of architectural acts, the renewed Boijmans van Beuningen Museum once again proves the selfless willingness of architecture to serve.

The museum is of course in the first place at the service of its visitors. This also underlies Chris Dercon's idea of expanding the museum into a centre of knowledge. This takes shape in the library, which was designed as a single piece of wooden furniture, taking as its example St. Jerome's study with its intriguing interior of wooden cupboards and seat. This library, located at the end of the new wing, occupies a strategic position between the more intimate life of the museum and the public bustle of the city.

Thanks to their consistent reinterpretation of the various wings of the museum and the fundamental transformation of the transitional zones, Robbrecht and Daem have succeeded not only in giving shape to the Boijmans van Beuningen Museum as a place of heterogenous fragmented space but also, and above all, as a place for art. This is also why it deserves a place in the short history of contemporary museum architecture.

Vertical section through facade

1 steel coping, 18 mm
2 wall build-up:
- reinforced concrete, cast in situ, 200 mm
- mineral wool insulation, 100 mm
- precast concrete facade panels, 130 mm

3 steel frame windows, double glazing
4 window linings in folded steel plate
5 glass screen:
- steel I-sections, 120 to 180 mm
- recessed stainless steel structural glazing fixing bracket
- 6 mm textured cast glass
  resin bonded to 10 mm toughened glass

6 18 mm folded steel plate
7 floor:
- polished concrete screed
- structural topping
- hollow precast concrete

8 18 mm steel plate
9 plinth:
- extruded PS foam insulation
- precast concrete plinth

10 retaining wall
- reinforced concrete, 250 mm
- 60mm extruded PS foam insulation
- bituminous membrane

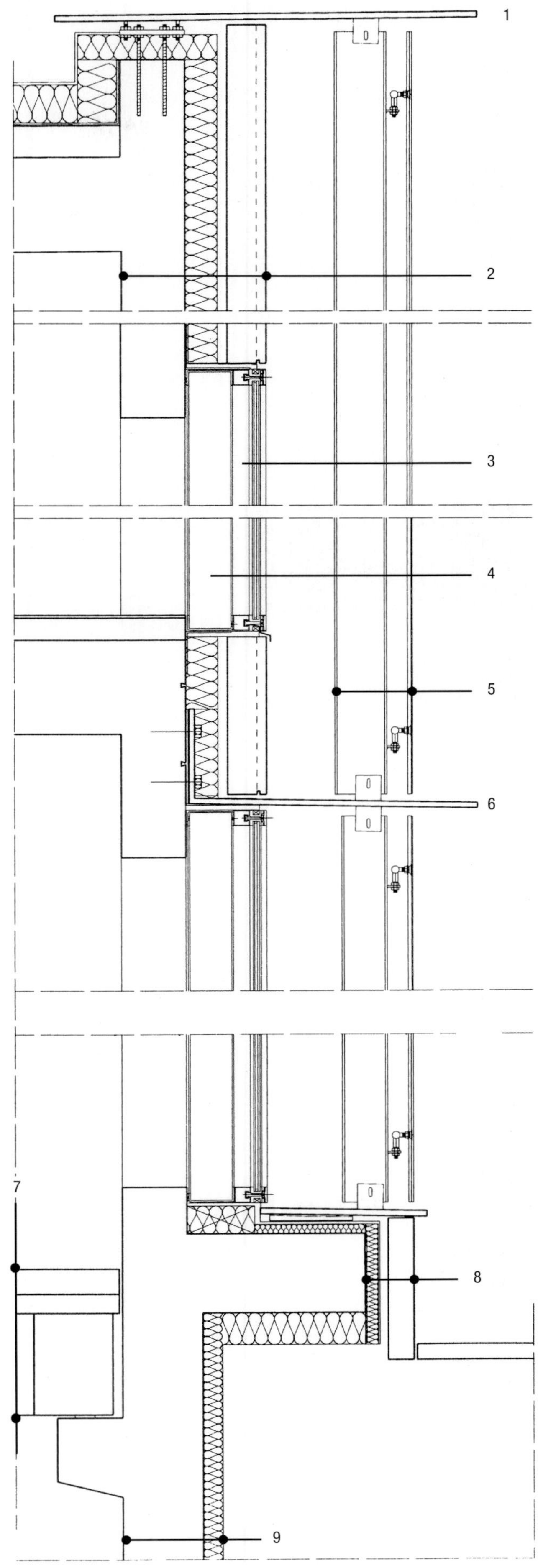

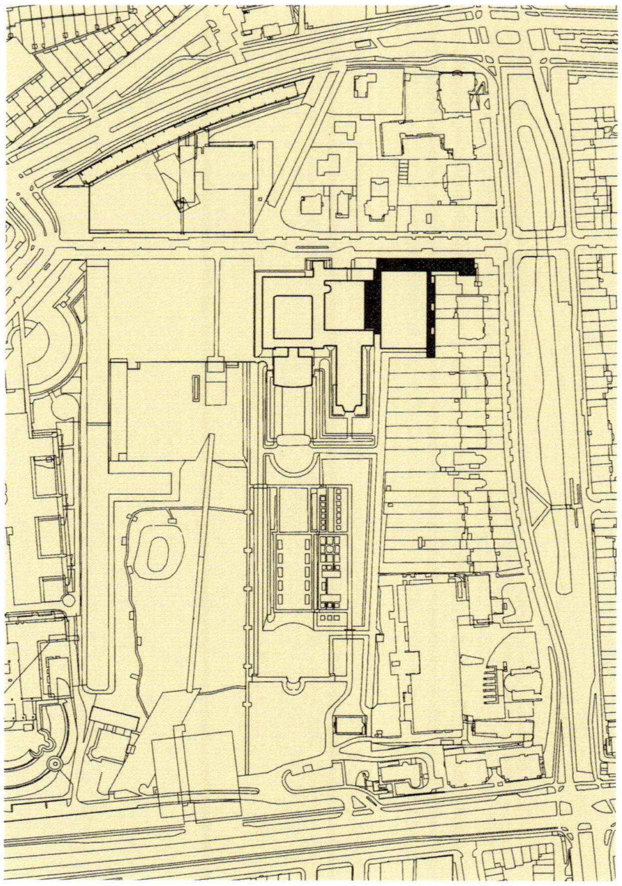

Situation plan

0 20 100 m

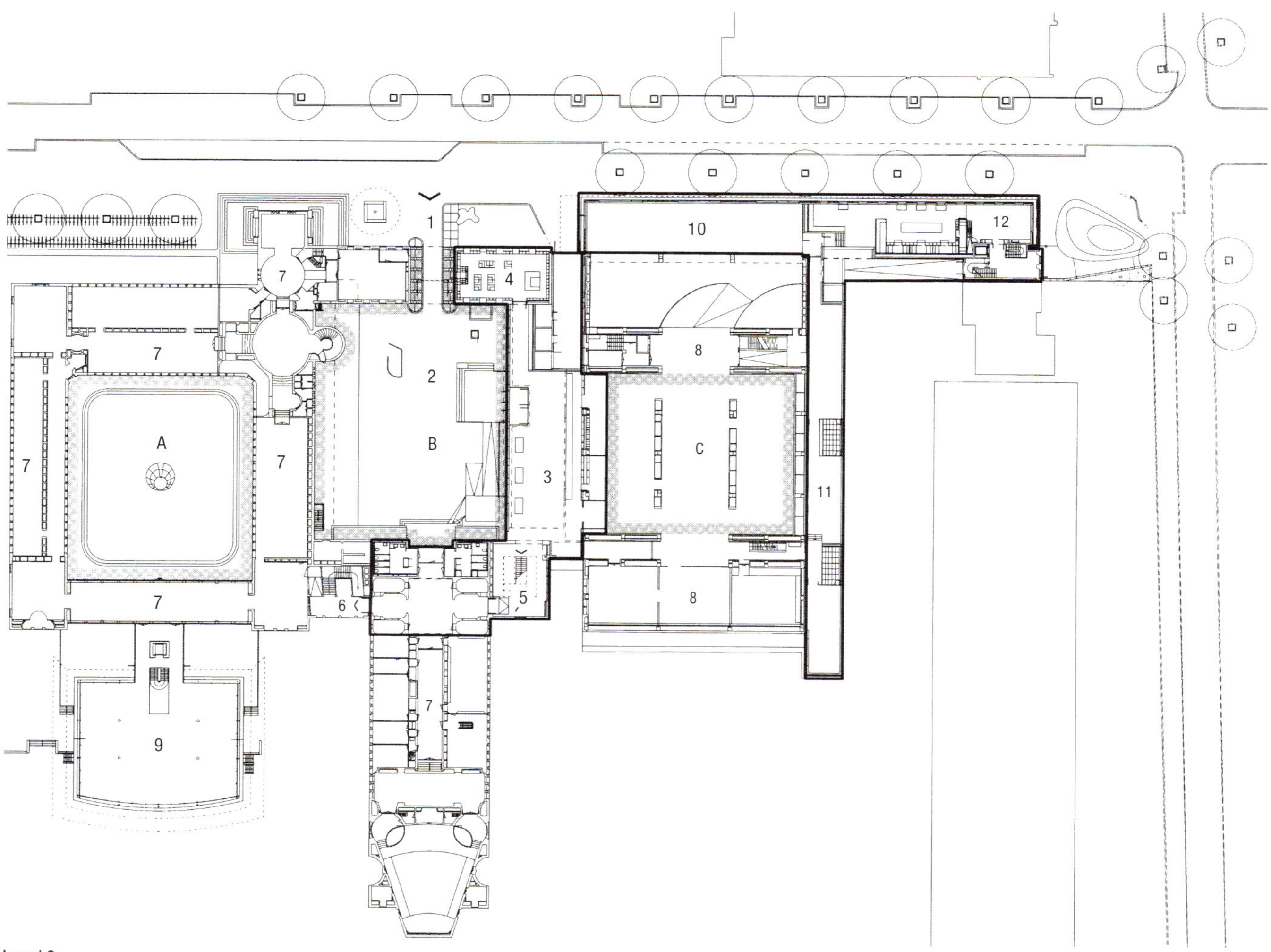

Level 0

System of courtyards

A enclosed courtyard in Van Der Steur building
B central square between Van Der Steur and Bodon
C covered square at Bodon wing

1 entrance
2 forecourt
3 entrance hall
4 new bookshop in existing building
5 new staircase in existing building
6 Old Dutch staircase in Van Der Steur building
7 exhibition area in Van Der Steur building
8 exhibition area in Bodon building
9 restaurant in De Vriese pavilion
10 extension of exhibition area
11 workshops
12 library
13 exhibition areas
14 new print room in existing building
15 offices

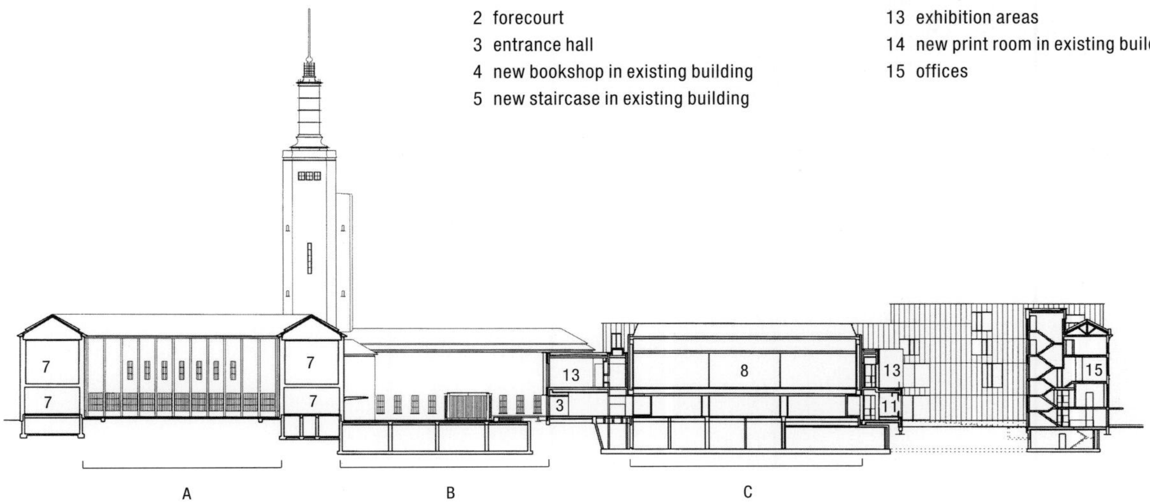

Section AA'

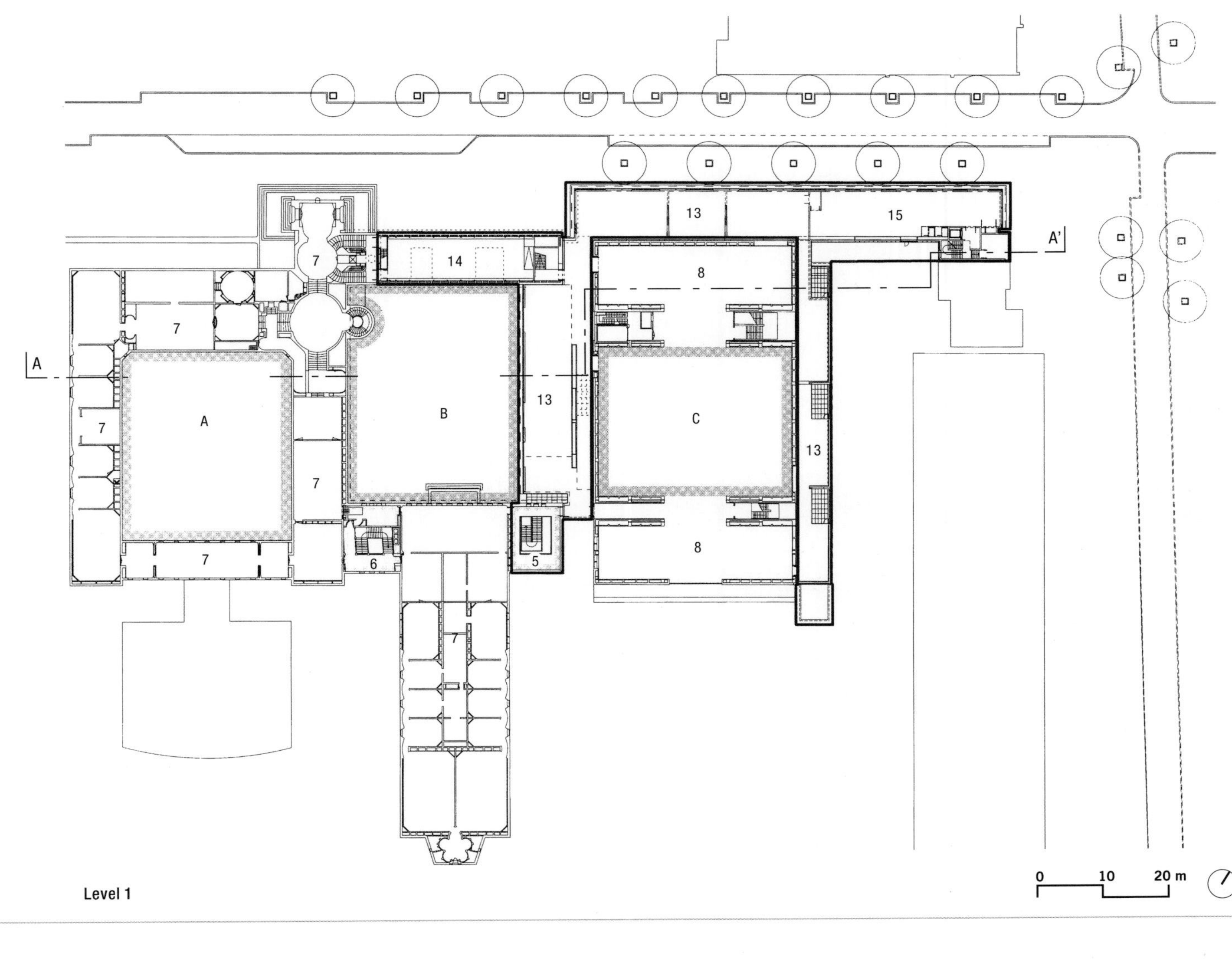

Level 1

I

IDENTITY AND DISPLACEMENT

▸ Ákos Moravánszky

The Concert Hall in Bruges
Robbrecht and Daem architects, 2002

How can we speak about the identity of an object, as if it were something that we could identify? By identity in the stricter sense, we mean that two (or more) things are indiscernible. But which properties should we compare to determine their identity? What if some of the most essential properties are hidden from our perception?

Despite such fundamental questions, identity plays the role of a joker card in discussions on topics such as globalisation or tourism. Ethnic minorities, geographical regions, religious groups and cities are working on the construction and adequate presentation of their real or perceived identities. Philosophers from Descartes to Husserl conceived identity as something essential and fixed, and tied the authenticity of life to the recognition of identity. The uncertainty regarding the 'true' identity is therefore the source of modern anxieties. Postmodern theorists, on the other hand, claim that identity is a myth, an illusion, and individuals can freely select or construct identities that are image-like and unstable.

In the case of a city, the construction of identity is not done by a single individual. Imagined identities are projected by local inhabitants and their organisations, politicians, tourism experts, preservationists and developers. More often than not, there are considerable discrepancies between these differing images. In the age of mass tourism, however, the difference between 'real' and 'invented' history fades away, and in some advertising campaigns, medieval European towns present a Disneyfied image of themselves. When Bruges became the Cultural Capital of Europe in 2002 and an international competition for a new Concert Hall was announced, the entries interpreted the issue of identity differently. The identity of Bruges as reflected in the proposals cannot be separated from the even broader issue of Flemish identity, a "thorny question" according to recent publication.(1) But the very title of that publication: *Homeward : Contemporary Architecture in Flanders* suggests that a question which is "deliberately not touched upon", focuses the eye on this very topic.

The history of Bruges shows that it is impossible to subscribe to an essentialist notion of identity. The extraordinary ebb and flow between opulence and poverty in the city is usually explained by natural events, such as the silting of the Zwin, the channel that connected the city to the sea. But even this very fact, which Belgian children learn in school, is called into question by recent research, which finds the reason for decline in political and economic circumstances.(2)

Like all cities, Bruges is a fabric of myths taken as reality, of a legendary Middle Ages in part invented in the 19th century. To

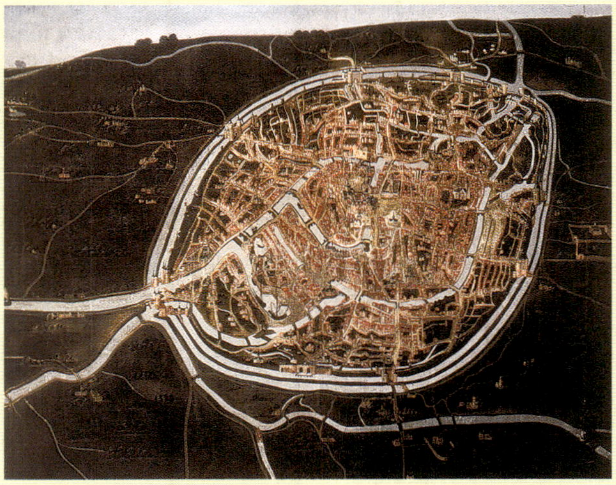

2

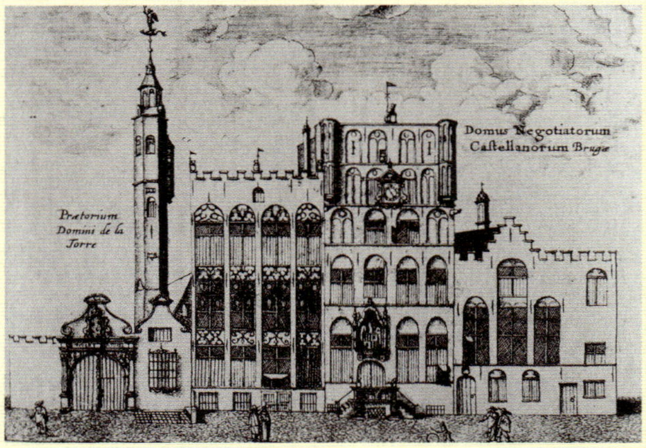

3

stage history in form of *tableaux vivants*, however, was part of the picturesque self-understanding (or rather self-mythologising) of Bruges as early as in 1515, when a pageant for Prince Charles's Triumphal Entry was organised. Still, even back then, the tableaux the city council was responsible for told a different story than those entrusted to the Franc of Bruges and the foreign merchant communities. (3) The uncertainty in Bruges regarding its relationship with Spanish Catholic rule resulted, with the help of troops from Ghent, in the installation of a Calvinist Republic in 1578, until Alexander Farnese forced the city to again embrace Spanish rule in 1584. The split from the Netherlands led to the decline of the city and although Bruges merchants still traded with England, the Spanish empire and the Indies, it slowly sank into poverty. In the mid-19th century Bruges was the poorest city in the country. French became the official language for public life in 1885, although many inhabitants only spoke their local dialect. It was at this time that Georges Rodenbach made the city famous in literature with his symbolist novel *Bruges-la-Morte* (1892). In this story, the city is the setting of an ill-fated love affair between the widower Hugues Viane and a young actress, and Rodenbach's evocation of the quiet streets and the dark, mirroring waters of the channels makes Bruges an allegory of past memories, but also of abandonment and amnesia.

Rodenbach here already raised the issue of the preservation of the medieval atmosphere of Bruges versus the practical benefits of an economical upswing. In Bruges, the Gothic Revival, which was seen as the only style adequate to the Catholic identity of the city, contributed to the present late-medieval image, which is a mixture of the 'real' Middle Ages and a revived (or rather restaged) Medievalism created in the 19th and 20th centuries (illustration 3). This image is successfully marketed by the city – millions of tourists come every year. When Bruges became cultural capital of Europe in 2002, a comprehensive new preservation programme was started which included the restoration of the Church of Our Lady, St John's Hospital, the Chapel of the Holy Blood and many other monuments. Nevertheless, the city council and the *Bruges 2002* organisation were keen to stress that new architecture must be part of the picture. Most of the new projects, like the pedestrian bridge by the Swiss engineer Jürg Conzett and the pavilion by Toyo Ito are on a smaller scale. The only large structure and the most important piece of contemporary architecture – as well as the largest investment – was the Concert Hall.

The competition called for a building for all kinds of musical performances: philharmonic concerts, opera performances and chamber music recitals – not an easy task, since they all require different acoustic conditions. The international competition was won by Paul Robbrecht and Hilde Daem over participants such as Neutelings Riedijk Architects, Stéphane Beel Architects, Kisho Kurokawa, Van Gerkan, Marg & Partner, Jo Coenen, Michael Hopkins and Peter Eisenman.

The most interesting proposals were submitted by Neutelings Riedijk Architects, Stéphane Beel Architects and Peter Eisenman. The proposal by Neutelings Riedijk was a 'decorated duck' (illustration 4) - a 'cartoon character' who had just arrived from the country, proudly wearing a lacy coat, sticking her neck out with some suspicion toward the city. A total solution indeed: the small footprint pulls the hustle and bustle of the square under the heavy body, which contains the auditorium and chamber music room as vital organs connected to a vertical core. The lacework pattern takes care of the identity issue as a veneer, which can easily be decoded by tourists who find the clichés reconfirmed, while ensuring that the architectural connoisseur does not miss the irony of the solution.

Stéphane Beel's solution (with Lieven Achtergael) (illustration 5) is elegant in an absolutely non-quacky way. His project shows his usual restraint: an elongated slab composed of sections of varying height. The *travertine antiquo* cladding heightens the effect of an urban wall. The range of well-calculated perforations and enclosed surfaces provides a common scale to negotiate between the small scale of the houses and the massive volume of the theatre block. In his review Geert Bekaert contrasted this project with the "two extremes" of Robbrecht & Daem and Neutelings Riedijk, emphasising Beel's resistance to "any temptation towards architectural coquetry or brilliance".(4) Beel shows the greatest reserve against any display of a Bruges iconography, operating entirely on the level of precisely calibrated geometries.

Peter Eisenman's waves (illustration 6), undulating all the way from Santiago de Compostela and Manhattan (cities for which comparable buildings were designed by Eisenman), remind us of the fact that the Golden Age of Bruges under the reign of the Dukes Philip the Good and Charles the Bold was inseparable from the waterway linking the city to the sea, until captains of Spanish ships had enough of running aground and decided to dock in Arnemuiden. It was not the Spanishness of the origin of Eisenman's waves that might have caused some irritation in Bruges, but rather the functional problems caused by putting the spaces underground – and the costs involved.

Obviously, the issue of how the new building should fit into the branding strategies of Bruges was a major issue. Instead of an iconic 'Bilbao effect', capable of attracting international perception and redefining the identity of the city (in which case, Neutelings' proposal would probably have stood out), the mayor spoke about a 'creative ode to Bruges and the dreams of this city'.[5]

Describing their project, Robbrecht and Daem anticipated this lyricism by conjuring up a bucolic vision: "...the building will be of the earth but will seem to float lightly above it: a pastoral building, carried into town on a tide of grass and leaves."[6] This is a world first described in Virgil's *Eclogues*, a middle land between the great city of Rome and the wild marshland, a promise of rural harmony amidst the Americanised Arcadia of Belgian countryside sliced up by efficient motorways.

The new Concert Hall, opened on 20th February 2002, stands quite firmly on the south side of the 't Zand, a large open square that functions as a boundary, a vestibule of the city. It was once the site of a railroad station that penetrated deep into the maze of medieval Bruges and left a void after its relocation. Motor traffic now flows along its Western edge and cars coming from the north enter an underpass near the 'lantern tower' of the new building. The long west façade with its heavy volumetrics serves as an announcement of arrival. On this side, the roof of a bus station and lines of trees underline the flow of traffic.

Flows determine the site: the linear movement along its west side and the organisation of the medieval town, encircled by water channels. The motorway has a tangential relationship to the old town; a roundabout directs the flow of car traffic close to the concert hall. This turbulence of encircling and intersecting movements is echoed in the internal topography of the building. The very first sketches by Robbrecht & Daem already show this idea of organisation, with the bottle-shaped large hall and the quadratic chamber music hall as an outpost, as one claw of a lobster. The unusual shape reveals that it is the result of understanding the urban form of Bruges as a 'shape of time', rather than an ensemble of individually crafted artefacts. Rodenbach already understood the loops of water encircling Bruges in this sense, as trajectories of events. The *'promenade architecturale'* is not a linear progress of time, but a circuitous journey with unexpected reappearances.

Rodenbach's *Bruges-la-Morte* was originally published with a careful selection of photographs relating to the text. A picture which resonates with the much-published view of the Concert Hall shows a large saddle-roofed house with the three towers in the background (illustration 7). It is associated with the following comment: *'Ah! ces cloches de Bruges ininterrompues, ce grand office des morts sans répit psalmodié dans l'air!'* [7] The quoted comment of the architects on the bucolic atmosphere of the Concert Hall shows a similar perception. The ringing of bells, floating gently yet mournfully over the fields, is evoked by the familiar image of the *campanile*, the start of a *largo*, a sweeping movement toward the fly tower of the large auditorium. This movement is augmented by the minor theme in the foreground: an embracing counter-movement concluding the flat-topped tower in the west.

4

5

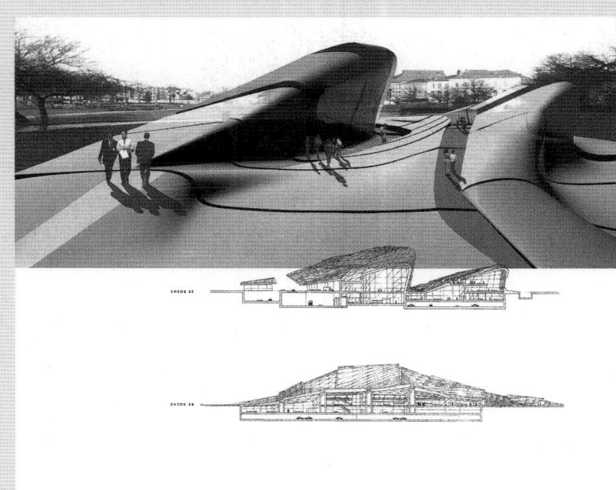

6

7

8

9

The interplay between 'foreground' and 'background' must be seen in a larger context. Seen from a distance, the volume looms large over the small medieval town of Bruges – a view presented in watercolour for the competition (illustration 1). The three slender towers of the Church of Our Lady, St Salvador and the Belfry, with their finely structured and nervous stone and brick architecture are still the dominant verticals in the view, while the flat roofs of the concert hall towers underline the horizon and create a stage for the three actors with clear physiognomies (illustration 8). The architects connected this image with the tradition of Bruges painting: "Coming into Bruges by car or train, one sees a scene like a medieval painting: a compact city encircling the three distinctive towers of the Church of Our Lady, St Salvador and the Belfry. The new concert hall will have a significant presence at the edge of the city, and for this reason we have formed its elements into a composition with an urban stature, which addresses and shapes the immediate vicinity, and joins in the dialogue between the major public buildings."

The reference to medieval painting is not coincidental. The 'ideal' lies in the background: the purple-coloured mountains with noble palaces and fragile church towers. Whatever takes place in the foreground is closer to us in space and time, although what is distant might be of great relevance. The juncture between foreground and background must be connected in our minds, since it is the atmospheric setting of the pastoral. At first glance, the concert hall emerges as an enclosed totality. The parts are all wrapped in terra-cotta so that the impression of a whole cannot be undermined by the fragmented character of the composition. Composition works with parts that are subordinated to a whole, and it is indeed easy to define the main components of the ground plan.

The reference to Bruges is not cartoon-like as in Neutelings' decorated duck; the observer perceives the ceramic substance of Bruges, but the terra-cotta is not *really* brick masonry, it does not support. We see no mortar joints, masonry is replaced by a smooth skin of ceramics that opens at places like a veil: pieces of terra-cotta are held in place by metal rods.

This solution is familiar and disturbing at the same time. The homogeneity of the volume goes against the analytical thinking that the German architect and theorist Gottfried Semper used to identify the ontological and phenomenological status of the elements of the architectural artefact. He distinguished between earthwork (terrace), wall, roof and the hearth (fireplace). Each of these elements corresponds with an archi-technology and a material. For instance, earthwork is a work of stereotomy, the layering of stones; the wall is woven and therefore its surface is 'textured' accordingly; and the roof is a work of tectonics, a wooden frame. The Semperian analysis requires a clear distinction between the building parts, paying particular attention to the juncture (or joint) between them, and a detailing that takes the origin of the element into consideration. But the Concert Hall goes against Semper's basic principles: there is no visible difference between roof and wall and even the rain gutter is well hidden.

Instead of providing a robust basis for the wall, the building rests on colours (illustration 9). *Levitation*, the miraculous appearance of a building floating gently above the spread of autumn leaves, is what the architects tried to conjure up. The inversion of heaviness into weightlessness brings the hollow bodies of musical instruments into mind, which for the sake of maximum resonance only touch the ground in the lightest of ways. The large cavities are tied together by wrapping a connecting layer around them, which makes the geometry ambivalent. The analogy between the layering of the building and the layering of the historical substance of Bruges is significant. The result is a specific object, whose identity – even its primary geometrical identity – cannot be easily determined by the observer. Walking around the building, a previous impression needs to be replaced by a new one: finally, the visitor tries to fit all of these impressions into one 'master view', reconstructing the 'true' volumetrics.

Our doubts regarding the dominance of the eye in the process of understanding (adequate in case of a concert hall) reappear when we look at the large funnel-shaped window on the north façade. Large 'picture windows' were important in modern architecture, as they allowed the inhabitant of a space inside the building to take visual control over the outside as well. Here the window is not simply a glazed opening in the façade but a window-object. In 1990, Robbrecht and Daem had previously used a large reflecting window-mirror on the façade of their BACOB bank building in Kortrijk. In Bruges, the protruding funnel-shape of the window, which corresponds with the geometry of the concert hall, reminds one of Russian revolutionary posters stressing the importance of broadcasting to the masses. The window indeed functions as a projection screen displaying the performance inside during concerts. At other times, one can look through and observe the movements and shadows of people strolling in the lobby. The framed picture was described by the inventors of perspective as an open window in a wall, dissolving differences between constructed perspective and real space, and inviting the observer to move into the depth. The strategically placed mirror in Jan van Eyck's portrait of the Arnolfini couple creates a telescopic extension of space like an endless tube, a tunnel that also reflects the 'outside' world in front of the picture, including the painter himself. The large window-screen in Bruges is an even more mysterious object than a mirror in a painting. As the perspective can no longer claim the status of the only 'true image' of reality, superimposed projections adequately express our understanding of the world, blurring the boundaries of commercial advertising and high culture.

Similarly, the movement inside the building is accompanied by a sequence of pictures: views of the surroundings, such as the tower of the Church of Our Lady, are treated as large illuminated transparencies of tourist sites. The picture frame is a device for estrangement, a strategy proposed by Russian formalists: living in a world full of images, it is increasingly difficult to distinguish between truth and representation. The rhetoric of the image that Dutch painters developed meant looking at the image as such, as representation executed with precision and virtuosity. Frames in a building designed for performance similarly make the claim that the observer must engage works of architecture, music and theatre on their own terms as autonomous forms of expression, rather than just 'looking through' them like panes of glass, searching for a hidden meaning.

The *promenade architecturale* inside the Concert Hall invites and rewards the visitor with views which are also directed at the raw concrete crevices, ramps and stairs of the interior. The dominant axiality of the structural walls emerges from the plan like a cross-hair: one axis is connected to the eastern wall of the chamber music room and with the western wall of the large auditorium and stage. The other axis is defined by the interior wall of the foyer. The origin of the cross-hair is a spatial pivot, accentuated by a concrete 'carpentry' that recalls monumental medieval tectonics as well as early experiments with concrete 'tracery' – to find the identity of the new material. The philharmonic auditorium and the chamber music room are two different ways of listening to music and two different concepts of the interior-exterior relationship. The chamber music room in the lantern tower, to seat 350, is inspired by models of the courtyard performance spaces in Italian palaces and Shakespeare's theatre. The audience is seated on balconies along a spiralling ramp – a solution which lacks the intimacy of a *cortile*. It is probably the result of the same process of dislocating Mediterranean images that Italian painters referred to as *alla ponentina*, to underline their strange Gothic appearance and lack of tactility.

The solution for the large concert hall shows Robbrecht and Daem's interest in Baroque lighting effects. The clerestories of this hall, which seats 1300, allow skylight to penetrate into the interior, not only to make it usable as a convention hall, but (thanks to the mixture of artificial and natural light) to create special atmospheres. The general mood of this hall is festive and sober, kept in tones of white, grey and black. To provide

10

optimal acoustics, Robbrecht and Daem designed, in cooperation with the engineers, a cladding of ridged wood and plaster punctuated with colour accents. We associate the use of patterns and colour systems with theories of harmony. The colour scheme in the Concert Hall is based on Le Corbusier's *claviers de couleurs* (illustration 10). The dominant tone, the terra-cotta of the outside cladding, is complemented by the grey of the concrete interiors. Between the two poles, the whole spectrum of colours is used on banisters, panelling and doors. This is the same scheme that – like the interior lining of a jacket – unexpectedly appears as a strip disconnecting the terra-cotta envelope from the ground.

The stripes on the furniture (illustration 11) (the benches are available now as the Ligeti bench) connect the colour scheme with Le Corbusier's *claviers de couleurs*: a keyboard of scales, rhythms and chords. Le Corbusier invented these colour keyboards for his clients. He writes: "All of us, according to our taste and reactions, favour one or more dominating schemes of colour. Each individual is drawn towards some particular harmony, which seems to accord with his inner feelings. The particular difficulty is to show colours in such a way that the individual can detect his own 'affinity'."(8) Rather than prescribing the colours, the client can use them with the guidance of the keyboard, to express 'his joy in life.'

Schelling called architecture "frozen music", and Goethe, referring to Schelling's remark, spoke of architecture as "spatialised music" (Musik im Raume).(9) It is easy to find musical references in the Concert Hall. Edgar Varèse's *Poème electronique*, composed for Le Corbusier's Philips Pavilion in Brussels, is one of the sound installations in the lobby and the architecture magnifies the expressive dimension of music. The building resonates not only with sound, but with memories of landscapes, towns, buildings and paintings. The architects use the term 'displacement' when they talk about the historic and contextual references that the building makes to Bruges, and to architectural history in general. In their description of the competition entry they explain: "Just as the Town Hall and Belfry recall with uncanny precision the Palazzo Pubblico in Siena, our concert hall can be seen as a further act of displacement, taking some of the formal and informal aspects from the city's centre, and forming a strong presence on 't Zand (...)" (10)

The lantern tower is related to the flat-topped church towers of the Bruges sea coast, which were used as beacons for ships; now it serves as a beacon for motorists. The complex concrete beam structure finds its predecessors in the masterful carpentry

11

of huge medieval barn roofs. Baroque precedents, Palladian memories, Semper and Garnier - the genealogy suggested by the architects in their statements reconfirms a reflective understanding of architecture, according to which "our time is the entire historical time known to us".(11) A very obvious reference to the building tradition of Bruges is the use of terra-cotta; a brick building would have been a too straightforward contextualism, resulting in a heavy masonry structure. Terra-cotta is able to maintain a clear connection, but in a much more indirect and subtle way.

Displacement as an interpretational model provided by Robbrecht and Daem raises interesting questions. Displacement confirms and denies the place at the same time. The idea that we are not in our 'real' place is as old as human history. The references to the 'real' place are plenty – just as in the paintings already described: the Arcadian landscapes, the paradise – the first and perfect space that is still undivided – exist as fragments that can be reinstalled in the framework of an artefact. In this sense, architecture is always dislocation. One can see the whole history of architecture as a chain of displacements, as references in architectural history are generally indirect; the individual talent of the architect can be seen in the originality of the interpretation of precedents: the antique orders displace the wooden posts of Adam's house in paradise or Solomon's temple. The *architecture rationelle* of the late Seventies reflected the nostalgia for re-location. But Robbrecht and Daem did not conjure up the image of an Italian town in Bruges; the multiplicity of their references gives the place an instability and multi-temporality. The image they present is blurred and diffuse, detached from any concrete place. They precisely locate the volume on 't Zand – and at the same time they succeed in 'escaping' from Bruges, in order to inhabit an ideal, floating, musical space.

This space is, of course, not permeated by the melancholy of *Bruges-la-Morte*, as today such a display of heroic identity (in a Don Quixote sense) becomes increasingly outdated, and even ridiculous. The irony in the image of Neutelings' decorated duck is a very clear display of the new pleasures of self-deconstruction. However, the 'pastoralism' of Robbrecht and Daem shows that there are other options that reflect our recent understanding of identity, without choosing irony as the main mode of rhetoric. A display of hybridity and fragmentation takes the place of earlier visions of integrity. It is probably less the strategy of displacement of historical precedents than the challenge to established models of perception that makes this building important. Transparency is challenged by the reestablishment of light as *lux* in its various appearances, isotropic space by the diversity of intersecting itineraries, block-like identity by a repertoire of possibilities. This does not mean that the idea of identity has been abandoned altogether, on the contrary: the identity of the object is the result of a non-monolithic, more complex understanding of the historic construction of Flemish identity.

Illustrations

1. Collage Concertgebouw, © Paul Robbrecht and Hilde Daem, Gert Swolfs.

2. Map of Bruges, Anonymous master after 1546. Bruges, Groeningemuseum, from: *Bruges and the Renaissance.* Exhibition catalogue Bruges, 1998.

3. The Castilian merchants 'Della Torre' house. Antonius Sanderus, Flandria illustrata, from: *Bruges and the Renaissance.* Exhibition catalogue Bruges, 1998.

4.5. 6. Illustrations in the publication on the competition of the Concertgebouw.

7. Photograph from Georges Rodenbach's novel, *Bruges-La-Morte*, reprint Paris, 1998.

8. View on Bruges from the Concertgebouw, © Karin Borghouts.

9. Detail Concertgebouw, © Karin Borghouts.

10. Le Corbusier's color keyboards from the first Salubra collection, 1931, from: Arthur Rüegg, ed., *Polychromie architecturale.* Basel, Boston, Berlin 1997.

11. Detail Concertgebouw, © Karin Borghouts.

Footnotes

1. Steven Jacobs, 'Introduction', in Kristiaan Borret et al, *Homeward: Contemporary Architecture in Flanders*, Antwerp, deSingel International Arts Center, 1998, pp. 14-15.

2. Roel Jacobs, *Brugge, een stad in de geschiedenis*, Brugge, Van de Wiele, 1997.

3. Wim Blockmans, 'Fondans en melencolie de povreté', in Maximiliaan P. J. Martens (ed.), *Bruges and the Renaissance*, Ghent, Ludion, 1998, pp. 26-32.

4. Geert Bekaert, 'Operating Instructions for Architecture: A Century of Architecture in Belgium', in Mil De Kooning (ed.), *Horta and After*, 2nd ed., Ghent, Department of Architecture and Urbanism, Ghent University, 2001, p. 45.

5. Patrick Moenaert, 'Voorwoord', in *Tentoonstelling Concertgebouw Stad Brugge*, p. 3.

6. Paul Robbrecht, Hilde Daem, *Bruges Concertgebouw*, text on the competition entry

7. 'Uninterruptedly, the bells of Bruges fulfilled their function of mourners, pouring without respite psalmody into the air.' Georges Rodenbach, *Bruges-la-Morte*, Paris, Flammarion, 1998, pp. 198-199.

8. Le Corbusier, 'Colour keyboards', in Arthur Rüegg (ed.), *Polychromie architecturale: Le Corbusier's Color Keyboards from 1931 and 1959*, Basel/ Boston/Berlin, Birkhäuser, 1997, p. 150.

9. Friedrich Wilhelm Joseph von Schelling, 'Philosophie der Kunst' (1802-1803), in Schelling, *Ausgewählte Schriften*, Band 2, Frankfurt am Main, Suhrkamp, 1985, p. 404.

10. *Bruges Concertgebouw* (see note 6).

11. Josef Frank, *Architektur als Symbol: Elemente deutschen neuen Bauens*, 1931, reprint Vienna, Löcker, 1981, p. 166.

The author thanks William Mann, the office of Paul Robbrecht and Hilde Daem and the Flemish Architectural Institute for their remarks and information used in this essay.

I

FLANDERS CULTURAL NEBULAR CITY

Cultural infrastructure in a Horizontal Urban Landscape

Wouter Davidts

"Passaic centre loomed like a dull adjective. Each 'store' in it was an adjective unto the next, a chain of adjectives disguised as stores. ... Actually, Passaic centre was no centre – instead it was a typical abyss or an ordinary void. What a great place for a gallery! Or maybe an 'outdoor sculpture show' would pep that place up!" Robert Smithson

In his 1967 essay *A Tour of the Monuments of Passaic*, the artist Robert Smithson reports on his trip to Passaic, a place in the suburbs of New Jersey.(1) Smithson lyrically describes the generic character of the post-industrial landscape he encounters on his 'suburban Odyssey'. Passaic doesn't offer picturesque views, iconic buildings or relics of a glorious past, only a juxtaposition of places and things that rival each other in their dullness and insignificance. This bit of suburbia exists without the 'big events' of history. Nor does it have an illustrious future.

According to Smithson it is doomed to bathe in a lethargic present. All you can find are 'memory traces of an abandoned set of futures'. The only monuments Smithson discerns in the 'zero panorama' of Passaic vary from a rusty steel bridge, a pumping derrick with a set of pontoons, a sand-box, gushing pipes to an extensive asphalt car lot. In comparison with the urban density of New York, the peripheral Passaic seems full of 'holes'. It does not have a centre: it is both unoccupied and absent. It triggers Smithson's imagination. The vacant centre is the perfect location for an art gallery. Or, even better, the ideal remedy for its lifelessness is an open-air exhibition.

BUILDING A CULTURAL IMAGE

At the start of the 21st century, there is not much irony left in Smithson's proposal. All over the world, art – or culture in general – is used as a lubricant for the revitalisation of post-industrial cities. To reanimate their centres, many cities no longer call upon their industrial or economic potential. Their capital has become ever more symbolic. Profitable cities need a specific image or profile, preferably cultural, commercial or recreational in nature. Since the early eighties, all manner of cultural programmes – infrastructure and/or festivities – have been employed to breathe new life into city centres and put the sparkle back in their faded blazons.

Many cultural institutions – headed by art museums – originate from the conviction and the wish that they can pep up the reputation of a city. Since the erection of the Guggenheim Museum in Bilbao city officials know the success formula: take the decision to build a new cultural institution, seek a strategic spot in the city, organise a large-scale architectural competition between the stars of the architectural firmament, and ultimately choose the design with the greatest iconic appeal. A competition that results in a signed landmark elicits considerable attention from the local, national and international press, perhaps even public controversy and, later, undoubtedly the expected tourism dynamic and the desired economic yield. A prestigious and powerful building such as the Guggenheim Bilbao puts a city 'on the world map'. Moreover, the building and the city are

2

constantly identified with one another. Whenever one mentions 'Bilbao', the building is always implied. The building operates as the icon, the sign and the logo of the city, all at once.

Buildings are not the only means of pepping-up waning city centres. For a few years there has also been an increasing 'festivalisation' of urban development. Such temporary events as world exhibitions, Olympic Games, football championships and cultural festivals provide the opportunity to focus on the 'unique assets' of a city, for a short time but with great intensity. Moreover, these events often function as a lever to realize missing urban or cultural infrastructure, such as a new subway line, a sports stadium, a station, a museum, a theatre or a concert hall. By means of an architectural competition the whole building process is guaranteed a place within the event logic. After all, a competition is an event in itself. A disgruntled participant, a controversial selection by the jury or a scandalised public may transform a competition into a real happening that, long before the actual event starts, is extensively covered by the media. Many still remember the public uproar concerning the competition for the Concert Hall in Bruges. But any forthcoming festival can use a little controversy. It draws attention and lets everyone know that something is about to happen.(2)

Over the last two years the Flemish architectural landscape has been enriched by a notable number of projects with a cultural programme or which ensue from a cultural event: the ModeNatie and the Winkelhaak design centre in Antwerp, the STUK in Leuven, the Beursschouwburg in Brussels, a temporary bridge for Anno '02 in Kuurne, and the Concert Hall, the pavilion and the pedestrian bridge for Brugge 2002. This range of projects raises several questions. It seems to insinuate that Flanders too is plagued by a cultural building boom. But is this really the case? Are we dealing with a trend? Do we really have a tradition in using prestigious cultural projects as city-marketing trumps? How does Belgium in general relate to its neighbours when it comes to cultural infrastructure and festivities? Aren't we fearfully attempting to catch up?

MUSEUM ARCHITECTURE IN FLANDERS?

There has never been anything like a 'museum boom' in Belgium. On the contrary, 'museum aversion' would befit us more. Compared to the neighbouring countries, which are undeniable leaders in this museum boom, the Belgian crop is rather thin. There is not a single Belgian city that is the proud owner of a prominent museum building by a well-known 'museum architect' like Alvaro Siza, Renzo Piano, Richard Meier, Frank Gehry or Hans Hollein. In the 1995 *Contemporary Architecture in Belgium*, Geert Bekaert counts just five museums worth mentioning: the Gallo-Roman Museum in Buzenol (Constantin Brodzki, 1960), the Museum of the Scheldt and Leie Area in Deinze (J. Van Den Bogaerde, J. Van Driessche and H. De Witte, 1981), the Museum at Mariemont (Roger Bastin, 1967), the Museum of Modern Art in Brussels (Roger Bastin, 1984) and the Gallo-Roman Museum in Tongeren (Alfredo De Gregorio and Michel Jaspers, 1994).(3) But none of these are architectural *tours de force*, let alone projects with an international reputation. Belgian officials refused to seize the opportunities.

One might almost suspect them of wanting to distance themselves from the museum boom. Why else did they, at such a strategic location as the Kunstberg in Brussels, bury a whole museum underground; and why else are the three museums of contemporary art housed in lamentable existing buildings – a supermarket, a grain silo and a casino? In a previous yearbook, Steven Jacobs rightly described the conversion of the Provincial Museum of Modern Art in Ostend (PMMK, F. Sohier and I. Morel, 1982 & 1990), the Museum of Contemporary Art in Antwerp (MuHKA, Michel Grandsard, 1987 & 1993) and the Municipal Museum of Contemporary Art in Ghent (SMAK, Koen van Nieuwenhuyse, 1999) as "a grotesque string of freaks."(4)

Prominent Belgian architects were forced to go abroad to get important museum commissions. Robbrecht and Daem transformed an old railway roundhouse into a showcase for the excellent Hauser & Wirth contemporary art collection in Sankt Gallen, designed the extension to the Boijmans-Van Beuningen Museum in Rotterdam and are working on the future expansion of the Whitechapel Art Gallery in London; Stéphane Beel designed the extension to the Central Museum in Utrecht. Beel also designed the only newcomer worth mentioning in Belgium: the monographic museum for Roger Raveel in the artist's native village of Machelen-aan-de-Leie. Here too, the international trends were challenged. The Flemish Government ultimately decided to build a new, high-quality museum, but it is devoted to the work of a single artist and located in an unsightly village halfway along the road from Ghent to Kortrijk; not exactly a metropolitan setting (illustration 2). Machelen-aan-de-Leie lies 'in the provinces', a stone's throw from Roeselare, Tielt and Oudenaarde. You simply can not reach it without a car.

The Raveel Museum lies in the midst of what is commonly called the Flemish 'nebular city'. This term has been used since the early nineties to describe the morphological structure of sprawl and the horizontal urbanisation of Flanders. The classical distinction between centre and periphery, city and country, has become utterly blurred by the decentralisation of living and working. Flanders is completely covered by a misty layer of urbanity that hardly has a centre. Nowadays one finds urban amenities in hangars just as much as in old city centres. However, the term 'nebular city' can be used to discuss the socio-cultural landscape of Flanders too. Sprawl befits not only Flanders' scenery, but its culture and cultural policy as well. The discursive potential of the term is threefold: it allows one to reflect on the amalgam of cultural institutions, on the accompanying infrastructure and on the overall policy.

BELGIUM, FLANDERS, ETCETERA

The widespread fragmentation of the cultural landscape goes back to the federalisation or decentralisation of cultural policy in Belgium in 1971. At that time the various language communities were given authority over their own cultural policy and financial resources. The consequences of this decision can still be felt in Brussels, where no less than six authorities hold sway. Any project concerning Brussels – and therefore by definition involves several communities – is, precisely because of this lack of an all-embracing cultural policy, doomed to fail. (5) In Flanders the situation is little better. The policy of most of its ministers of Culture has always been characterised by a search for 'broadening'.

A recent Flemish Government campaign was headed with the slogan that 'Culture is a feast for everyone' (illustration 3). In order to enable as many people as possible to actively experience culture, the government is investing in local initiatives and institutions. "It doesn't always have to be *culture with a capital C*," was the noteworthy subtitle. This credo automatically reminds us of the ideology behind one of the most remarkable cultural projects of the past: the mass construction of cultural centres in the late sixties. Even before cultural autonomy was introduced, a group of sociologists carried out an in-depth study of the cultural infrastructure throughout Flanders, not just in the major towns and cities.

They inevitably came to the conclusion that it was virtually nonexistent and full of shortcomings. Stimulated by the then Flemish minister of Culture, Mr Van Mechelen, a major building programme for cultural centres in small and medium-sized towns was initiated. Culture had to be brought to the people and – similar to politics, economy and education – democratised. It was against this background of cultural dissemination and the nascence of a provincial network of cultural centres that the present nebular city took shape (illustration 4). After homes and jobs left the core cities, the cultural centres initiated the suburbanisation and sprawl of cultural life. (6)

The cultural centre project was the first and last time the government coupled an ambitious vision with an actual investment in infrastructure (in this case new). Therefore the whole operation is even more typical of the overall policy of the Flemish Government. It has never distinguished itself when it comes to coherence. Nebulous spreading is probably more appropriate. Something for everyone: some a little more, some a little less. After all, the construction of cultural centres took place without consideration of the existing network of cultural institutions, such as theatres and museums.

They represented a middle-class, asocial and elite culture and were thus neglected, although the infrastructure of the museums had always been rather restrained. In 1971 the notorious museum advocate Karel Geirlandt rightly labelled the museums the 'Cinderellas' of the cultural family, in terms of both resources and infrastructure. (7) The result was that until the late eighties Flanders suffered from a structural deficiency of official exhibition spaces and that contemporary art was forced by sheer necessity onto the fringe. Before such institutions as the PMMK, MuHKA and SMAK were able to enjoy definitive and, above all, their own accommodation, they led, of necessity, a ghostlike existence in other buildings, even in other cities. As a result of political unwillingness and policy tussles, each of them suffered a series of temporary homes, successive moves and vain plans for 'new buildings'. The three 'conversions' that ultimately took place were in fact stopgap solutions rather than the result of articulate policy decisions. In Brussels there is still no official institution that guarantees a long-term and structural commitment to contemporary art. So an *Einzelgänger* like the Raveel Museum cannot disguise the fact that the balance of artistic infrastructure in Flanders is still extremely poor. (8) It took a long time before we had fully-fledged institutions, let alone appropriate buildings.

TWO HOURS WIDE OR TWO HOURS LONG (9)

Because of the structure lack of important cultural institution, the artistic sector of Flanders has always been marked by a marginal position and identity. Flanders, and by extension Belgium, is at the heart of Europe, but on the periphery of the international art world. In relation to such artistic capitals as New York, Paris and London, Flanders was and still is an artistic suburbia. We lack such major institutions as the Museum of Modern Art, Tate Modern and the Centre Pompidou. On the artistic world map Belgium is, to borrow Douglas Coupland's description, nothing but "a drive-thru nation". (10)

Many interesting people pass through, but they don't stay long. In a special Belgian issue of the art magazine *Studio International* in 1974, Barbara Reise, in her article '"Incredible" Belgium: Impressions', linked Belgium's status as an artistic suburbia to its dense highway network. She thereby grasped the problem from a double perspective. While the highway network generated the spatial nebular city, it perpetuated the fragmentation of the cultural landscape as well: according to Reise, the great advantage of the Trans-European highways is

3

4

that they allow people "to pass through Belgium without stopping" (illustration 1). [11] When Reise did at long last stop in Belgium, she was full of praise for the 'social aesthetics' to which she was treated. Belgium has always enjoyed a hearty reputation as a result of its many eccentric personalities – artists, private collectors, gallery owners and curators – and unorthodox places. The nebulous government policy has never really stood in the way of a dynamic bottom-up artistic climate. The reception of modern art in Flanders simply took place away from the museums. Flanders – and the cities of Brussels and Antwerp in particular – is widely known abroad for its sparkling artistic scene and its lively activities in contemporary art. However, closer scrutiny of the output reveals that the scene is largely characterised by a well-developed private sector, comprising a great many private initiatives of a temporary and changing nature. [12]

These organisations are valuable, but rarely transcend their alternative and improvised character. Moreover, their private basis reinforces the nebulous quality of the Flemish cultural landscape. A mist of initiatives hangs constantly over Flanders, but it rarely gets to solidify. Various organisations sponge on institutions and buildings, but they do not install any proper network that guarantees durable operation. Because of unstable subsidy policy or the simple reason that curators seek out more lucrative and more reliable positions (abroad), foreign art lovers frequently encounter closed doors or a deserted building. Major players disappear from one day to the next, and with them the 'institution' they had founded and developed. This ever-fluctuating web of places is often designated as the key to Flanders' exciting and dynamic artistic scene. But this argument conceals the fact that the government continues taking *ad hoc* decisions, does not make structural commitments and thus only simulates a policy. Symptomatic of this was the collectively reviled system of Cultural Ambassadors which was introduced for some time in the mid-nineties. Flanders' cultural reputation was created by personalities instead of by institutions. The elected ambassadors were supposed to hold up the image of a culturally active hinterland, even if they lacked any proper infrastructure at home.

MISS EUROPE

Once in a while Flanders tries to lift the mist by turning the cultural spotlight on one particular town or city. It is at the very least remarkable that in the relatively short history of the system of Cultural Capitals of Europe, no less than three cities in the 'Flemish diamond' have been nominated: Antwerp in 1993, Brussels in 2000 and Bruges in 2002. Even though Flanders is no bigger than a handkerchief, it has been a three-time prizewinner in the Urban Miss Europe contest.

There may be an overall poverty of infrastructure, there is certainly no lack of festivities. [13] Exhibitions, recitals, open-air concerts, fireworks and other shows are mounted with bravura. Over recent years our cities have been reigned over by such figures as Tintin, Rubens, Van Dyck, Charles V and Jacques Brel, phenomena like fashion and design, and events like the Battle of the Spurs, the birth of the Belgian railways and the construction of the HST line. In these festivities art always plays a major role. There's always at least one art exhibition that brightens up the event and thematises the occasion. Flemish people seem to be endowed with a genuine cult of and expertise in artistic festivities. Strikingly enough, this 'gift' once again originated in the nebulous nature of the artistic infrastructure. Flanders was a cultural Passaic: there were no buildings or institutions to occupy the 'centre'. Therefore people became competent in the second option that Smithson put forward: the organisation of large-scale artistic events.

The obvious absence of any well-developed institutional platform – it was nothing but periphery – or the lack of a high-quality circuit of official museum or exhibition spaces, forced curators in Flanders and Brussels to work 'temporarily' and 'on location': in attics, cellars, flats, abbeys, factories and even churches. Flanders has a remarkable tradition of temporary exhibitions, epitomized by the exploits of Jan Hoet and his Museum of Contemporary Art in Ghent. Acting from his headquarters in the rear of the Museum of Fine Arts, Hoet had a double agenda: his activities in the city and abroad had to establish both a home *and* an identity for his museum. During the exhibition 'Chambres d'Amis' (1986), the undeniable climax of this enterprise, infrastructural shortcomings were adroitly charged with artistic ambitions *and* civic chauvinism. Jan Hoet wanted not only to win an autonomous museum but also to give the city of Ghent national and international artistic status. By putting art into the citizens' houses, the whole city was put on show: its streets, its squares and its parks.

'Chambres d'Amis' was undoubtedly an international trendsetter in the policy of city-marketing. Nowadays, every cultural festivity is accompanied by at least one art exhibition in the public space, in the hope that the site-specific efforts of the artists will highlight the specific cultural character of the town or city. The original artistic and institutional motives have yet surrendered to more worldly ones. The rhetoric of crossing boundaries and breaking down the walls of the museum now only serves, in a roundabout artistic way, to brighten up and draw attention to the urban space for a few months. The main outcome of 'Over the Edges', the miserable successor to 'Chambres d'Amis' in the heart of Ghent in summer 2000, was the large number of visitors and the spectacular turnover by the city centre's commercial enterprises.

In the meantime the format has become so well established that just about every small to medium-sized town in Flanders – from De Panne and Watou to Borgloon, from Tielt and Grimbergen to Zoersel – organizes its own open-air or promenade exhibition: in municipal parks, on abandoned industrial sites, on the sea-front and even in roadside chapels. All these exhibitions and art events produce an overfull summer calendar, but disguise the fact that they merely simulate an artistic platform. Only a haze of artistic activity hangs over our region, which immediately evaporates as soon as the shows conclude. For example, every summer Watou is baptised as the centre of poetry and art. For the rest of the year the silence is audible. In wintertime the stables and farmsteads share the same fate as the pavilions at the Giardini in Venice: only animals are there to occupy them.

NOTHING REALLY ENDS [14]

A nomination as Cultural Capital is highly prized by cities that are not especially noted as vibrant centres of culture. Brugge 2002 aimed for example at a "cultural revaluation", or in other words a release from the city's reputation as a medieval Disneyland for foreign tourists (illustration 5). The European cultural crown provides the licence to deliberately act too big for its boots. But this only becomes a problem when one wants to maintain the 'same elan' afterwards. At the start, every 'intendant' loudly proclaims that the cultural project will not end when the festive year comes to a close. On the contrary, the aim is always to install a long-term cultural platform. The most appropriate medium to achieve this is architecture: it leaves 'lasting traces'. What is more, contemporary architecture 'rejuvenates' a city. Brand new buildings can be used to re-inject a failing architectural policy, or at least give the impression that it is 'under construction'.

Furthermore, when architecture is brought in to create the urban infrastructure that is missing, the return is doubled. The city gets the concert hall, art gallery or museum it always lacked, while simultaneously the image of architectural renewal is conveyed. This procedure however runs the risk of taking the festivities as the yardstick. You cannot create architecture overnight nor do you get rid of it so easily. By contrast, festivities are exceptional situations. They suspend everyday life for a while and have their own temporal and spatial logic: they take place somewhere and they go by. Then routine takes over again. When compiling the brief for a building in the heat of the preparation of a festivity, one quite often overestimates the actual cultural needs and sensitivities or local capacities and expertise. Afterwards, the programmers lack both the indispensable finances to manage and run the institution, and a sufficiently broad social base or the necessary public to fill the space. One only has to think of the purposelessness of the Millennium Dome in London and the recent problems of viability at the Concert Hall in Bruges. What's the use of a spectacular dome construction, when you don't know what to do with it afterwards; why does a concert hall need 1200 seats when, after the opening concert, you can hardly, if ever, hang the 'sold out' sign on the door?

Because of their scale, impact and prestige, this sort of commission is very popular with architects. 'Big buildings' allow them to make urbanistic statements, reconfigure the appearance of the city and at best even change the skyline. However, when the institution is later experienced as misplaced or superfluous, architecture inevitably takes its share of the blame, whether it is a high-quality project or not. Any building gives shape to the ambitions of the client, regardless of how unrealistic they are. So it is up to the architects to decide whether they consider a critical questioning of the client's institutional motives to be part of their design task.

In Bruges, the nomination as Cultural Capital was used as a catalyst for contemporary architecture in the city centre. The intention was to enrich the existing heritage with a few high-quality contemporary buildings and thereby cast off the nostalgic and historicist reputation of its architectural policy. The development of a theoretical discourse was discarded in favour of achieving immediate results 'on the ground'. The result of this ambition is all in all unbalanced. In addition to the impressive concert hall, which was forced through at exceptionally high speed for the start of Brugge 2002, Toyo Ito designed an elegant reception pavilion on the Burg, Jürg Conzett designed an ingenious pedestrian bridge over the Coupure and West 8 reorganised the Canal Island together with Poponcini & Lootens. While many people believe 'a miracle has happened', the Flemish Government Architect, bOb Van Reeth, even trumpeted that Bruges had "finally" put itself on the architectural map of the world. [15] But is this really such a groundbreaking accomplishment? Regardless of their architectural qualities and functional location, have these projects really brought about the desired about-turn in architectural thinking in Bruges? None of the three showpieces – the concert hall, the pavilion and the bridge – fit in with prevailing building practice in Bruges city centre – the first because of its scale and the last two because of their exceptional nature and status. This building practice is still dominated by the renovation of terraced houses and plagued by a compulsory facadism. In addition, the three projects clearly participate in event logic: they are outstanding, symbolic and iconic, they occupy unique locations and are designed by top architects.

So the question is whether they will generate the desired effect in the long term. Does a project like the Concert Hall really get anything moving in Bruges? To what extent does Ito's pavilion succeed in breaking down the fixation on the image of the typical Bruges terraced house? A project that makes a much more significant contribution to this, though it is not one of list of achievements of Brugge 2002, is the Pandreitje housing complex (Haverhals-Heylen) (illustration 6).

This ingenious stacking of homes with courtyards proves that in Bruges' city centre, only a stone's throw from the Burg *and* visible from the Halletoren, there is space for contemporary architecture that does not lapse into an historical pastiche of the brick step-gable and red roof-tiles. This project probably brings about the intended change of mentality in the municipal departments, much more than the 'follies', large and small, built for Bruges, Cultural Capital 2002, would ever do. But a housing project is no obvious choice within the logic of events (cultural or otherwise). Housing is not exactly an exceptional programme, and therefore earns the architect little prestige. Even if there's spectacular architecture involved, this often

5

6

conflicts with the private use. However, an important precedent was provided by the *Blue Moon* project in Groningen in summer 2001, for which no less a person than Toyo Ito conceived the master-plan (illustration 7, 8). Groningen, comparable to Bruges in scale, has a lively tradition of events that put the city and its architecture up for discussion. After a number of events for which top international architects including Zaha Hadid, Bernard Tschumi, Rem Koolhaas and De Solà-Morales were asked to design urban landmarks, mobile theatres *(A Star is Born)* or video pavilions *(What a Wonderful World)*, the organizers decided to change course. For the *Blue Moon* project the centrifugal logic of the city festival – both organisational and infrastructural – was completely reversed. The festivities and accompanying festival architecture were given a place on the periphery, on an abandoned industrial site outside the city.

In addition, five architectural firms (Toyo Ito, Xaveer De Geyter Architects, Foreign Office Architects, Space Group Architects and Tony Fretton) were commissioned to design a home with a semi-public programme for vacant lots in the inner city (illustration 9). [16] For spectacular events you had to go to the outskirts. The city centre only offered five sincere architectural schemes that proposed inventive solutions for the combination of housing and urban functions. A housing project like this would have been truly pioneering and revolutionary in Bruges. The results would probably not have been as eye-catching as the current new buildings, but it would have had a more structural, and certainly a more insistent impact on the urban, primarily residential, fabric of Bruges. But anyway, we can be fairly happy that apart from the oversized concert hall, no new cultural programmes with accompanying buildings have been completed in Bruges. They might just as easily have founded and built a museum of contemporary art. And that would have been the umpteenth small and inevitably provincial museum on Flanders' minuscule territory. It would have perpetuated the Flemish nebular city on both the cultural/institutional as on the urban/infrastructural level.

WHAT NOW?

Up to the present, an *ad hoc* cultural policy with limited resources has been pursued in Flanders. The abundance of regulations that currently apply in this field hardly indicate an overall vision. In the Ministry of the Flemish Community, the same policy material is worked on by a great many actors at an equal number of government levels, so that there is little or no possibility of mutual rapport, let alone an integrated policy plan. This is reflected in the deficient state and miserably low architectural allure of the cultural infrastructure.

But the question is whether we should continue lamenting all this. Six editions after the first architectural year book (of complaints), it is perhaps the moment to take a different tack. Is there any credit to be gained from an epithet like 'Flanders Cultural Nebular City'? A recent report by the Centre for Cultural Sociology at the University of Leuven, commissioned by the Flemish Visual Arts Initiative (IBK), discusses the possible direction Flanders might take in terms of culture, and the visual arts in particular, in the future. [17] How do we deal with the present patchwork of museums, collections, artists, curators, galleries, artists' initiatives, magazines, private collectors, foundations and so on? Should we still try to go against the tide, or can we turn the present situation to our advantage? In other words, should we still try to occupy a central position in the international art world or can we resign ourselves to our present peripheral situation? Can we instrumentalise the suburban status and nebulous nature of artistic Flanders? According to the authors of the report, Pascal Gielen and Rudi Laermans, it is of little avail to compare the Flemish art scene with London or New York.

These world players offer no useful measure. They plead (with a deliberately paradoxical formulation) for the development of a 'central-peripheral' position *and* identity. This does not mean that the cultural nebular city has to be maintained, but rather that a number of its crucial features need to be settled in the overall policy, the amalgam of institutions and their infrastructure. We should no longer try to compete with eminent artistic capitals when it comes to institutions and events. It may be a pity that we have no Tate Modern, Museum of Modern Art or Centre Pompidou in Flanders, but we should no longer moan about it. The basic fact that Flanders lies at the 'centre of Europe' but on the 'periphery of the international art world' sets out the basic markers for a different and perhaps much more interesting mental framework.

Gielen and Laermans suggest that Flanders no longer has the desire and ambition to develop into a capital of the contemporary art world. It is possible to exploit the disparate qualities of the Flemish artistic scene, but only if the region as a whole presents itself as a transit zone and residential area. It is time we take advantage of Reise's insight that the highway network is Belgium's greatest asset. We have to make sure that the interesting people who pass through Flanders *do* stop and interrupt their journey for a while. Hence they need reasons and amenities that distinguish their residency in Flanders from both their starting point and destination. This first and foremost requires a thorough change of mentality at the policy-making level. The decision to consolidate Flanders as a nebular city for the visual arts implies that we programme accordingly. The centre remains vacant and is no longer defined by major institutions. Big events also decline in importance as, following Smithson's remark on Passaic, the suburbs exist without them. [18] The emphasis is put on less spectacular things such as the establishment and validation of study, research and discourse. Instead of competing in the exhibition rat race, Flanders can present itself as a place where the hellish tempo of the art industry is briefly suspended.

In the other sectors of the cultural scene, such as dance, theatre and music, it is of equal importance that one examines *and* decides to what extent the nebulous articulation can be exploited. These sectors also need a coherent vision of future policy, on both the institutional and infrastructural level. However, if all the cultural actors support the project for Flanders Cultural Nebular City, this will have considerable consequences for architectural practice and production. It simply means that in the future we will also miss out on the prestigious cultural projects. But the question is whether we thereby lose that much. Will the decision to erect no more major cultural buildings in Flanders indisputably signify a loss for architecture? We probably have to alter or learn to rethink its role in the cultural landscape. Flanders is in any case the clearest proof that in cultural policy architecture is always both at play and at stake.

7

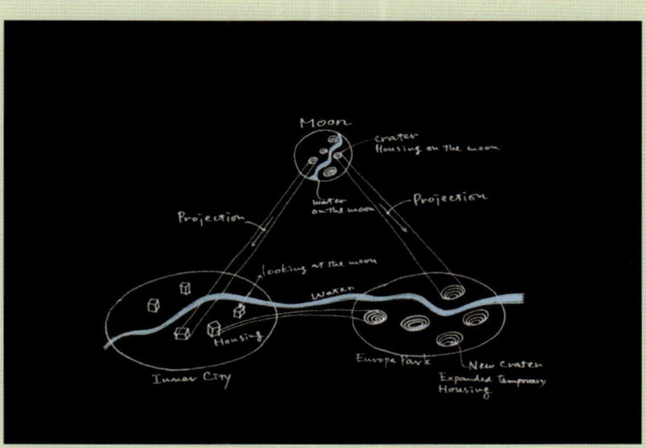

8

9

Illustrations

1. Antwerp, © Jan Kempenaers.
2. Machelen aan de Leie, © website Raveelmuseum.
3. Image of a campaign of the Flemish Community: 'De Vlaamse Overheid. Tot uw dienst', 2003.
4. Ganshoren, © Jan Kempenaers.
5. Poster Brugge 2002, Cultural Capital, © LG&F Advertising.
6. Housing 't Pandreitje, Haverhals-Heylen architecten, © Koen de Waal.

7. 8. Masterplan Blue Moon, Groningen, Toyo Ito.

9. Blue Moon Café, FOA, © Christian Richter.

Footnotes

1. Robert Smithson, 'A Tour of the Monuments of Passaic, New Jersey (1967)' in Jack D. Flam (ed.), *Robert Smithson: The Collected Writings*, Berkeley, University of California Press, 1996, pp. 68-74.

2. In addition, competitions have frequently been employed to legitimise the often still uncertain construction, to mobilise political will or even to generate public support. It is a common fact that organisers hope that as soon as a project has assumed concrete form, vanity and desire will take the upper hand and transform into the will to build. Large budgets are often put by for a competition, while the budget to build the institution and to let it function afterwards are by no means assured. This strategy is extremely popular in Belgium, as demonstrated by the competition for the new KunstenForum De Krook in Ghent. Despite the fact that the minister considered "the dossier for the Forum not yet to be ripe for a definitive decision" and that "the basis is interesting", "but that the project is "not yet fully-matured," a budget of half a million Euro was still made available for an international architectural competition (*Beleidsnota Culturele Infrastructuur 2002-2004*, pp. 5-6). The participants in this competition are Rem Koolhaas, Toyo Ito, Claus & Kaan, Samyn & Partners and Neutelings-Riedijk. The last of these must nevertheless be aware of the disadvantages of this scenario, since it was also used for the Museum aan de Stroom or MAS in Antwerp. Neutelings-Riedijk's design, which was proclaimed the winner of the final stage as early as 2000, is for many reasons, mainly budgetary and organisational, still waiting to get under way.

3. Geert Bekaert, *Hedendaagse Architectuur in België*, Lannoo, Tielt, 1995, p. 57. In the meantime, to this list must be added the ModeNatie (Marie-José Van Hee, 2002) in Antwerp and the MAC's (Pierre Hebbelinck, 2002) in Le Grand Hornu. An examination of the successive Architecture Yearbooks yields an equally short list. The only museums included are the Stedelijk Modemuseum in Hasselt (Simoni, 1995) and the Raveel Museum in Machelen-aan-de-Leie (Stéphane Beel, 1999). One notable 'laureate' is the renovation and conversion of the Belgian pavilion in the Giardini in Venice (Georges Baines, 1997).

4. Steven Jacobs, 'Bakstenen in de Vlaamse nevelstad', in *Jaarboek Architectuur Vlaanderen 1998-1999*, Ministry of the Flemish Community, Brussels, 2000, pp. 39-42.

5. On the dream of a bicommunal cultural project and a bicommunal centre in Brussels in particular, see Dieter Lesage, 'De bicommunautaire conditie/La condition bicommunautaire', in Bert Balcaen, Wouter

Davidts, Dieter De Clercq, Lieven De Boeck and Tijl Vanmeirhaeghe (eds.), *B-SITES. Over de plaats van een kunst- en onderzoekscentrum te Brussel / A propos de la place d'un centre d'art et de recherche à Bruxelles*, Brussel/Bruxelles 2000, Vakgroep Architectuur & Stedebouw, Ghent University, Brussels/Ghent, 2000, pp. 19-26.

6. For this see Maarten Delbeke, Arthur Wortmann, 'Architectuur in Vlaanderen: vechten tegen onveranderlijke scènes en ongeboren catastrofen', in *Archis*, no. 10, 2000, pp. 8-9; Paul Vermeulen, 'Culturele Centra. Een reis door de nevelstad', in Archis, no. 10, 2000, pp. 12-22.

7. Karel Geirlandt, 'Belgian Commentary', in *Studio International*, 183, no. 937, 1971, pp. 148-149.

8. In the Ministry of the Flemish Community's *Beleidsnota Culturele Infrastructuur 2002-2004*, the Raveel Museum is even referred to as a "happy exception".

9. From the title the curator Barbara Vanderlinden gave the contemporary art section in 'The Fascinating Faces of Flanders' exhibition, organised on the occasion of the world exhibition in Portugal in 1998. See the catalogue The *fascinating faces of Flanders : 58/98 two hours wide or two hours long*, Stad Antwerpen, Antwerp, 1998.

10. Douglas Coupland, 'The New Season / Architecture', in *The New York Times*, 11th September 1994: *Drive thru-ness and fluidity*: 'Steven drives along the conveyor belt hyperfreeways of the new Europe and thinks of Belgium as the first drive-thru nation.'

11. Barbara Reise, ''Incredible' Belgium: Impressions', in *Studio International*, 188, no. 970, 1974, p. 117.

12. For an analysis of the role and influence of private initiatives in the Belgian art world, see Koen Brams & Dirk Pültau, 'Het sublieme succes. Over de popularisering van de hedendaagse kunst in België sinds 1992', in Bart De Baere, Jan Denolf, Luk Lambrecht & Paul Tanghe (eds.), *Decennium II*, Ludion, Ghent, 2004.

13. Nor did this escape the attention of Barbara Reise (*'Incredible' Belgium: Impressions*, p. 118). According to some of the people she encountered on her way through Belgium, this is a question of a broadly recognised *'savoir-vivre'*: '... the only thing Belgians automatically agree on is the value of living the good life. "What's that?" I asked. "Good food, good drink, and a festive celebration whenever possible.'

14. From the song title by the Belgian rock group dEUS. This song was played at the close of the farewell ceremony for Bruges Cultural Capital 2002 in the new concert hall.

15. The Flemish Government Architect bob Van Reeth, as quoted in Hugo De Greef (ed.), *Een verhaal in feiten*, Brugge 2002, Bruges, p. 10; *De Volkskrant* headline was 'the three wonders of Bruges'

16. These semi-public programmes comprised, among other things, a creche, an IT company and a café. Only the homes by Foreign Office Architects, Space Group Architects and Tony Fretton have so far been built. For a description of the *Blue Moon* project see Harm Tilman, 'Potenties van vergeten plekken. Het versterken van multifunctionaliteit', in *De Architect*, October 2001, pp. 28-43.

17. Pascal Gielen & Rudi Laermans, Een omgeving voor kunst. *Een toekomstperspectief voor het beeldende kunstlandschap in Vlaanderen*, Lannoo/Centrum voor Kunstsociologie KULeuven/Initiatief Beeldende Kunst, Tielt/Leuven/Ghent, 2004.

18. Robert Smithson, *ibid.*, p. 72.

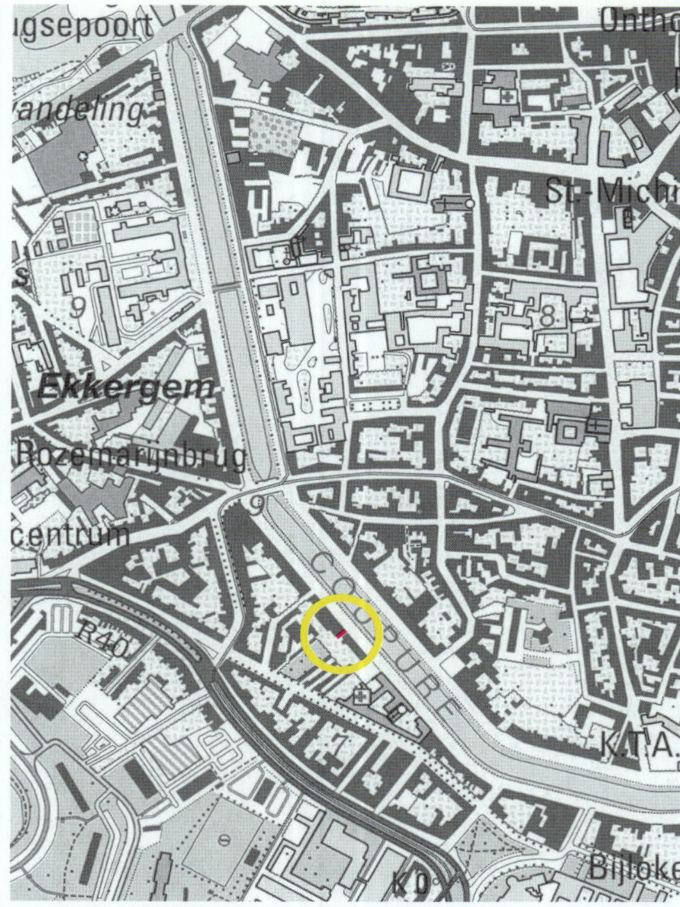

EXTENSION OF HOUSE WITH SCULPTOR'S STUDIO

architect **KRISTOFFEL BOGHAERT**

location Coupure Links 289, 9000 Ghent

client	Philip Van Isacker
design - building	2000-2002
project-workers	Bureau voor Architectuur en Stabiliteit Dirk Jaspaert, Leuven
contracted work	Structural work: Bekaert Betonbouw, Wondelgem
	Woodwork: De Meersman & zonen, Aalst
	Steel: Framac, Temse
area	50 sq. m.
volume	190 cubic. m.
building costs	62,500 EUR
building costs/sq. m	1,250 EUR/m^2
project description	Katrien Vandermarliere
photography	Kristien Daem p.82b,83,85 I André Nullens p.84,86
	Stefan Vandermeulen p.82a

Nothing in the exterior of the fine 19th-century mansion on Coupure leads one to suspect that an exceptional sculptor's studio has been added on in the lower-lying garden at the back. The client, Philipe Van Isacker, previously had a studio elsewhere in the neighbourhood, but had for a long time cherished the desire for a workspace in his own quiet garden. The artist called in Kristoffel Boghaert, giving as his only requirements height and top light. Whereas at first sight the architect's response to the brief appears simple, one gradually becomes aware of its complexity and the intriguing play of light and space.

The classic first floor of the house, in three bays, retained its original function and division after the building work. The one-storey difference in height between the street and the garden was left as it was. However, a change to the circulation means it is used in a completely new way. At the garden level are the secondary living and working functions, and at street level are two study/workrooms running into one another. The first and second floors are for living and sleeping. Two new openings and one blocked-off window give the house a completely new relationship with the garden behind. The new studio appears like a stacking of two concrete volumes cast on the spot. Since the lower building was constructed against the outside wall of the house and the upper building is separated from it, a sort of light court is created between old and new. The position of the windows has been very

precisely defined from inside the studio and in addition to the working light requested they make for a contemplative atmosphere.

This also emphasises the studio as a freestanding volume. The window in the topmost volume is exactly opposite the window of the study/workroom. The short distance between the two does not allow one to see the wooden cladding of the new building. Through the workroom window one sees the window of the studio and the glass surface reflects a brick wall. The view through and the reflection create an interesting visual effect.

In the studio, the rough finish of the concrete walls, with traces of the formwork and untidy joins, are left visible, as a reference to the sculptor's struggle with his material. The floor also has a neutral anthracite-grey polished concrete surface, which is resistant to dust and dirt. The light transforms this hard concrete shell, marked by random graphic patterns, into a serene place. It is only from the garden that one has a view of the overall transformation. The offset between the two new volumes leaves space for an L-shaped terrace that serves as an intermediary between house and garden. From here, open steps descend into the garden. The terrace and the house are connected by a small concrete staircase. The cladding in Afrormosia slats gives a precious impression to the outside of the studio. Six-centimetre slats

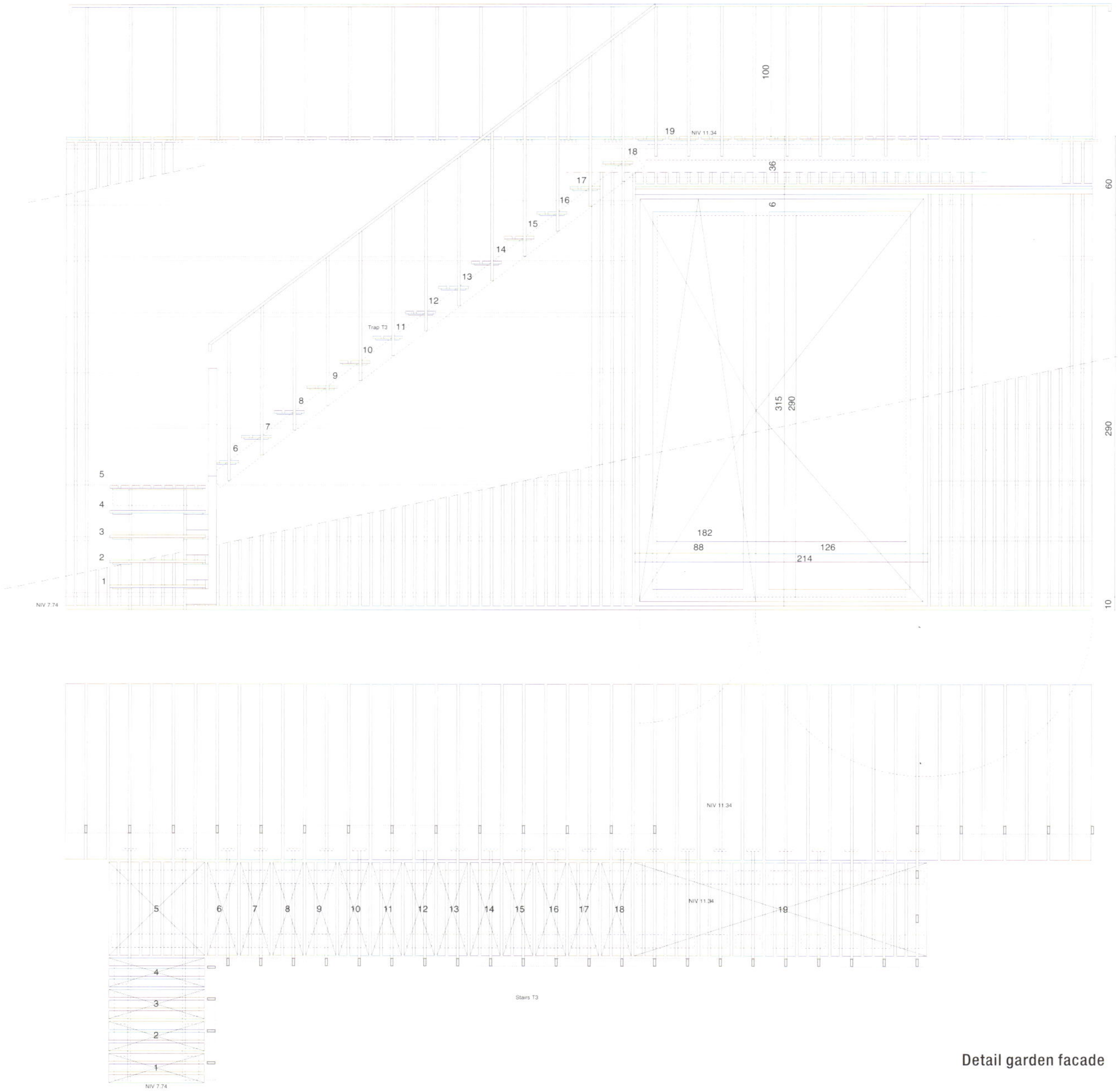

Detail garden facade

alternate with a two-centimetre join. The measurements of the facades, windows, stair-treads, landings, balustrades, parapet and terrace are all multiples of these dimensions.

The corner of the wooden volume was taken as the reference point for setting-out. Both vertically and horizontally the slats run on from each other and fit together perfectly. The railings of the terrace and the steel supporting sections of the treads are inserted into the joints between the wooden slats. They are welded on to a section that is concealed in the batten structure of the facade.

The balustrades and the structure of the stairs are in galvanised steel. All details: wooden slats, supporting sections, railings and woodwork, are characterised by correct proportions, perfect joints and Swiss precision. The tactility of the materials, the play of light and volumes, the proportions, the interaction between solid and void and between inside and outside are features we consider typical of the realm of sculpture. This means the studio is much more reminiscent of a sculpture than of an extension. This simple and sober addition gives the house a new richness and freedom. The existing view is enhanced; new and surprising relationships are created. The concrete shell concealed in its linear wooden grid forms a hidden gem in the garden.

1 studio
2 storage
3 passage
4 entrance hall
5 office
6 void studio
7 terrace
8 garden

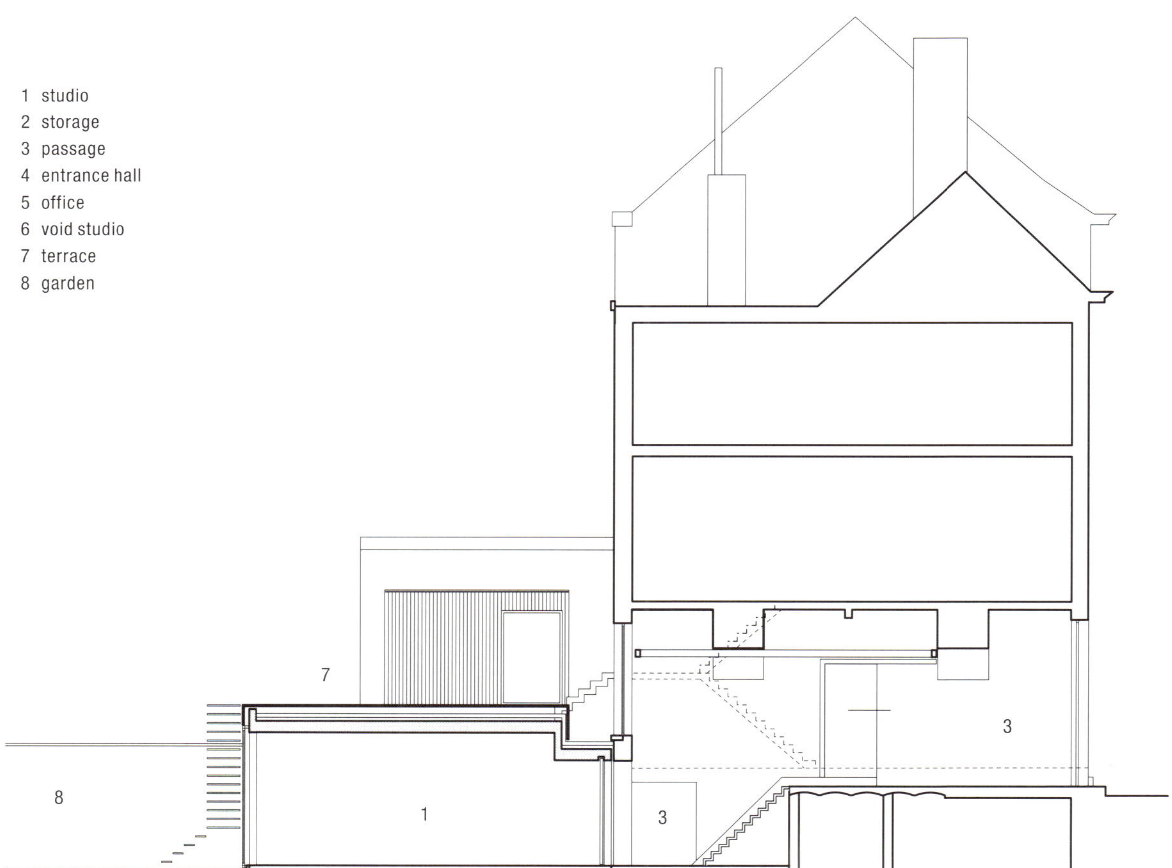

Section AA'

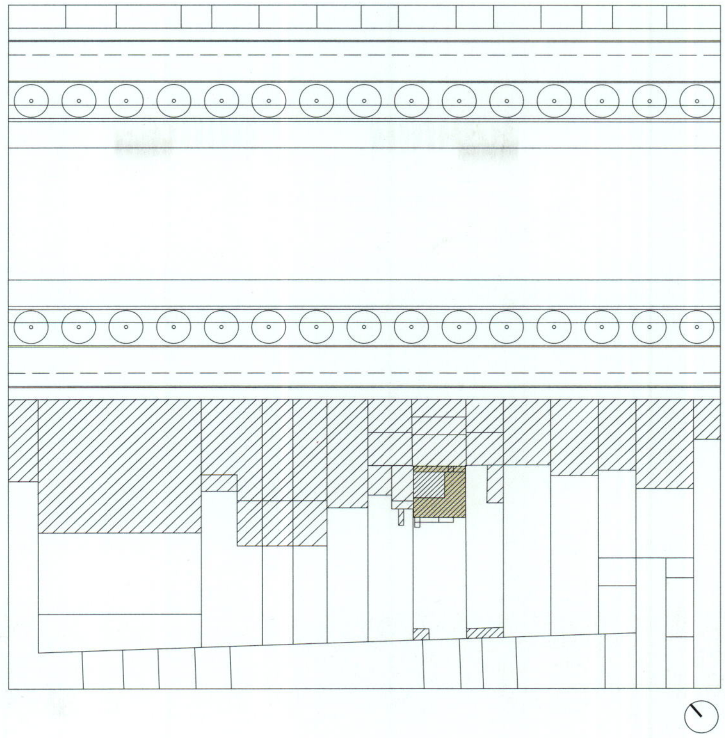

Situation plan

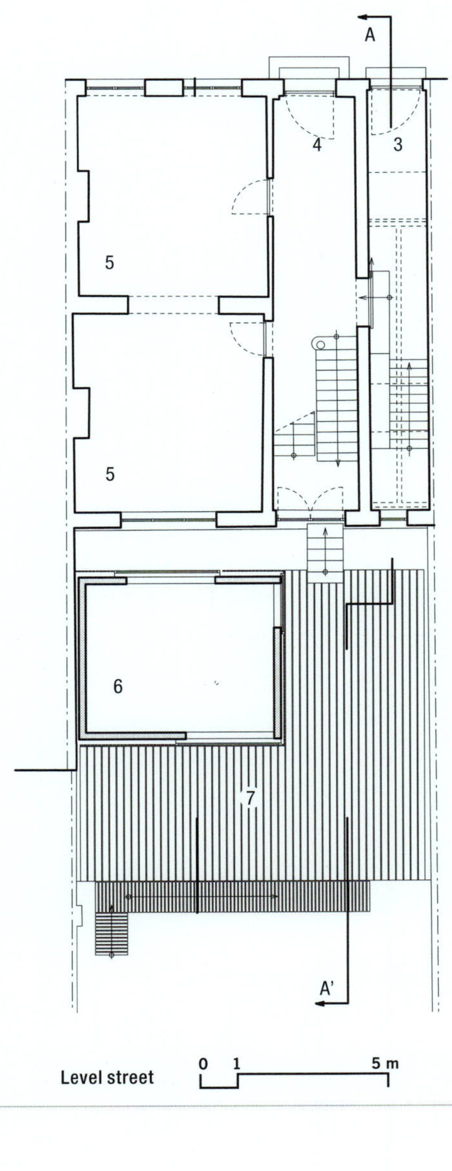

Level street

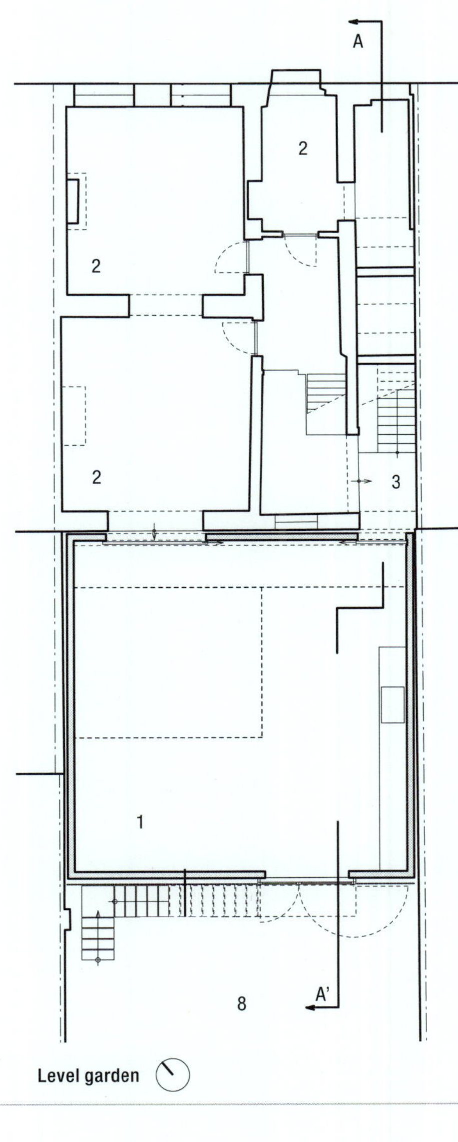

Level garden

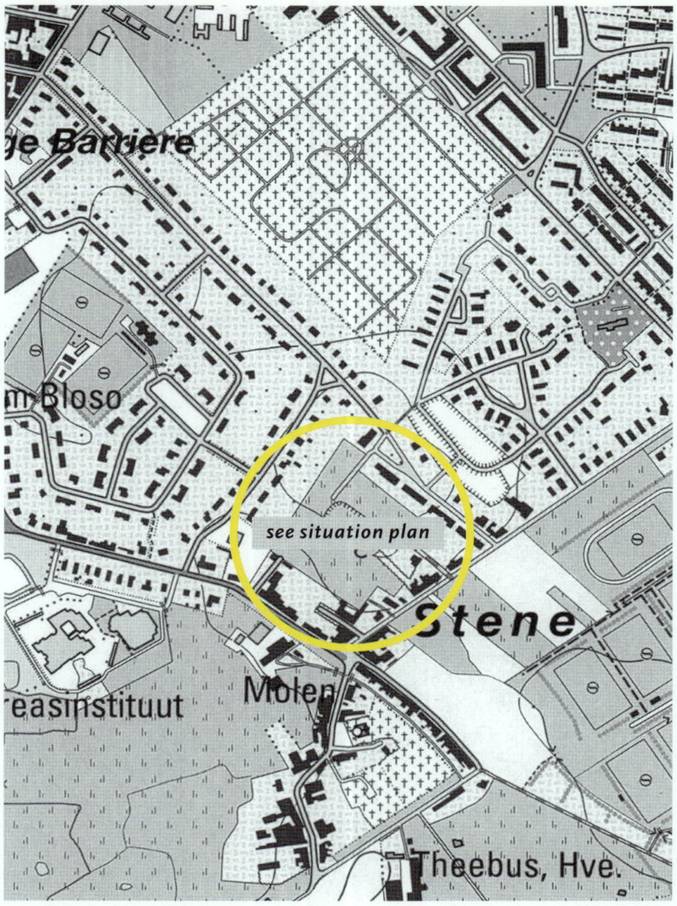

STUDIO HOUSE

architect **AN FONTEYNE AND JITSE VAN DEN BERG**

location Melkerijstraat 24, 8400 Ostend

client	Ronald and Magda Fonteyne-Verbeeren
design - building	1999-2002
engineers	Studium - engineer Hugo Zwaenepoel [stability]
contracted work	General building work: Ronny Mylle, Ichtegem
	Steel joinery: Lootens Line, Nazareth
	Woodwork and carpentry: Vandaele, Ostend
	Plumbing, heating and electricity: Wilfried Naessens, Leffinge
	Paintwork: Freddy Arnou, Bruges
	Kitchen: Jan Vanden Berghe, Poelkappelle
	Garden: Chris Noppe, Oostkamp
area	104 sq.m.
volume	429 cubic m.
building costs	96,720 (excl. VAT and fees)
building costs/sq. m	930 EUR/sq. m. (excl. VAT and fees)
project description	Hera Van Sande
photography	Karin Borghouts p.91,94,95 I Stefan Vandermeulen p.90

STUDIO HOUSE ▸ architect AN FONTEYNE AND JITSE VAN DEN BERG

The terraced house for which An Fonteyne was commissioned to design an extension lies on the outskirts of Ostend. It is on a suburban estate built in the eighties, a monotonous row of low houses in a quiet street. The building meant as a printmaking studio (with guest accommodation) is intended to be an independent extension of an existing house. The new house is situated on a plot, bordering the one of the existing house, and is 12 m. deep. In future this building can function as a fully independent home. The front facade, with its austere design, cornice height and sloping roof, is absorbed into the street scene. But this is an illusion. It soon turns out that, without pretension, this simple facade transcends the street's gloomy face. The grey, cement-painted facade in long building blocks is interrupted by a single large, off-centre wooden frame in which a wooden, almost rustic front door has been hung. This gives it the air of a simple farmhouse as one might find in the Flemish countryside.

Although the facade already indicates that something special is going on here, one gets a complete surprise on entering this small building. One comes into a bright space with the natural colours of the roofs and walls set against the vividly-coloured sliding panels, and spaces are formed by a play of staggered walls and volumes. Even so, this dynamic radiates a restful feeling. The abundant light comes from three sections of saw-tooth roof that are hidden behind the facade. This unexpected apparition results from playing with the building regulations, which are intended for conventional housing types. The combination of the urban planning requirement for largely sloping roofs and building on the plot to a depth of 12 m, and the desire to accommodate the brief in a single storey with north-eastern orientation, resulted after a long search in the use of sawtooth roofs. The slope of these roofs diminishes the further they are from the street and this limits the height of the rear facade so it fits the scale of the adjacent houses. By constructing this rear facade entirely in glass, the interior is open to the garden and merges into it. One can here in fact no longer talk of space in the accepted sense of the word, nor about interior and exterior. It seems as if one were standing, screened off, in the open air.

A number of decisions that arise from the composition of the plan add dynamism to the house. Since the area that can be built upon is used to the maximum, the side walls of the house extend beyond the rear facades of both neighbouring houses. At this point the party wall becomes a insulated, entirely outside wall. The architect aligns the staggering in the wall with the boundaries of the roof zones. The zoning of the sawtooth roof is reinforced in yet another way. A number of white-painted geometric brick volumes are playfully scattered around the space, housing the classic subsidiary functions of a home (storage, heating, WC, etc.).

Each volume has been placed within the bounds of the roof zone, creating a succession of equivalent zones whose use the occupants are free to determine. So the living activities can be swapped around at will. In addition, these volumes play a constructional role. They support the concrete beams that bear the lowermost parts of the sawtooth roof structure. This makes it an economic structural composition.

The beams and lintels are in bare concrete, which emphasises their presence. The sloping sides of the sawtooth roof are clad in the same rough, unplaned planks as used for the formwork of the concrete beams. The grain of the planks is repeated in these beams, which makes for a certain ambiguity between the two materials. The studio shows itself openly, without ornament. The floors and roofs are in black slate.

The walls are in building blocks with visible rough pointing, painted white. In the austerely decorated living area, large bright yellow, orange and red wooden sliding doors make it possible to change the relationships between the various spaces. The design balances between the roughness of the bare concrete, the texture of slate and the rough pointing of the painted building blocks on the one hand, and the refined finish of the sliding doors, facades and jointing on the other. The architect has a sort of no-nonsense attitude to the generation of design decisions, but has a subtle range of means for making them material. The bold attitude to

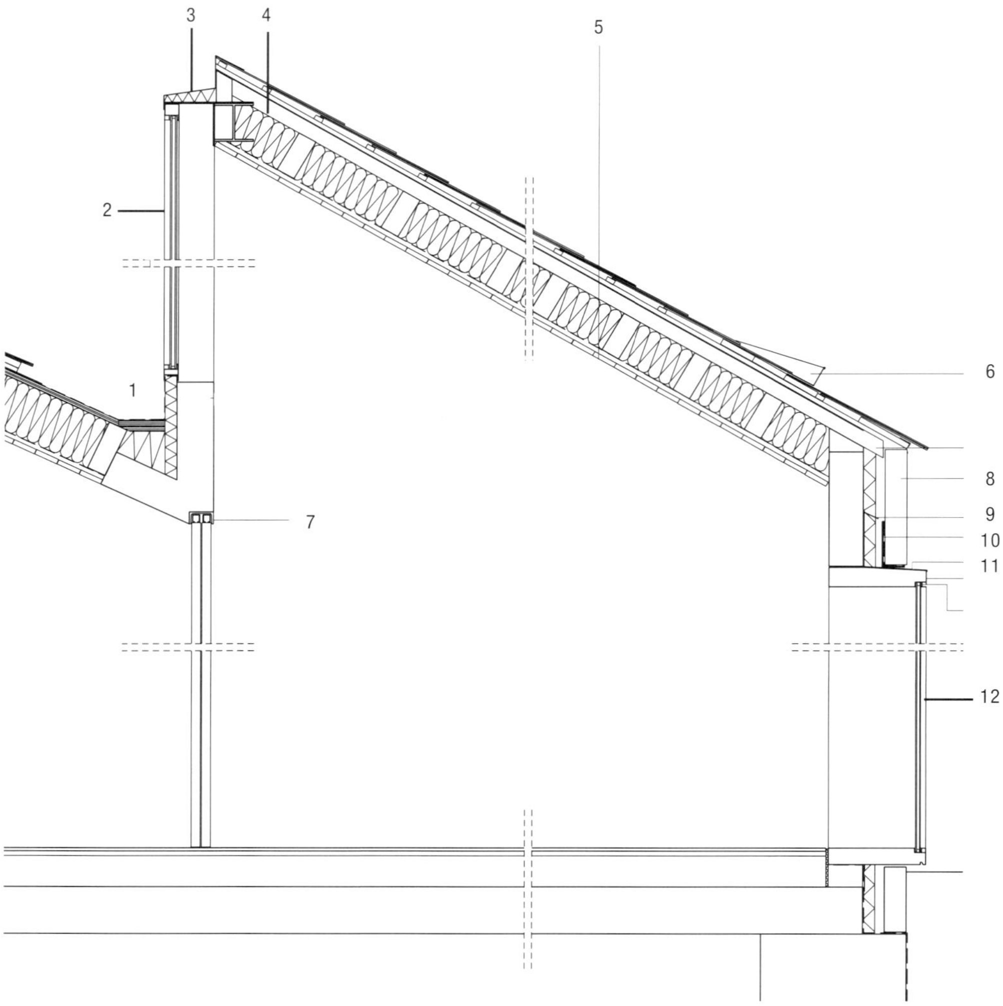

Detail

1 gutter: EPDM bonded to WBP plywood
2 steel windows,
double glazing
3 ridge flashing in folded aluminium,
anodised
4 steel ridge beam, HEB 160
5 roof build-up:
- slates, 300 x 600 mm
- battens
- counterbattens
- 3mm fibre cement sheet
- rafter, 60 x 60 mm +
60 mm insulation
- timber purlins, 180 x 70 mm +
180 mm insulation
- vapour barrier
- wood boarding on battens
6 concealed gutter in zinc
7 UPN 100, galvanised steel U profile
to receive sliding door tracks
8 brickwork, 290 x 90 x90, mineral paint
9 damp proof menbrane
10 steel lintel
11 lead flashing
12 hardwood window frames,
weather to greystainless steel
beading, security fixing

colour, materials, design and division of space enables this studio home to develop real vitality. When one looks from the existing house towards the studio in the evening, the house's third dimension appears to transform into an abstract composition of lines, planes and colour. In the garden facade, the repetitive play of lines in the balanced composition of steel window frames is broken by a single extra window in the top left-hand corner. In the background appears a play of large and small rectangles in white, yellow and orange.

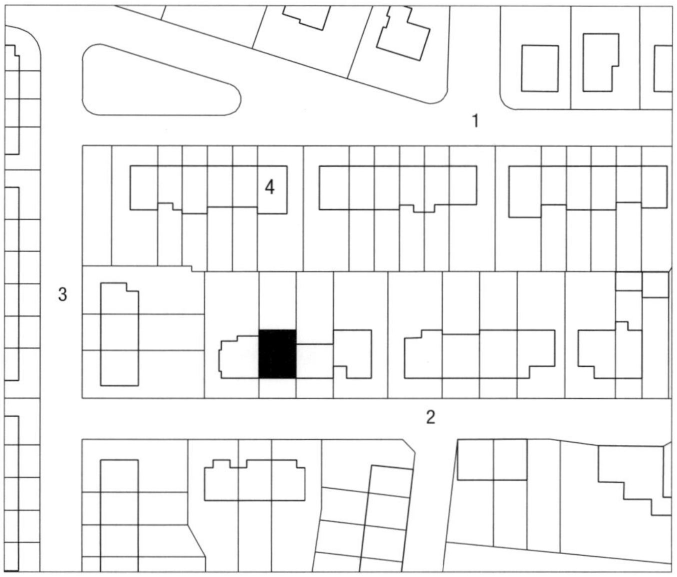

Situation plan

1 Heidebloemstraat
2 Melkerijstraat
3 Brugstraat
4 existing house

0 10 20 m

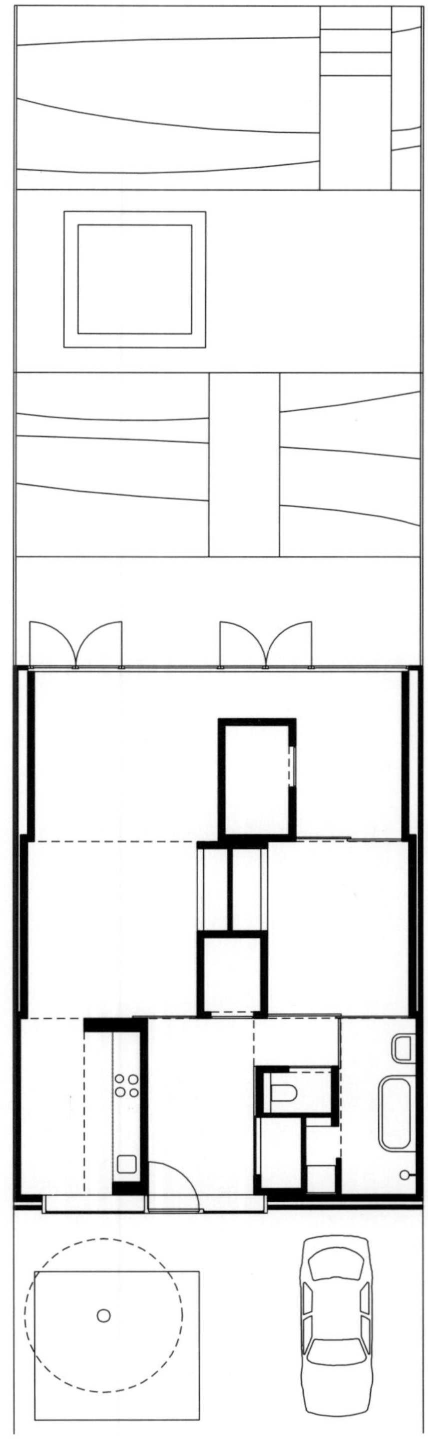

Level 0

0 1 5 m

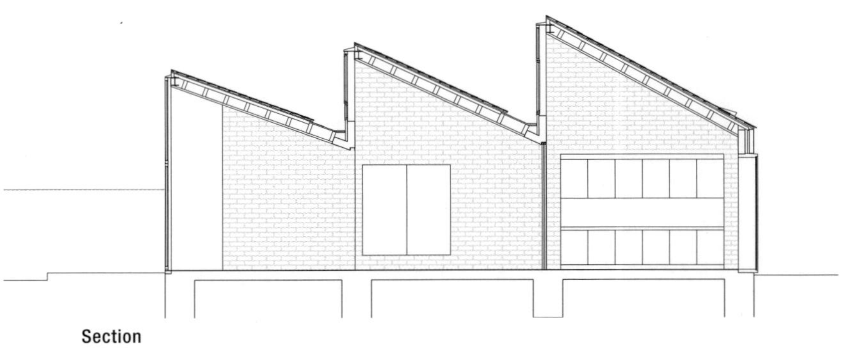

Section

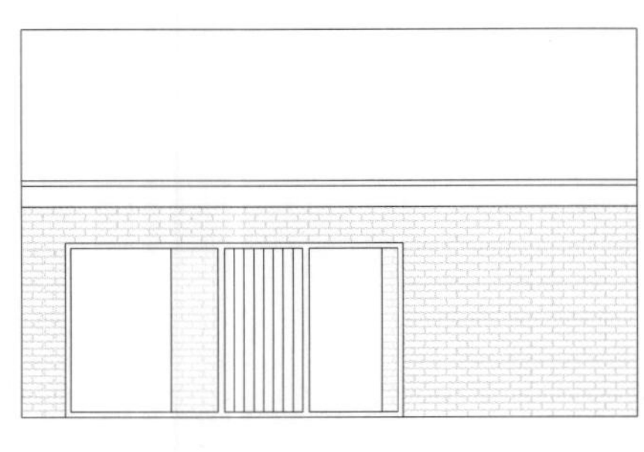

Street facade

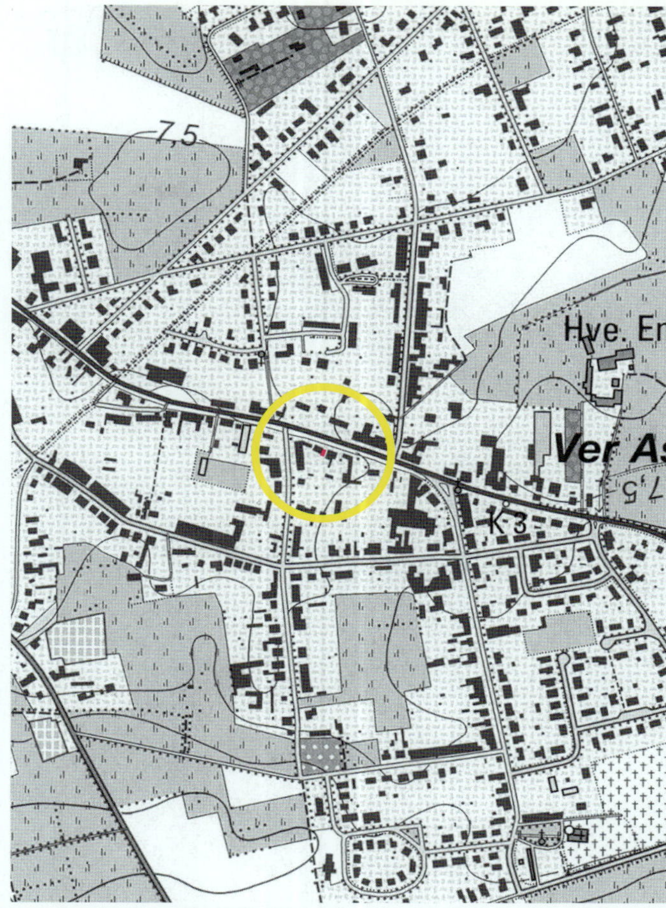

TERRACED HOUSE

architect **TOMAS NOLLET AND HILDE HUYGHE ARCHITECTS**

location Astridlaan 408, 8310 Bruges

client	Tomas Nollet and Hilde Huyghe
design - building	2000-2002
engineers	Stability: Engineer De Muynck, Izegem
contracted work	Structural work: Bouwteam Mylle-Teerlinck, Eernegem
	Carpentry: Schrijnwerken Speeckaert, Knesselare
	Technical installations: Chauffage Bral, Maldegem
	Polished concrete: Durmuline Guido Steyaert, Ghent
area	195 sq. m.
volume	553 cubic. m.
building costs	126,750 EUR (excl. VAT)
building costs/sq. m	650 EUR/sq. m. (excl. VAT)
project description	Adam Caruso
photography	Karin Borghouts p.100b,104,105 | Paul d'Haese p.99,100a
	Stefan Vandermeulen p.98

TERRACED HOUSE ▸ architect TOMAS NOLLET AND HILDE HUYGHE ARCHITECTS

The road is very long and straight and feels like a direct line between the historic centre of Bruges and the more ordinary inter-urban landscape of contemporary Flanders. The house is in a small narrow terrace squeezed into the side garden of one of its older and fatter neighbours. The front façade is rather blank. There is a door-proportioned opening on the right side of the ground floor, and a very wide first floor window shifted to the left beneath a full storey of blank wall.

It is a careful composition in an understood modernist language. There is also a way through at ground level, a sort of tradesman's passage that gives access to the back of the site and at its mid-point provides an entrance to the house. The ground floor has a central service core pushed forward in the plan to define a small entrance and toilet lobby, a kitchen and a larger dining room that faces south towards the long, long garden.

The tradesman's passage is a semi-enclosed space that excuses the interior of the small house from providing a dedicated internal foyer. Instead, it makes a covered outdoor entranceway at a scale that would be the envy of a far larger dwelling. This sensitivity to practical matters is evident immediately as one enters the house and suggests that this design has engaged with themes of domesticity and use in an unusually direct way. The interior is arranged so that each room benefits from the daylight and the airiness of the house as a whole, while affording an appropriate degree of privacy. At ground level, the displaced core accommodates wet services in and around its volume at the same time as shielding the dining room and garden from the presence of the street. At the first floor level, the core reduces to a stair and a wall. Like a miniature warehouse, the full sweep of the interior from north to south is revealed, but sliding panels held within the thickness of the wall can separate the studio, which overlooks the street from the south facing living room.

The stair emerges into a small hall on the top floor that extends into an 'L' accommodating the bathroom which, along with children's bedrooms, faces south to the garden. The master bedroom is nestled behind the blank upper portion of the street façade and is oriented west towards an intimate patio.

This exterior room has a shower on one wall and looks back to the bathroom on the south side of the house. A large window from the patio allows natural light to fall onto the top flight of the stair. This internal arrangement has a spatial precision and sensitivity to propriety that is reminiscent of an almshouse or a monk's cell in a charterhouse. The efficiency of the interior has not come about as a result of an abstract plan or a complex spatial composition, but has been achieved by paying close attention to matters of use

and by a profound sense of how these have been accommodated in the long history of urban dwelling.The house would not be so redolent of these archaic typologies if the organisation of the interior were not sustained by an equally precise materialisation. The shell of the house is made in one material, concrete.

This is not a case of formal reduction. Rather, by using one material in its different forms – concrete blocks, concrete planks, concrete slabs – the creation of this simple structure becomes more than just construction: it is intimately linked to giving scale and character to the interiors. The vertical structure is made with concrete blocks laid in a simple stretcher bond. The size and pattern of the masonry unit sets the depth of the floor structure and the position of the walls. The care with which the blocks are laid out (very few are cut) lends this material an unexpected precision and delicacy that is in sympathy with the scale of the house. The floor structure is made of pre-cast concrete planks that span about four metres from one party wall to the other.

The small gaps between the planks make a serial pattern on the ceiling, a dry counterpoint to the concrete block and mortar stacks of the walls. All the planks are identical and their modular form is reconciled to the depth of the house by an in situ concrete beam that ties the whole structure together and trims the openings at the stair. The pre-cast floor structure is topped by a power-floated concrete slab containing underfloor heating. The surface of the floor is soft and shiny: it reflects light at the window edge and is warm underfoot. The secondary elements in the construction – windows, doors and built-in furniture – are simple and mostly painted white.

They are remarkable for the way in which they relate to the primary construction. The fact that the junctions between window frame and masonry openings, stair stringer and floor structure and the integration of services occur naturally and without any fuss is a testament to the way even the smallest requirement of the house has been anticipated in the concept and detailed resolution of the shell. The incredible care with which spaces and materials have been handled imbues this house with an extraordinary dignity. This is a dignity that results directly from the project's engagement with habitational matters, and its enjoyment of the possibilities afforded by extremely restricted means.

This seriousness stands in stark contrast to so much contemporary housing. Whether it is responding to the basest demands of the private housing market or is the product of brand-name architects, the result so often represents, rather than embodies, what is at the core of valuable housing. Historical housing typologies have proven to be remarkably robust in accommodating new lifestyles and uses. This is

because of their economical use of available technologies and their diagrammatic and flexible organisation. One fears that much current housing will prove barely suitable for a single generation of habitation. Consumer choice, lifestyle and luxury are not qualities that naturally encourage long-standing and rich habitation to take hold. This project, behind its taciturn face, possesses qualities that do.

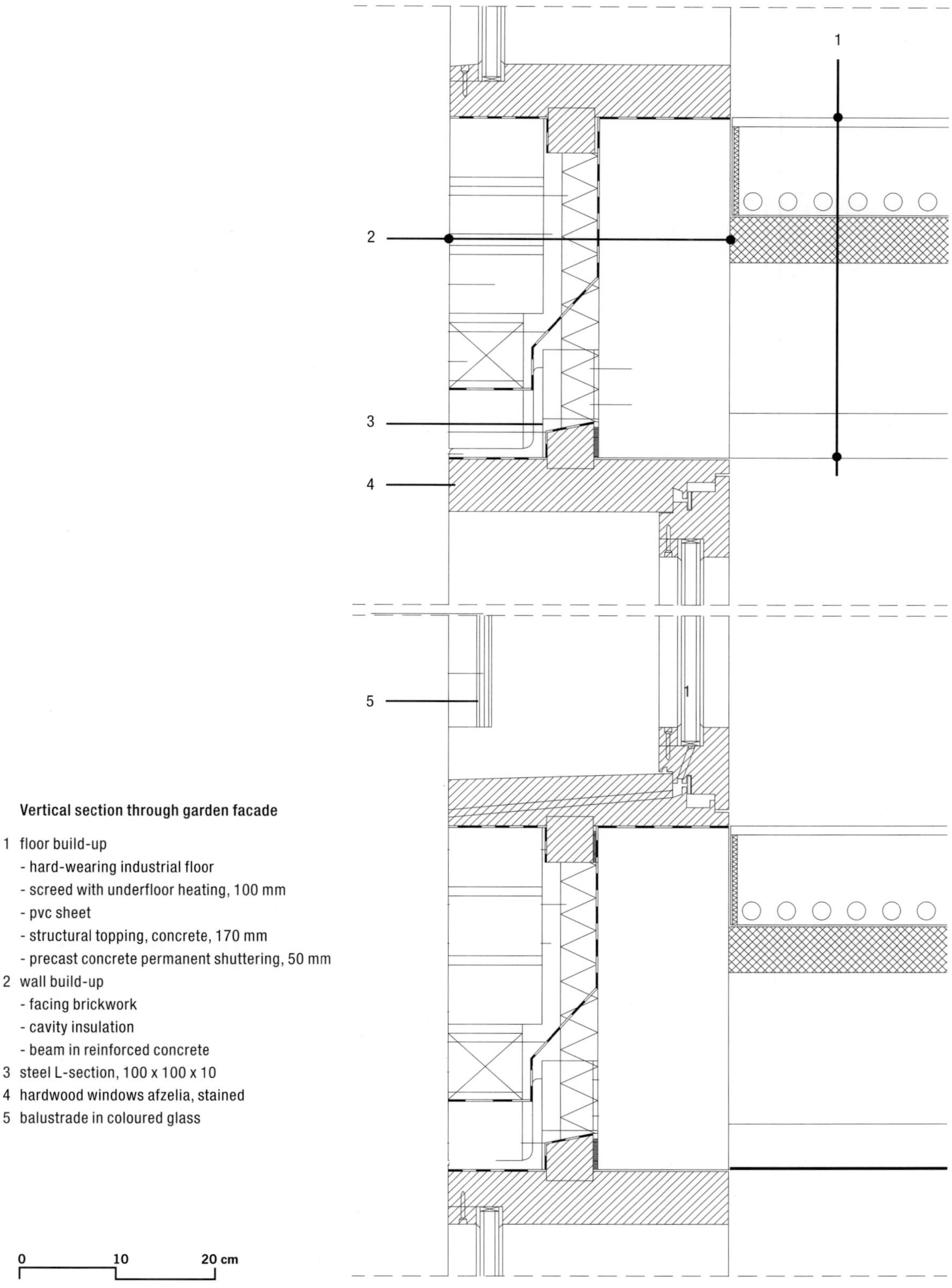

Vertical section through garden facade

1 floor build-up
- hard-wearing industrial floor
- screed with underfloor heating, 100 mm
- pvc sheet
- structural topping, concrete, 170 mm
- precast concrete permanent shuttering, 50 mm

2 wall build-up
- facing brickwork
- cavity insulation
- beam in reinforced concrete

3 steel L-section, 100 x 100 x 10
4 hardwood windows afzelia, stained
5 balustrade in coloured glass

Situation plan
1 Astridlaan
2 Meersenstraat

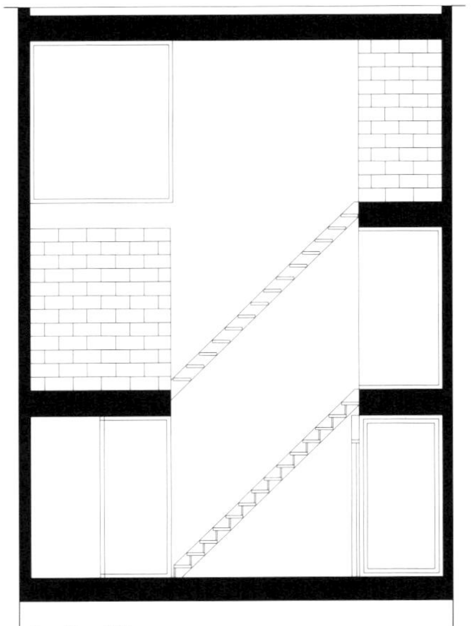

Section AA'

Level 0
1 covered entrance passage
2 front door
3 backdoor
4 passage door
5 private part of entrance passage
6 toilet
7 storage
8 kitchen
9 dining area
10 garden

Level 1
1 office
2 sitting area

Level 2
1 landing
2 children's bedroom
3 bathroom
4 shower
5 master bedroom
6 patio

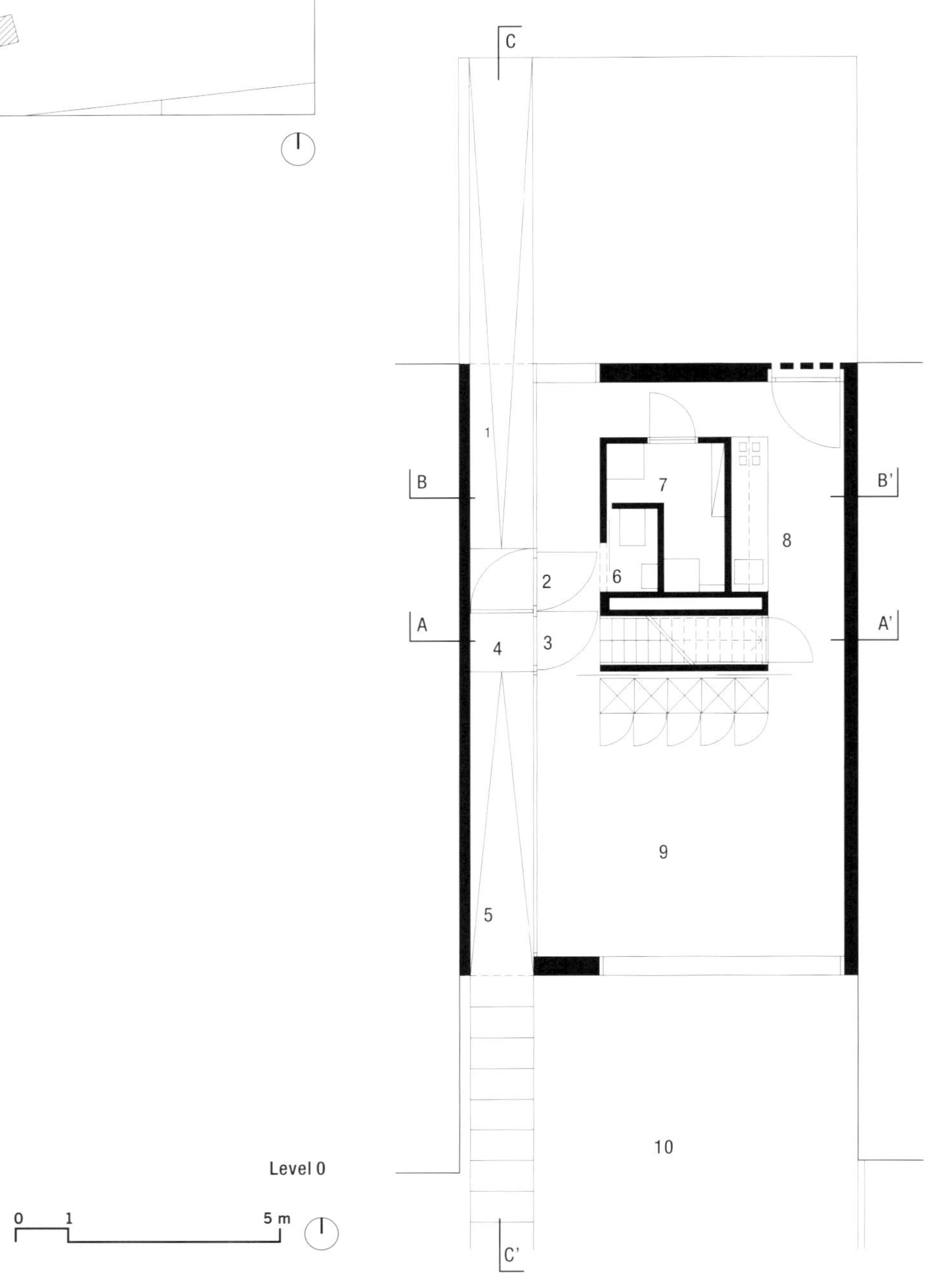

Level 0

Section BB'

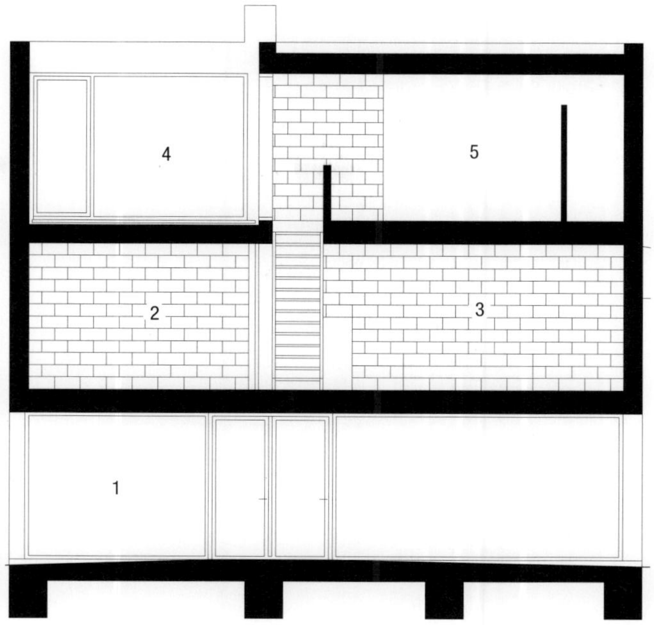

Section CC'
1 entrance passage
2 office
3 living area
4 patio
5 bathroom

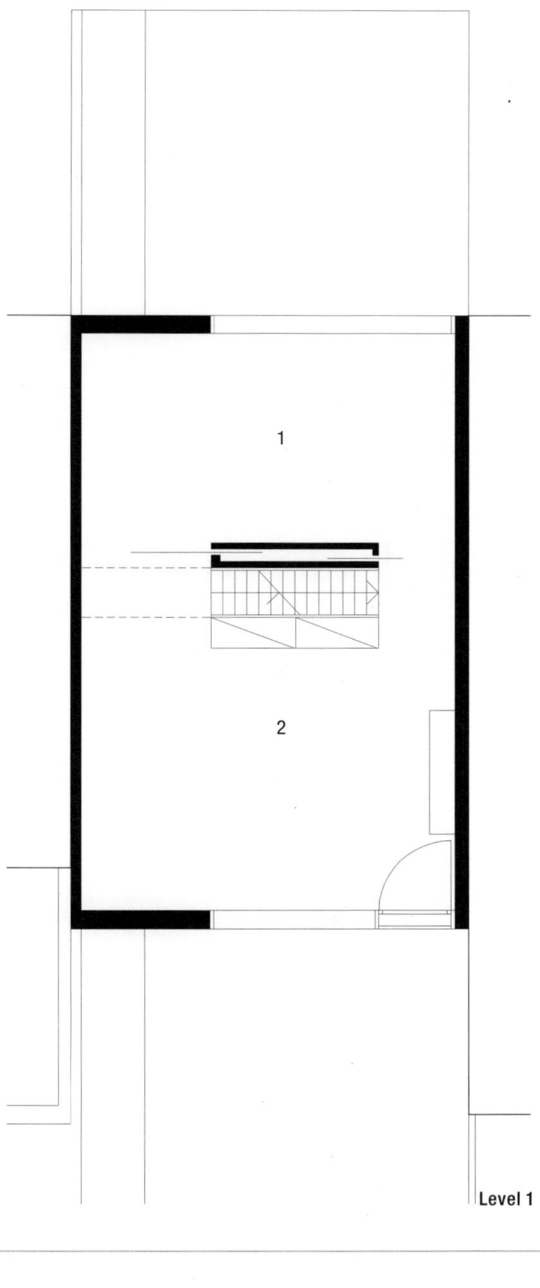

Level 1

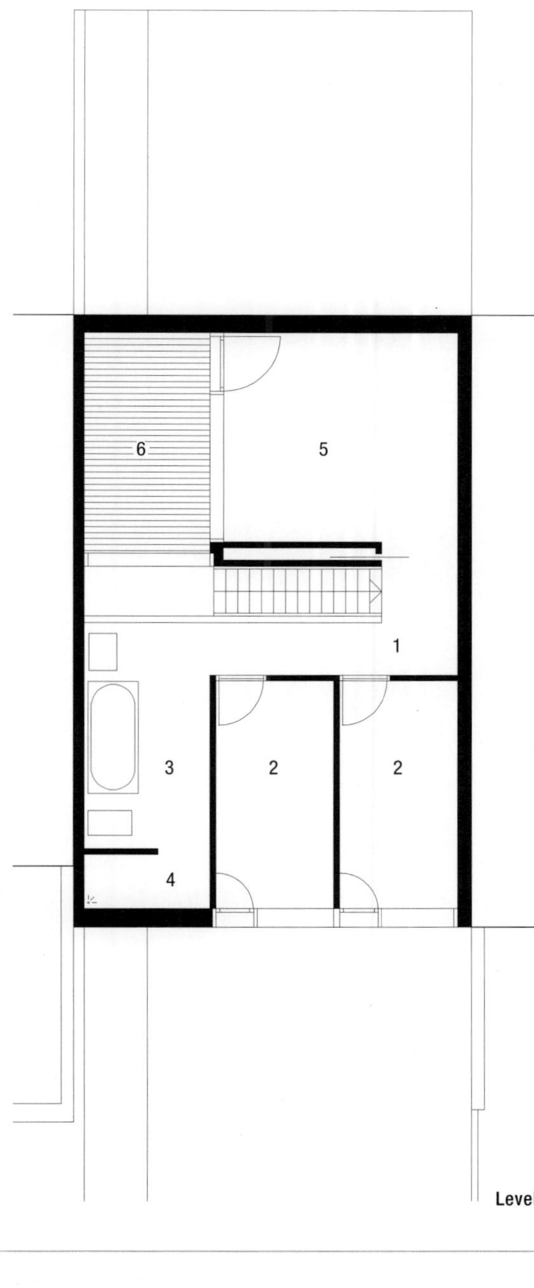

Level 2

LEEUWS-CROES TOWN HOUSE

architect **MARIE-JOSÉ VAN HEE**

location Pluimstraat 7, 9000 Ghent

client	Stanny Leeuws and Jeannot Croes
design - building	1997-2002
project-workers	Filip Reumers
engineers	Bureau voor Architectuur en Stabiliteit Dirk Jaspaert
contracted work	Gebroeders Pijnaert nv I nv Van Tornhout P. I Natuursteenbedrijf Eggermont nv
area	160 sq. m.
volume	476 cubic. m.
project description	Tom Avermaete
photography	Peter Lorré p.110 I André Nullens p.109,114,115 Stefan Vandermeulen p.108

LEEUWS-CROES TOWN HOUSE ▸ architect MARIE-JOSÉ VAN HEE

Pluimstraat, an L-shaped street connecting Zilverhof and Tinnenpotstraat, is to be found in the medieval urban fabric of Ghent. It is a narrow lane whose low, narrow workman's houses define its appearance. Somewhere halfway down the first part of this street there is an inconspicuous plastered facade which fits in naturally with the adjoining buildings. It is the Leeuws-Croes house, designed by Marie-José Van Hee and built on a plot of 120 square metres on which two dilapidated workmen's houses had previously stood. The house is composed of two connected three-storey volumes each with its own ridge roof.

The foremost volume covers half the width of the plot, while the one at the back covers the entire width. This creates a forecourt on the street. A narrow alleyway at the side links the forecourt with an 'outdoor room' at the back which extends across the full width of the plot.

The three-part composition of outdoor room, front volume and back volume is the basic figure onto which Van Hee has designed a variety of transitions between indoor and outdoor spaces, and between the private and public domains. She uses spatial composition, details and the materials of the building to add nuance to these transitions. She introduces a game of confirmation and denial of boundaries. For instance, the first floor in the front volume, combined with the rendered street facade, creates a distance between the public domain of the street and the private sphere of the house. However, along the forecourt the same volume is designed as a wooden wall with cupboards that continue into the entrance hall, which by contrast creates a connection with the domestic sphere and activities.

Access to the home is also a complex play of transitions between the public and private domains. It is approached via a path in the forecourt which is interrupted by a simple threshold and a large wooden door that leads into the hall. The next door leads into the dining area and the kitchen which looks out onto the outdoor room.

This succession of spaces might lead one to suspect that there are clear barriers between the street and the house. Nothing could be less true. Van Hee has designed the various spaces so that they can merge into one another. The doors are designed as large pivoting surfaces, which can fold away entirely, thereby connecting the forecourt and the dining area with each other.

This continuum between the forecourt and living area is enhanced even more by the floors of the entrance hall, the dining area and the kitchen, which run seamlessly into one another. The result is a complex and contradictory link between the public and private domains which can adapt to the way the occupants live.

Inside the house Van Hee continues playing with the boundaries between spaces. The central open staircase plays an important part in this. In the tradition of Adolf Loos, this staircase is not an independent element but much more a sculpture that winds past and through the many and various spaces, entering into a different relationship with each one. For example, in this house the staircase, by means of through-views, ensures a spatial relationship between the dining room in the rear of volume and the sitting area higher up in the front volume.On the first floor the living room stretches out over the full width of the site. The precisely located windows, whereby all possibility of seeing or being seen by the neighbours is carefully eliminated, the sense of space is shifted far beyond the boundaries of the plot. A broad, narrow window in the rear facade frames the weathered garden wall as if it were a still-life. The space above the alleyway to the outdoor room is designed partly as a storage space in which to keep the wood for the hearth, and partly left open to allow the sun to penetrate deep into the forecourt.

A window on the front gives a view of the roofs and chimneys on the edge of the city. The views through from one space to another, the alternation of short and long perspectives, the varied play of light and shade the windows provide, the diagonal effects through the house and the secure feeling with regard to the street, transform this relatively small area

into a spacious domestic world. The top floor is designed in a completely different way. From the living area the staircase first goes up through a service zone including the bathroom, washroom and storeroom, and then divides into two staircases, each of which serves a separate bedroom volume. On this floor the two building volumes with their pitched roofs are easy to see. They remind us of the original scale of the surroundings and fit into it seamlessly. The horizontal strip window from one party wall to the other provides a broad view of the roofs and towers of the city. Both rooms isolate themselves from the continuity of the rest of the house.

With this house, Marie-José Van Hee has made an important contribution to the development of high-quality contemporary housing types in the existing fabric of the historical city. This house is an interplay between an ingenious use of space and a skilful positioning of rooms, open spaces and windows. However, it is above all the result of an exceptional sensitivity to the individual nature of contemporary ways of living and their spatial and material implications. The urban home is rethought and redefined against the background of the complex character of these ways of living.

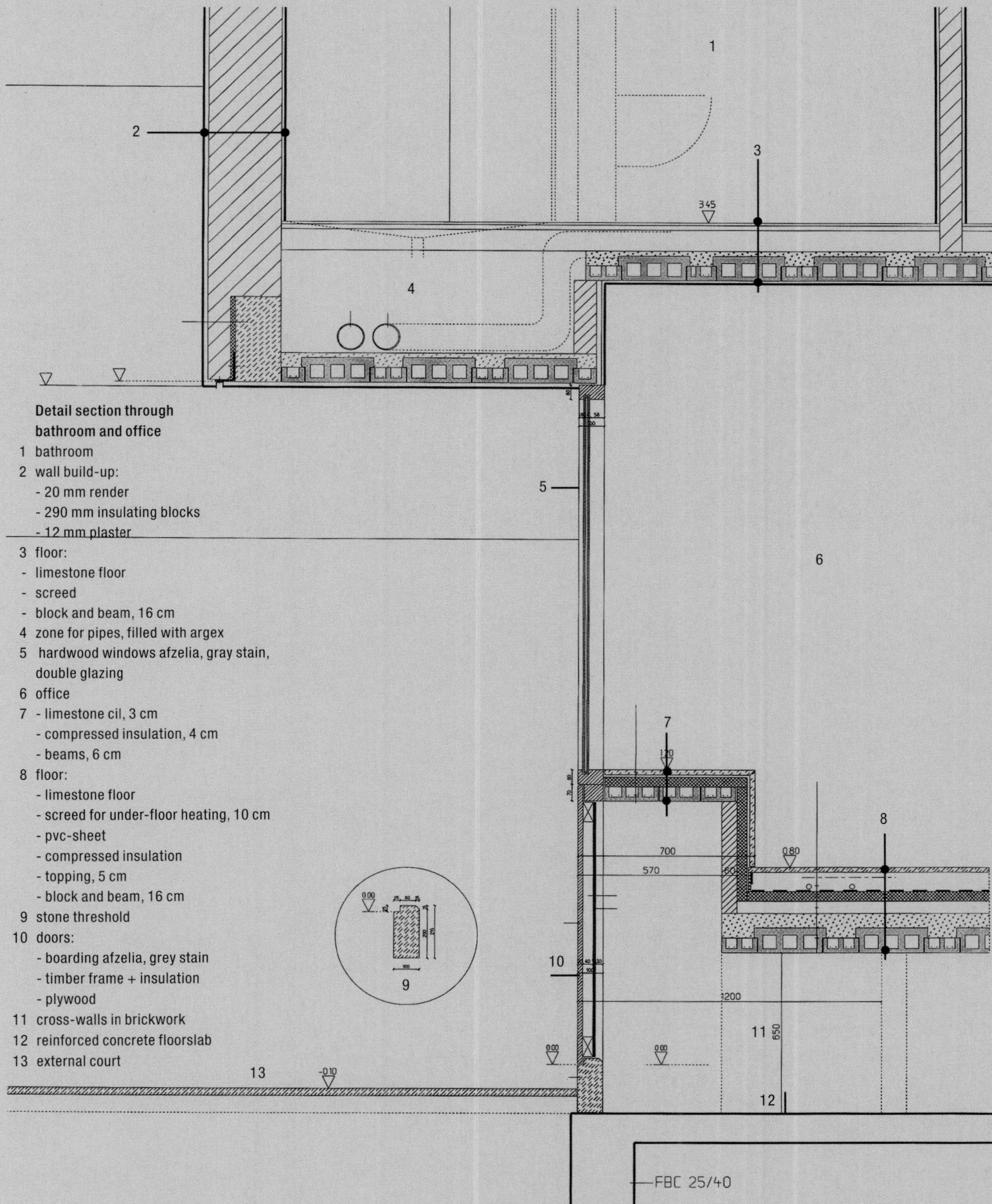

Detail section through bathroom and office

1 bathroom
2 wall build-up:
- 20 mm render
- 290 mm insulating blocks
- 12 mm plaster
3 floor:
- limestone floor
- screed
- block and beam, 16 cm
4 zone for pipes, filled with argex
5 hardwood windows afzelia, gray stain, double glazing
6 office
7 - limestone cil, 3 cm
- compressed insulation, 4 cm
- beams, 6 cm
8 floor:
- limestone floor
- screed for under-floor heating, 10 cm
- pvc-sheet
- compressed insulation
- topping, 5 cm
- block and beam, 16 cm
9 stone threshold
10 doors:
- boarding afzelia, grey stain
- timber frame + insulation
- plywood
11 cross-walls in brickwork
12 reinforced concrete floorslab
13 external court

Front facade

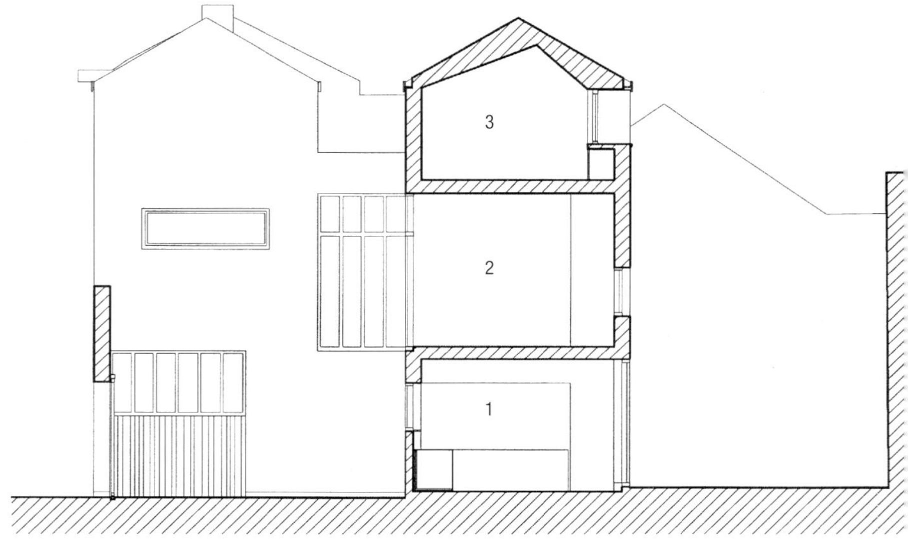

Section AA'

Section AA'

1 kitchen
2 living room
3 bedroom

Section BB'

1 dining room
2 office
3 passage
4 living room
5 bedroom

0 5 m

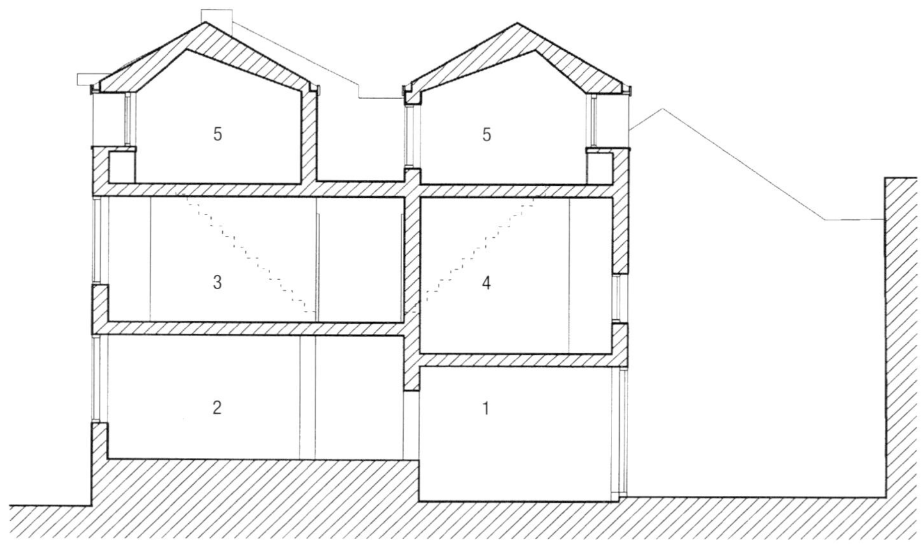

Section BB'

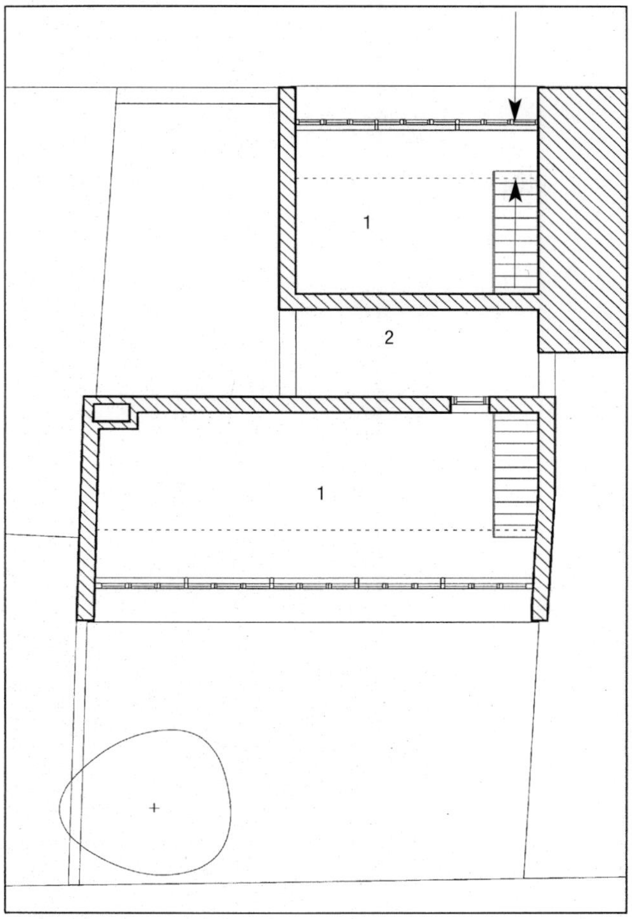

Level 2

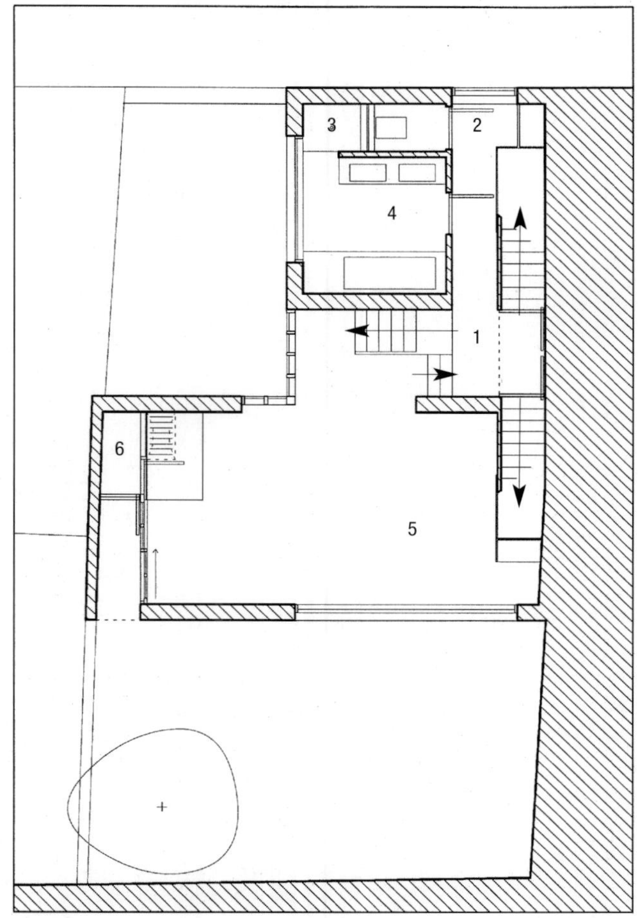

Level 1

Level 2
1 bedroom
2 flat roof

Level 1
1 staircase
2 passage
3 shower
4 bathroom
5 living room
6 storage

Level 0
1 hall
2 office
3 dining room
4 kitchen

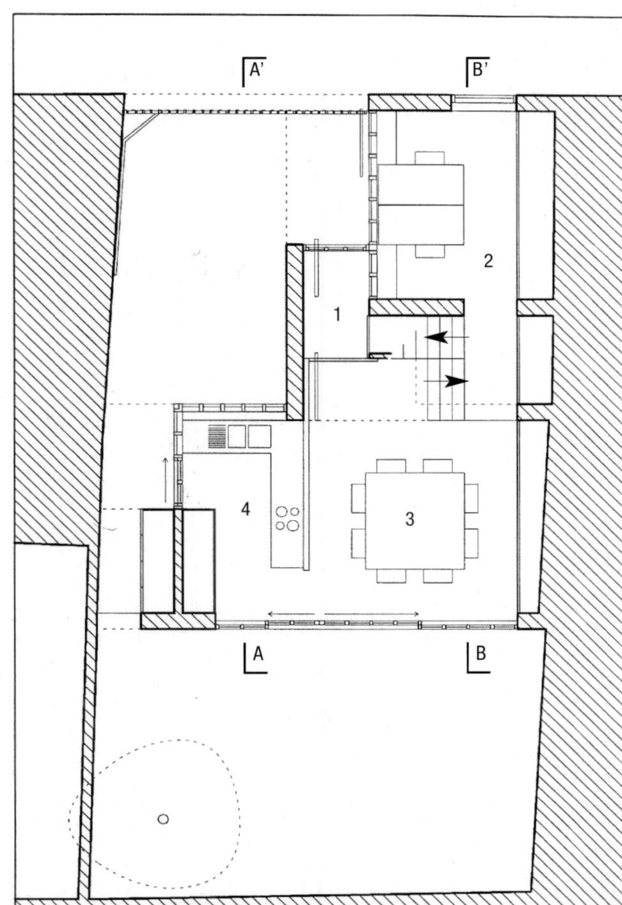

Level 0

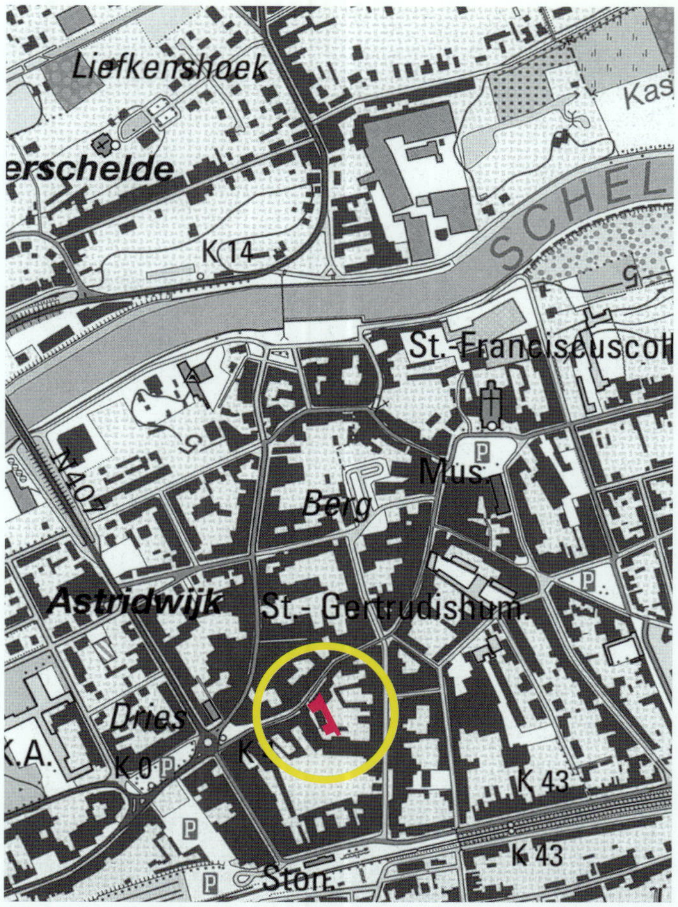

VAN LEEMPUT - OOSTERLINCK TOWN HOUSE

architect **MARIE-JOSÉ VAN HEE**

location Hoenderstraat 41, 9230 Wetteren

client	Peter Van Leemput and Griet Oosterlinck
design - building	2000-2003
project-worker	Filip Reumers I Dietlinde Verhaeghe
engineers	Bureau voor Architectuur en Stabiliteit, Dirk Jaspaert
contracted work	nv Luc Scherpereel I bvba André De Witte Kristof Dewitte I Natuursteenbedrijf Eggermont nv
area	486 sq. m.
volume	1,333 cubic m
project description	Koen Van Synghel
photography	Wouter Rawoens p.119,120,123 Stefan Vandermeulen p.118

VAN LEEMPUT - OOSTERLINCK TOWN HOUSE ▸ architect MARIE-JOSÉ VAN HEE

How do you create good-quality living in a cheerless shopping street which, like so many typical streets in urbanised Flemish boroughs, has to cope with the negative conditions of the city? How do you counterbalance the lack of open space and greenery, the oppressive proximity of adjacent buildings, and a shortage of parking? How do you incorporate rights of way and rights of light? How do you create privacy and an outdoor space for two housing units, a small one for a live-in parent and one for a family with children? How do you include three parking spaces in all this? And how do you translate all this into space, rhythm, light and material; or in other words into a natural form of architecture?

The architect Marie-José van Hee faced no shortage of challenges on this brief. For example, a very specific aspect of this house was the integration of a passage through to the neighbour's workshop. A driveway for a truck had to be left free over the full depth of the site, about 35 metres. Van Hee made organisational use of this right of way by placing the occupants' parking spaces at the rear of the site. In spatial terms too, she transformed this negative condition into a masterly architectural gesture.

By raising the house up on an arcade that derives its rhythm from rough concrete columns, she created a monumental semi-public space. Van Hee placed the row of columns about a metre from the party wall and thereby simplified not only the technical aspects of the foundations but also used this distance to allow light in under the arcade. The interaction between the old brick wall and the concrete arcade structure makes for a new sort of experience of nature whereby the smell of rain, the play of light and the blowing of the wind can be sensed intensively. In essence, Van Hee is here using architectural means to transform a banal easement into an original covered play-space for bikes, skates, and so on. Without detracting from the privacy of the flat and the house, the various external rooms, from the concrete passageway, through the studio's somewhat higher patio garden, to the even higher terrace of the flat, are all visually linked.

In this way, subtle spatial and social relationships are made possible between the children's play area, the grandmother's garden and the parents' terrace. So this is not a case of virtuoso architecture pour l'architecture, but architecture where living as a family, beyond the limits of the nuclear family, can develop unimpeded. In this house it is striking to note that the dwelling begins right on the public street and subtly slips into the arcade/alleyway to then enter into the house itself by way of the garden and the patio garden.

This is in fact the route the occupants take when they arrive home at their miniature urban *woonerf* (residential com-

pound) by car or bicycle. This townhouse, like every country home, has, thanks to the arcade, a front door and a backdoor, which enables it to offer the freedom of a so-called formal (front door) or the more informal (backdoor) approach to the house. This aspect is exceptional in the urban context, but it gives the dwelling a remarkable freedom and generosity.

This is expressed in the walk from the carport, up some steps, to a raised garden, from where a second set of steps leads to the sun terrace higher up. From this terrace one can go in two directions. Either a few steps higher, straight into the bedroom passage, or taking a long bridge along the party wall, that leads to the terrace outside the living room of the flat. These many options may make a somewhat complex impression, but Van Hee is here not just laying out a '*promenade architecturale*' in order, *à la* Le Corbusier, to admire the marvellous play of volumes and light, but rather to make routes grafted onto the natural lines of life in this home.

The rooms fold around the garden and terraces in an L-shape. While the bedroom area has opal glass on the north-east side, on the south-west side, the study/bedrooms, are bathed in a sea of light. The living and dining rooms occupy a strategic position both on the street side and looking out over the terrace and garden and enjoy light from both the south-east and north-west. Raising this flat up to the first floor means that light is given the chance to enter all the rooms generously. Van Hee composes the street facade of this complex house in layers with the same subtle mastery with which she allows the public nature of Hoenderstraat moderately into the back gardens. For example, the gigantic railings in front of the alleyway dissolve into the bend in the street that occurs almost halfway along the facade.

The monumental scale of this gateway is given a counterpoint in the horizontal balcony on the first floor. It is intriguing to see how, as a result of the bend in the site, this balcony transforms at an angle into the bay window of the living room. In this bay window, as in those Van Hee designed for the house next door, one recognises the concern not to optimise the house at the expense of the street, but on the contrary to create space for the natural interaction between private and public, interior and exterior, intimacy and the expressiveness of the house.

The facade also reveals that the small studio is on a mezzanine. This gives this compact home not only the distinction of a *bel-étage* but also the privacy it requires with regard to the hubbub of the street. What the facade does not lead one to suspect is that the raised floor of this studio can easily be removed, so that this studio space can later be made part of the adjoining shop. The client for the Van Leemput-Oosterlinck house in fact works in this business, a shop building

that incorporates her parents' home, which Van Hee also converted in the nineties. It is precisely the success of this conversion that lay behind the building of this townhouse. It also explains the analogous materials, which lead to a naturalness of texture and colour, while in terms of rhythm the option was rather for a tense contrapuntal harmony. The consistent choice of such materials as concrete, white stone and wood are evidence of a timeless vision and also explain the absolute lack of fashionable affectation.

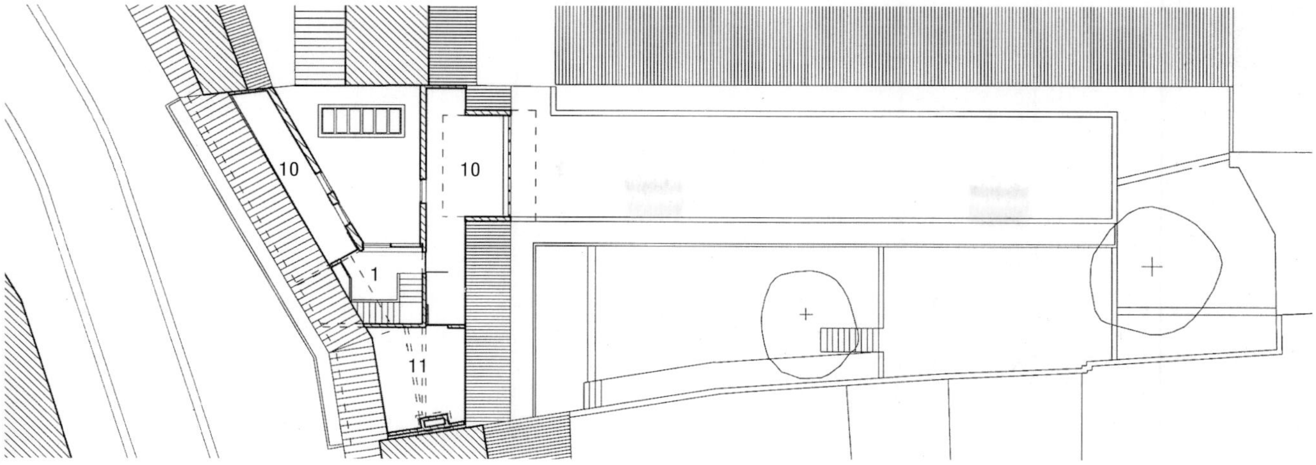

Level 2

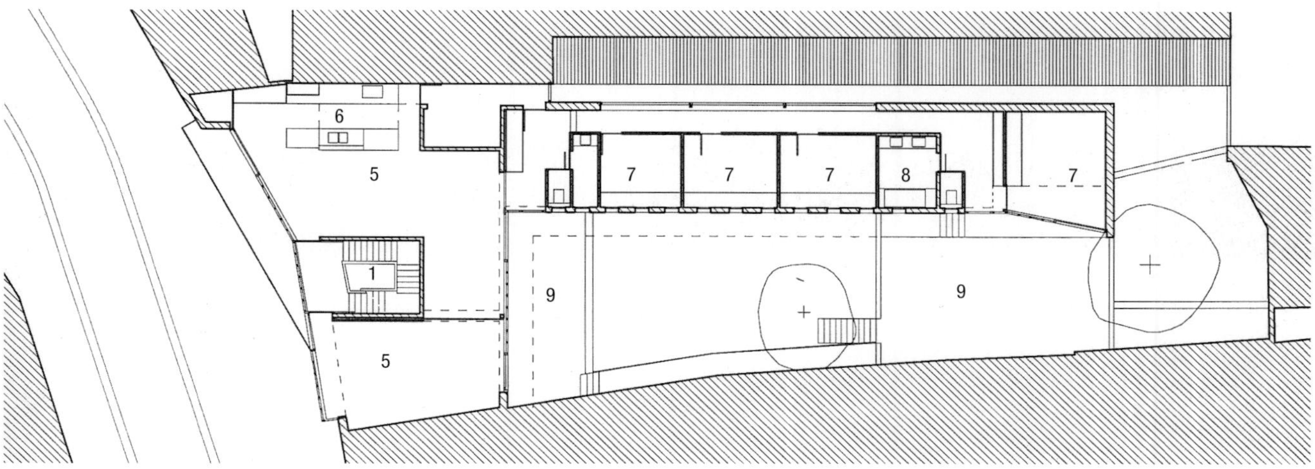

Level 1

Level 0,1 & 2

1 entrance hall / staircase
2 passage
3 carport
4 patio
5 living room
6 kitchen
7 bedroom
8 bathroom
9 terras
10 playroom / office
11 attic

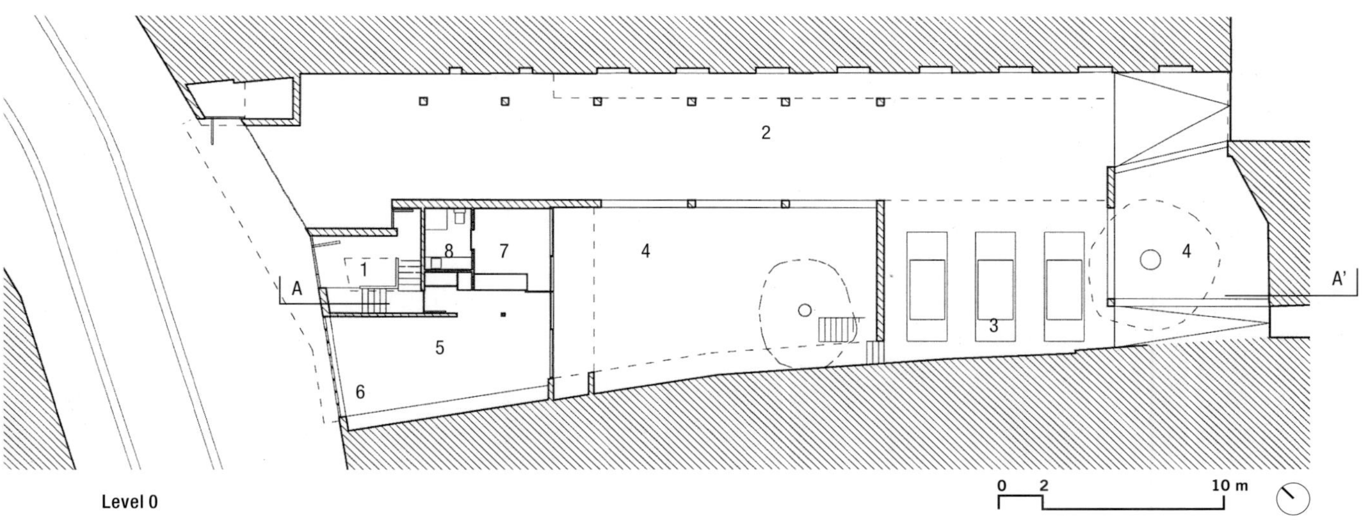

Level 0

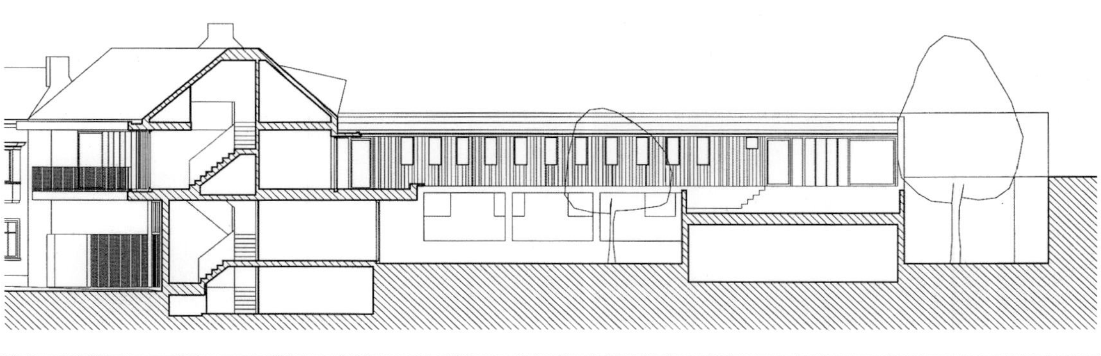

Section AA'

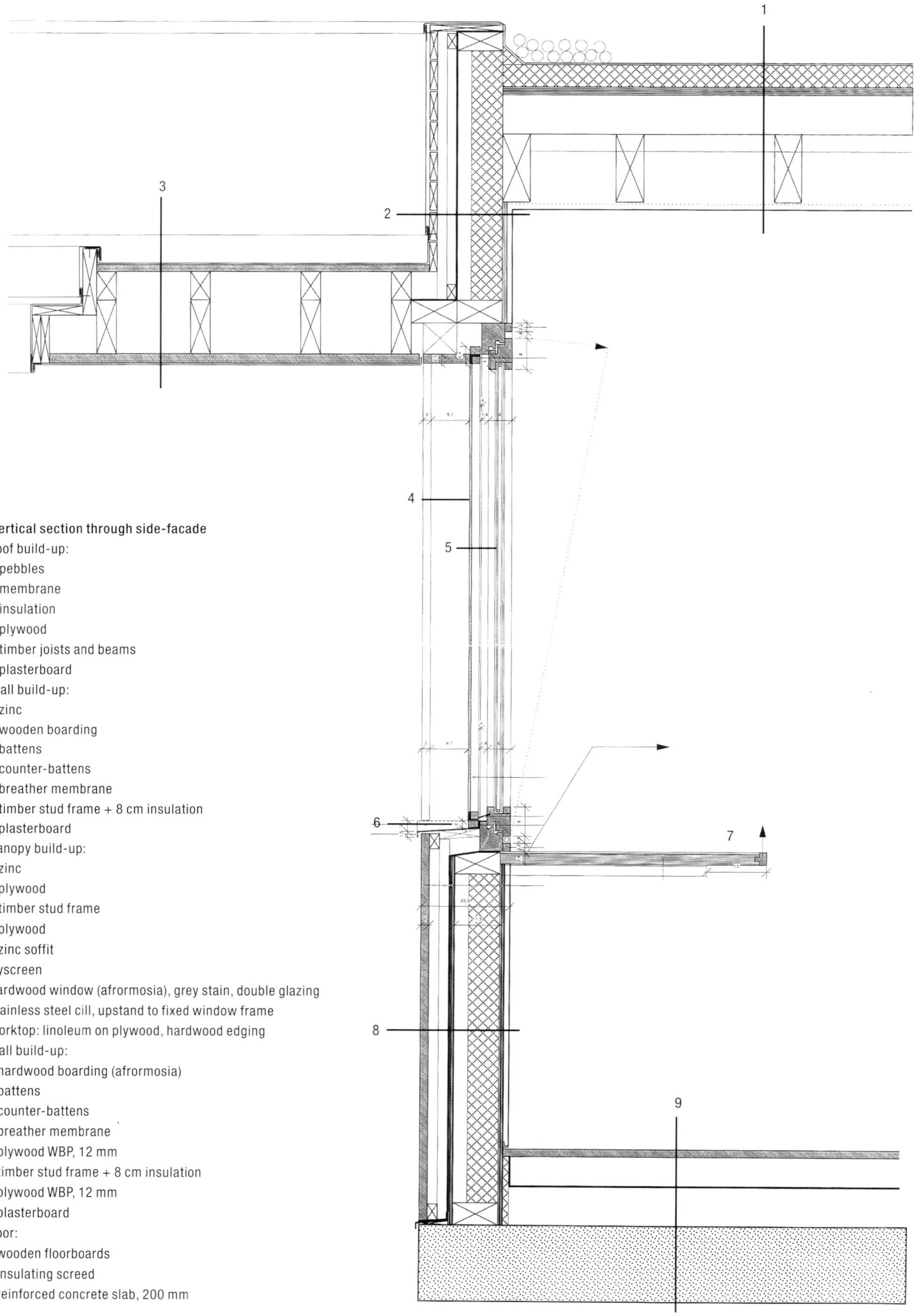

Vertical section through side-facade

1 roof build-up:
  - pebbles
  - membrane
  - insulation
  - plywood
  - timber joists and beams
  - plasterboard

2 wall build-up:
  - zinc
  - wooden boarding
  - battens
  - counter-battens
  - breather membrane
  - timber stud frame + 8 cm insulation
  - plasterboard

3 canopy build-up:
  - zinc
  - plywood
  - timber stud frame
  - plywood
  - zinc soffit

4 flyscreen

5 hardwood window (afrormosia), grey stain, double glazing

6 stainless steel cill, upstand to fixed window frame

7 worktop: linoleum on plywood, hardwood edging

8 wall build-up:
  - hardwood boarding (afrormosia)
  - battens
  - counter-battens
  - breather membrane
  - plywood WBP, 12 mm
  - timber stud frame + 8 cm insulation
  - plywood WBP, 12 mm
  - plasterboard

9 floor:
  - wooden floorboards
  - insulating screed
  - reinforced concrete slab, 200 mm

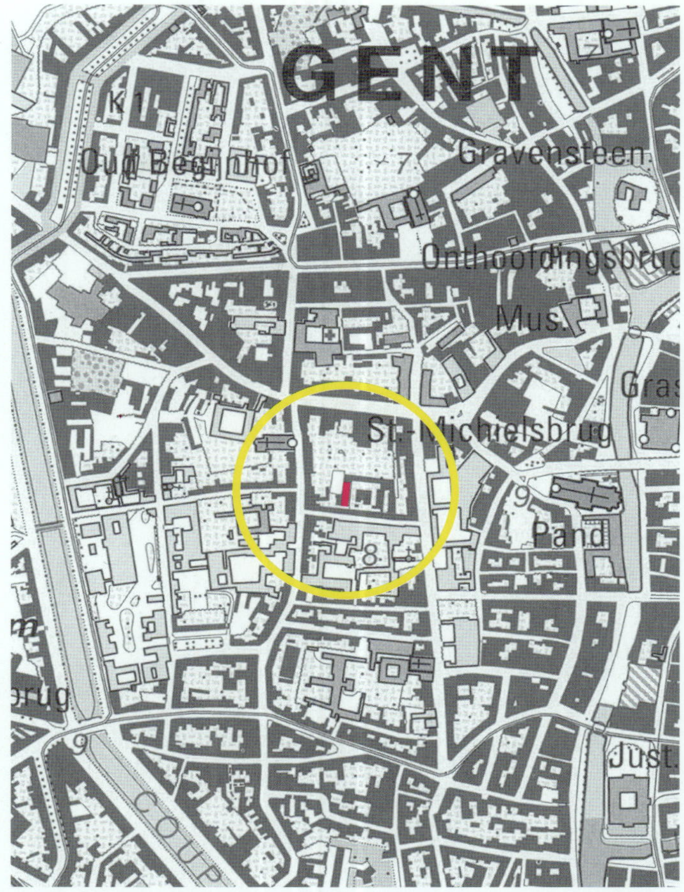

DVH HOUSE

architect **JAN DE VYLDER AND TRICE HOFKENS**

location Schouwvegersstraat 20a, 9000 Ghent

client	Jan De Vylder and Trice Hofkens
design - building	First option on buildings and land: october 1996
	Actual purchase of buildings and land: december 1999
	Occupied: december 200
project-workers	Jan De Vylder I Trice Hofkens
	Bert Van Boxelaere [assistance in execution of communal areas]
contracted work	Bouwonderneming Verfaillie bvba I ICC nv Industrial Cleaning Company
	Dak- en Gevelwerken bvba Ducla I De Loof R. bvba I Camerlynck lastechniek bvba
	Van Eeghem bvba I Wer-bouw bvba I Stroming bvba I Bart Slosse I
	Decolust nv I Serrenbouw De Clerq gebr. bvba I Renoir I
	Piet De Vylder tuin- en landschapsarchitect I ABC design bvba
area	420 sq. m. interior area, 90 sq. m. enclosed gardens
volume	2,500 cubic. m.
building costs	150,000 EUR
building costs/sq. m	350 EUR/sq. m., including exterior spaces
project description	Koen Van Synghel
photography	Jan Kempenaers p.127,128 I André Nullens p.129,132,133
	Stefan Vandermeulen p.126

DVH HOUSE ▸ architect JAN DE VYLDER AND TRICE HOFKENS

The DVH house in Schouwvegersstraat in Ghent is part of a collective renovation project. The architects, Jan De Vylder and Trice Hofkens, bought a complex of nineteenth-century workshop spaces behind a series of workers' houses together with their fellow architects Bert Van Boxelaere and Axel Devroe. As a team, they were able, on the basis of a master-plan, to convince the local council of the feasibility of a *woonerf* (residential precinct). The site was divided into three zones, each with a more private outer area, but all looking onto a communal inner garden.

The master-plan laid down from the very beginning the outlines within which housing for three families would find a natural balance between collectivity and individuality. Despite the dilapidation of the part they were to convert, De Vylder and Hofkens were able to start from the rational column and beam structure and draw inspiration from the industrial construction of this factory building.

The steel columns and beams give the space a grid pattern which immediately provides the designers with a certain spatial division which they have reinforced by dividing the large hall entirely into strips. To do this they used greenhouse walls as interior walls. The choice of these prefabricated industrial greenhouse elements was prompted by an extremely limited budget. While being cheaper than a plastered wall, these glass panels additionally have the advantage that the space remains visually open. What is more, depending on the season, they can be slid open or closed, making the rooms generous or compact. The striking thing here is that the radically economic interpretation of a construction element like a wall opens the way to a surprising form of sustainable architecture. This is because, by using these elements for an actual sun-lounge on the south side, a thermal buffer zone was created between the interior and the exterior.

In essence, De Vylder and Hofkens have created architecture more by leaving out than by adding. For example, by removing the roof from one bay on the south side of the block they created a patio garden which, enclosed by the outer walls of the old factory, enjoys a certain privacy. Something comparable was done at the back. The only difference is the breadth of roof that was removed. In fact in this case one can hardly call it a patio since the outdoor space between the new full-length glass window and the existing wall is no more than a metre. But it turns out to have been a strategic move. On the ground floor this one-metre outdoor strip both gives the bathroom a certain intimacy and at the same time creates the illusion of being outdoors. What is more, the distance from the wall and the full glazing of the rear facade reveals a view of a magnificent tree in the neighbouring garden.

The striking thing about this home is its pronounced and infectious informality, which enables the boundary between inside and outside, bathroom and light-giving yard, kitchen and living area, working space and sitting area to be constantly shifted. The space, which can be adapted to wants and needs by means of the sliding glass walls, is an open invitation to habitation. You can live here as a *homo ludens*. Here, you are free in everything, in the true sense of the word: the space is freely available and you are free to arrange and rearrange depending on the time of day or night, summer or winter, childhood or old age. This is why the architects who live here now occupy half of the home with their working space, and the space now full of computers can be effortlessly transformed, so that the space can at any time be made available to live in.

In their raw beauty, the industrial materials, due to their repetition and pattern, provide sufficient repose, while their roughness gives this urban home a sort of rural quality. Here, one can so to speak come into the house in one's boots. Details in the construction also tell us a lot about the attitude with which the architects have given shape to their concept of architecture for the home.

Where the old structure of columns and beams had to be removed, they replaced them with props: column-like steel supports. Work implements in other words. The use of implements as columns, as structural elements to support the floor of the upper storey, has the feel of improvisation. As if this building were not complete. As if it had not yet outgrown the stage of building and construction.

On closer consideration, this unorthodox use of the prop says a lot about the logic of building, about literally building up and propping up. It seems as if De Vylder and Hofkens have appropriated the props improperly, a sort of artistic appropriation by which means they expose the history and genesis of their building.

The treatment of the storey under the roof does not have the same complex and generous spatial interaction of the greenhouse walls downstairs. The uniform woodwork of the walls, floors and ceilings in rough chipboard retains all the visual qualities of the material, which was chosen for its very economic price. The construction does not succeed in transcending this economic factor or matching the spatial interaction of the light sliding walls below.

This does not detract from the fact that it is precisely the contrast between the 'log cabin' stability, the determinacy of the wooden walls, and the lightness of the ground floor that provides a livable balance. In any case, the quality of living created here is high. A quality that has nothing to do with the luxury of unusual materials and gadgets, but relies

on a spatial freedom that is created both in the home itself and in the layout of the communal garden. What's more, the cars stand casually in the yard, the scrap wood lies ready for the winter hearth... Living in this house means living naturally in the city.

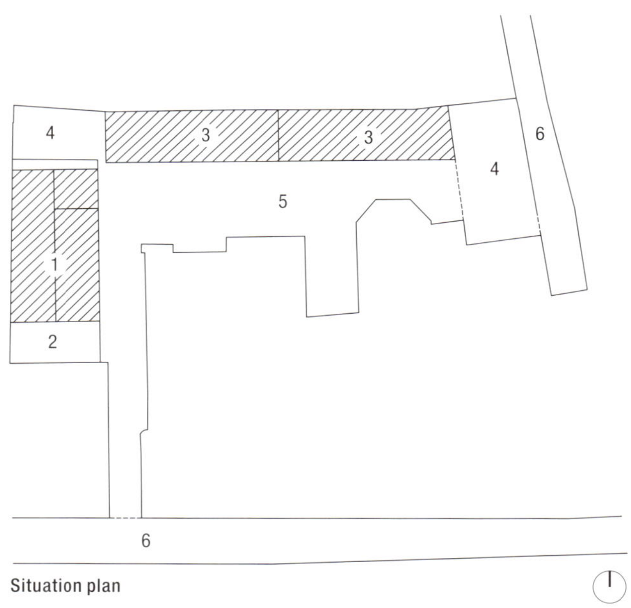

Situation plan

1 DVH house
2 DVH patio
3 house
4 patio
5 communal internal garden
6 street

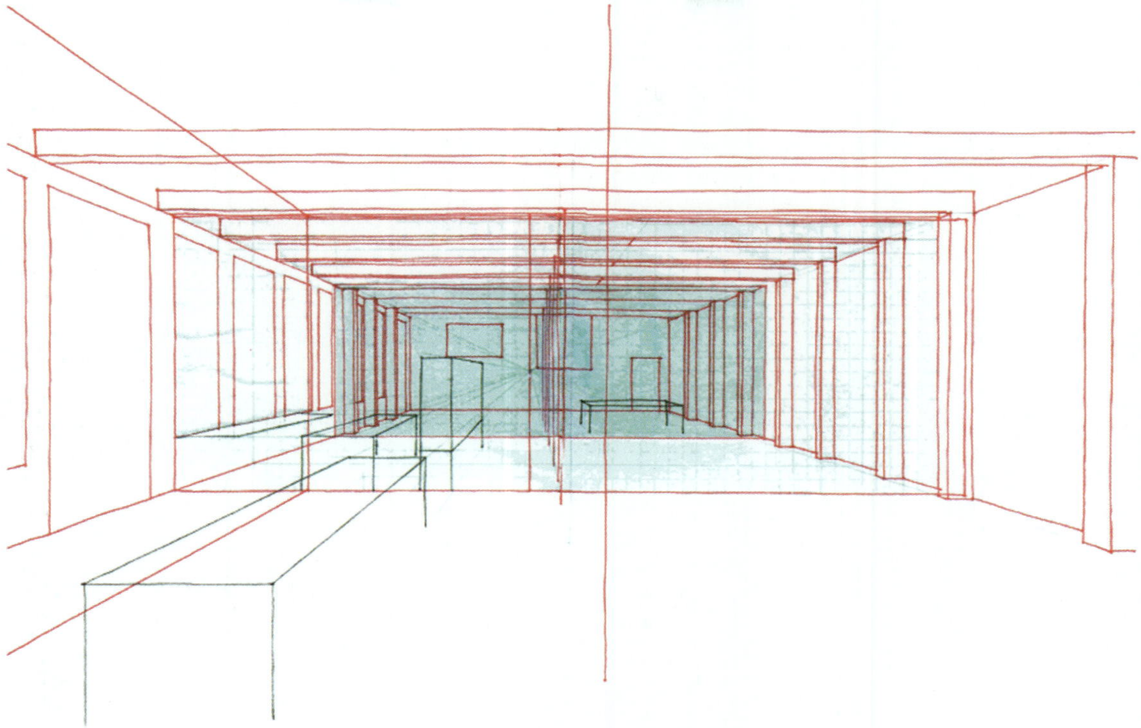

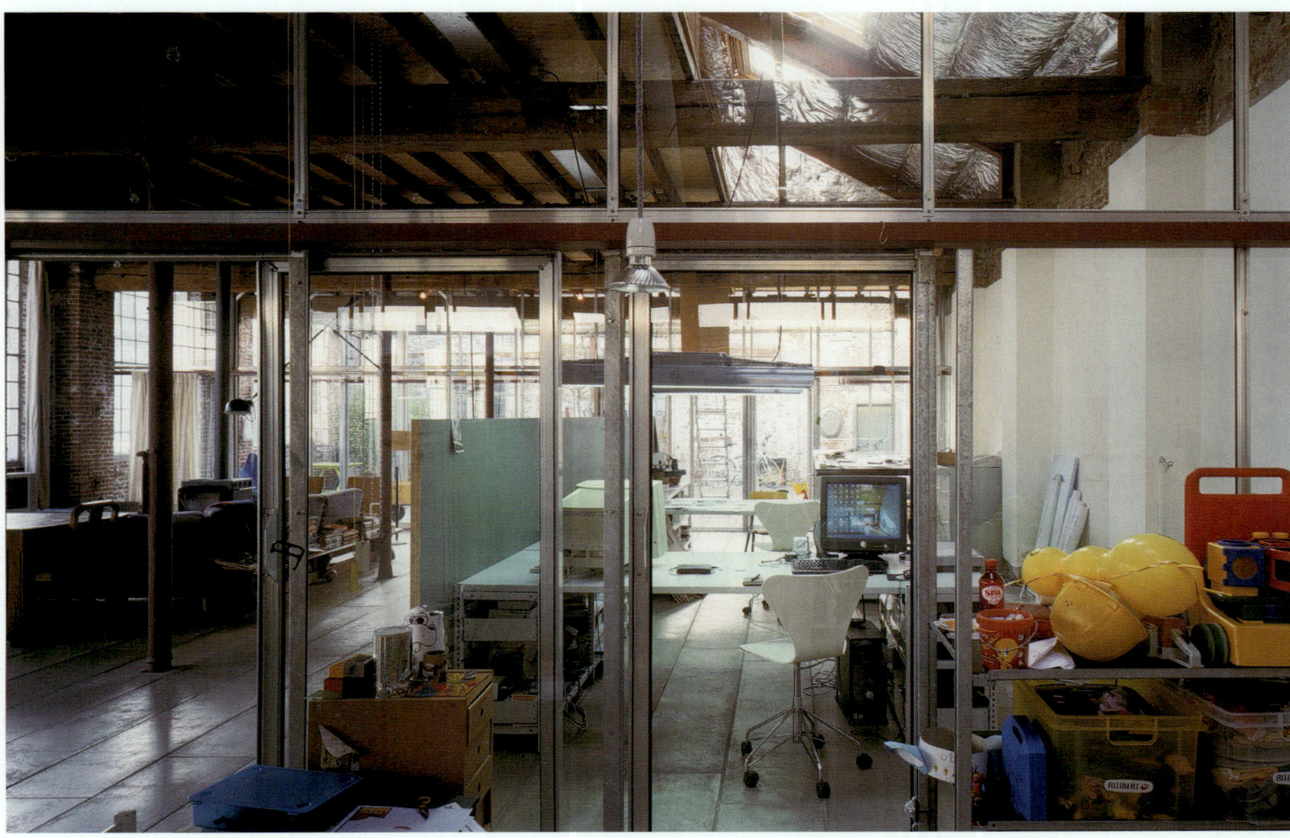

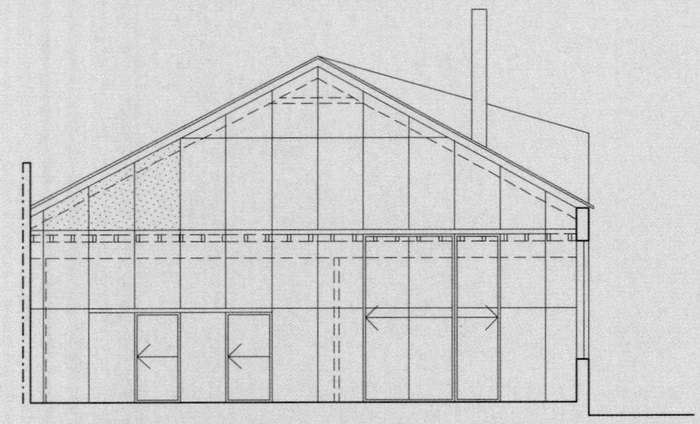
Section DD'

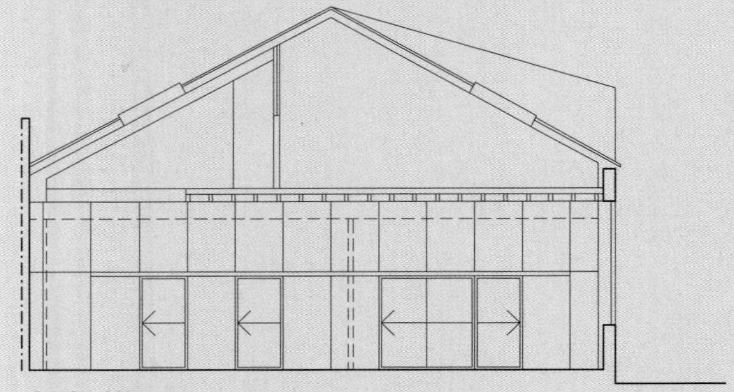
Section CC'

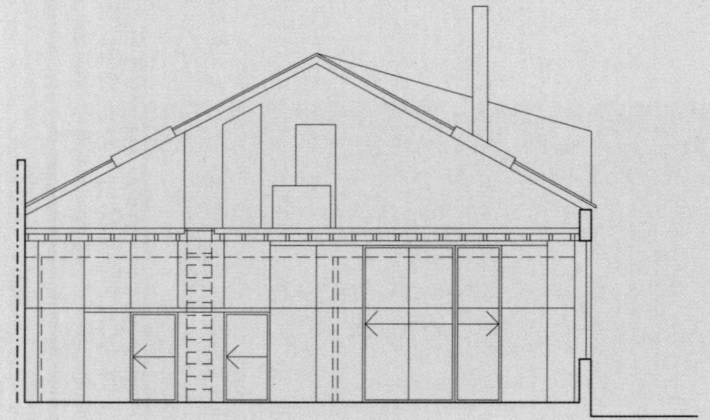
Section BB'

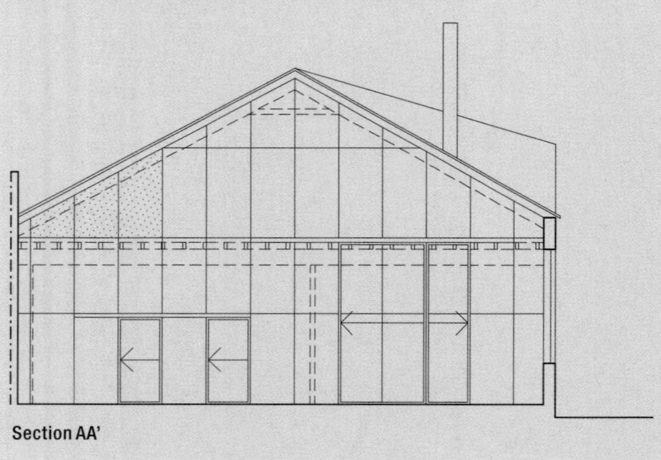
Section AA'

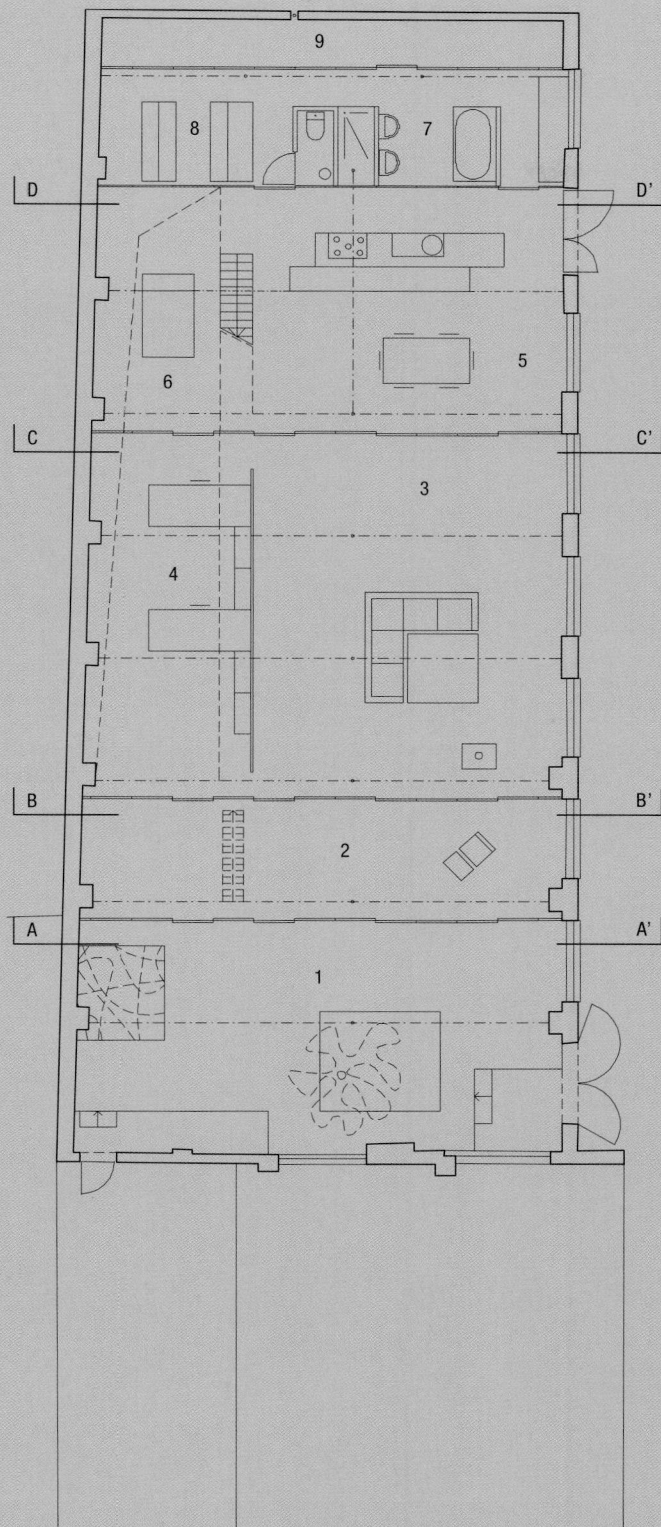

Level 0

1 entrance patio
2 sun lounge
3 living room
4 workroom
5 kitchen
6 play area
7 bathroom
8 storage
9 patio

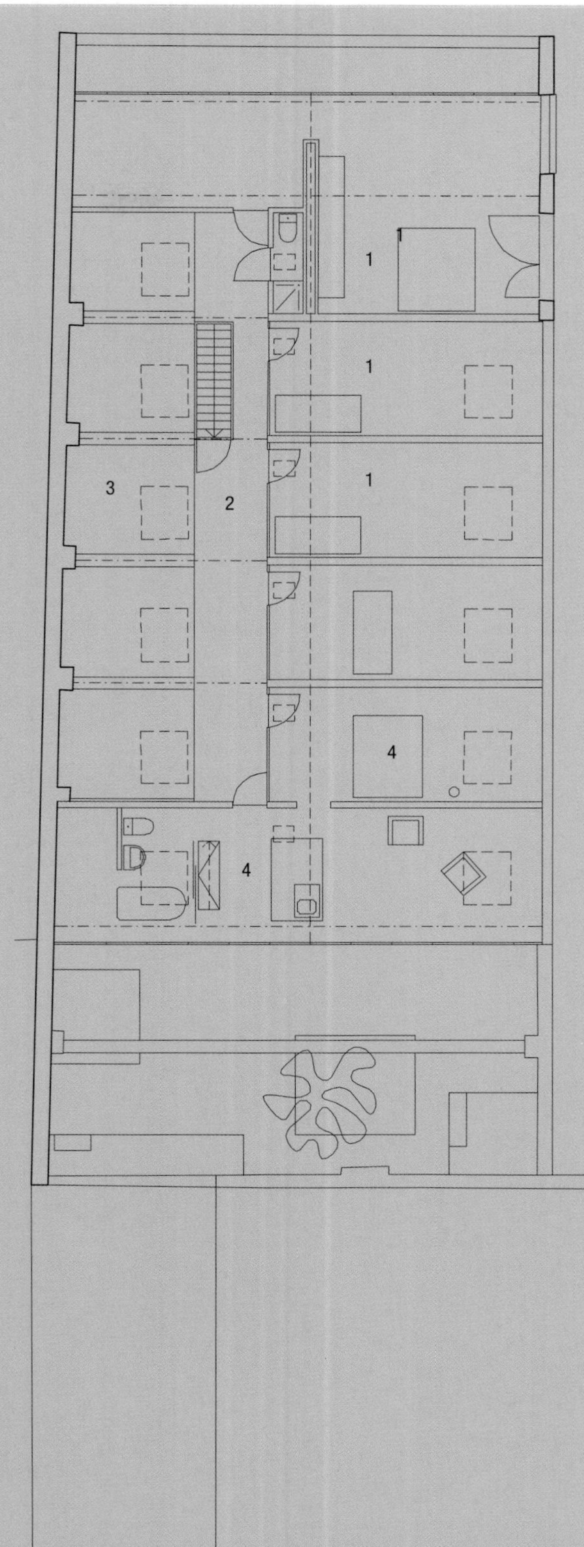

Level 1

1 bedroom
2 night hall
3 void
4 studio flat

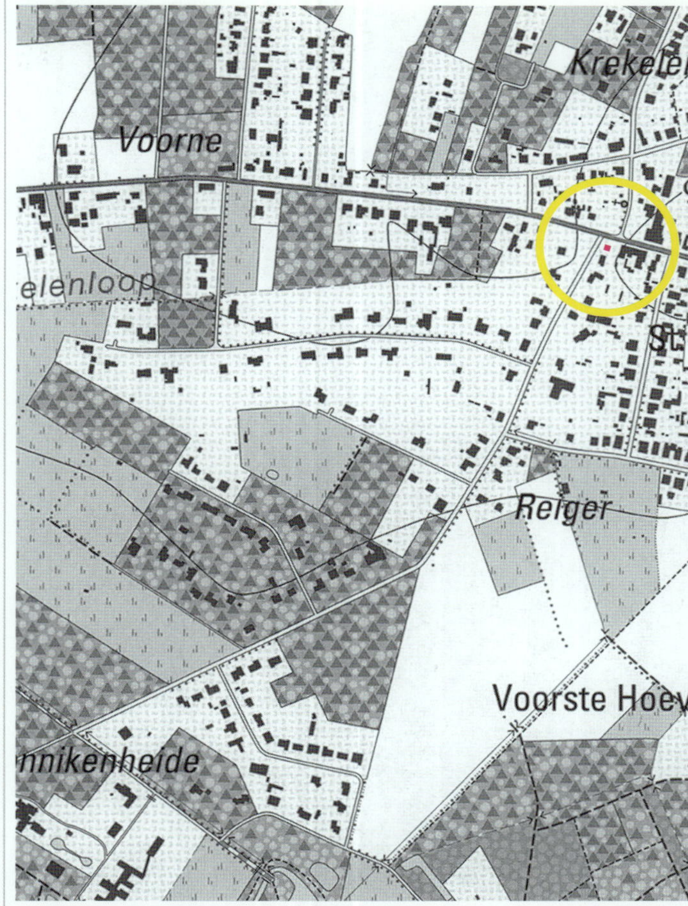

HOUSE ON THE VOORNE – MONNIKENHEIDE, ZOERSEL

architect	**HUISWERK ARCHITECTS**
location	Voorne 1, 2980 Zoersel

client	Monnikenheide vzw
design - building	2000-2003
project-workers	Dirk Somers I Eric Wieërs
engineers	Newton bvba
contracted work	Bouwonderneming Dillen bvba
area	365 sq. m.
volume	1,130 cubic. m.
building costs/sg. m	1,300 EUR/sq. m. (excl. VAT and fees)
project description	Raf Snoeckx
photography	Karin Borghouts p.138,139 I Paul d'Haese p.142,143 Huiswerk Architects p.137 I Stefan Vandermeulen p.136

 HOUSE ON THE VOORNE ▸ architect **HUISWERK ARCHITECTS**

The Monnikenheide organisation's domain lies withdrawn in the woods of the rural district of Zoersel, between Antwerp and Turnhout. It was founded as a private initiative thirty years ago and its creation of a short-stay centre made it a pioneer in the individual approach to providing services and accommodation for people with a mental disability. The domain was later expanded to include an occupational home and a day centre offering permanent care, and the quality of the housing became a major point. Housing in this context means collective living under supervision, shielded from the village and wider community.

The residents requested more independence and so in spring 2000 a pilot project was set up offering an alternative to eight of them: more independent and closer to the life of the village. The House on the Voorne, named after a local stream, thereby became the first project under the name 'Sheltered Living'.

It was a large house on the edge of the village, where mainly small-scale terraced building gives way to large villas on land carved out of the wood. It has adopted the scale of the villas and the form of the village houses, it accommodates eight residents and thus achieves its collectivity in an atypical house. The house seems to be aware of its position on the edge of the village and makes use of it by adopting a number of typical elements from the different forms of housing and letting them clash with each other: from the village it takes the gable clad in slate (with windows!) From the wood the panoramic window with a view of nature; the minimal bathroom windows are drawn from the collective housing block and the brick from the postwar workman's house; lastly, the asymmetrical roof in zinc is quite hard to place. The entity created out of all this transcends the banality of the individual parts. They are stuck together to form an apparently untidy volume and in so doing their significance changes as soon as one views them from another angle.

Just as a badly moulded pot on a potter's wheel seems to be constantly changing shape, this house too is always showing a different face. Making stately eyes at the village, stretched out in the grass or just inconspicuous at the side of the road. As a result of these changing impressions, the house seems to come to life, to move in its surroundings and to be almost absorbed by them, as if it shared something with a common lot on this site. A building can integrate too. It did not want to demand a place in the village, it just occupied it and tells us precisely what its residents want to say: that they just want to belong.

This 'making its mark' is not limited to the expression of its relationship to its surroundings. From the inside too it says something about itself and its residents. The whole programme – eight individual studios, a communal kitchen/

breakfast room and a bathroom – is organised round a three-storey hall. By pushing the stairs and the lift to the perimeter, this space like an oversized void bathed in white light in an otherwise compact volume.

Behind the closed and almost invisible doors on this hall lie eight different, highly personal private lives, two on the ground floor and three on each of the upper floors. Each studio has its own sanitary unit with toilet and shower, a kitchenette and a small sitting area. They have plenty of windows, and are oriented more towards their surroundings and themselves than the interior of the house. Here the individual comes first.

From the hall, the kitchen-cum-breakfast room is much more conspicuous. With its large doorway, which is probably only closed on cold days, it connects with the hall and uses its spaciousness to spread its sphere of influence over the whole building. As such, the hall functions as a buffer between the individual aspect, which lies behind its walls, and the collective, with which it shares its space. But the void can also be charged with other meanings. The sterility of the white walls and doors, reinforced by the solid parapets upstairs, makes us aware of our position as intruders in a clinical set-up. Because, however independent these people with mental disabilities may be, they always have the air of needing help and of vulnerability. Nothing here is

more linked to this than the 'white'. But it is not 'fridge' white that reflects everything: the plastering has the fragile and porous appearance of a sugar-cube and is thereby in keeping with the ultra-domestic check pattern of red and white tiles that cover the floors and stairs. In this way, in addition to the arrangement of the spaces, the treatment of the surfaces also helps weave together the intimate aspect of domestic living and the clean, impersonal nature of collective care provision.

The complexity of these unusual relationships is entirely concealed behind the naturalness with which the designers have been able to achieve it. They appear not to have had the ambition of entertaining us with surprising perspectives and inventive details. Nowhere does our gaze linger on anything that is not familiar to us. This upgrading of what is ordinary and banal, which is in fact characteristic of all Huiswerk's work, appears to be fully reconciled to the exceptional nature of the brief, which could not tolerate architecture of any weight.

Of particular note here is that this building might provide a model for the whole institutional sector. Whereas accommodation in rooms in old people's homes, youth institutions, reception centres and so on - arranged along long corridors in wings of sombre buildings or housed in pavilions on enclosed domains - is always secondary to accommodation in 'the institution', here the domestic is equal in status to the institutional aspect, and one can truly call it a 'home'. A home in a highly condensed setting. Because, whereas for the client it started out as an experiment in giving their familiar collective living a more individual character, the designers were able to turn this to their advantage and, using the form of the individual village house, have carried out an experiment in more compact collective living.

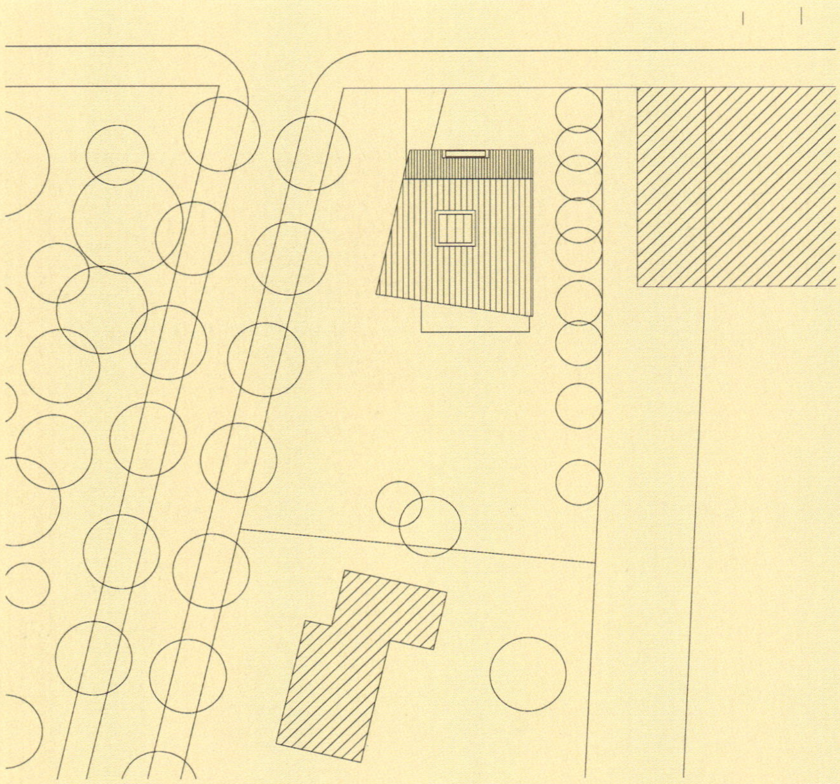

Situation plan

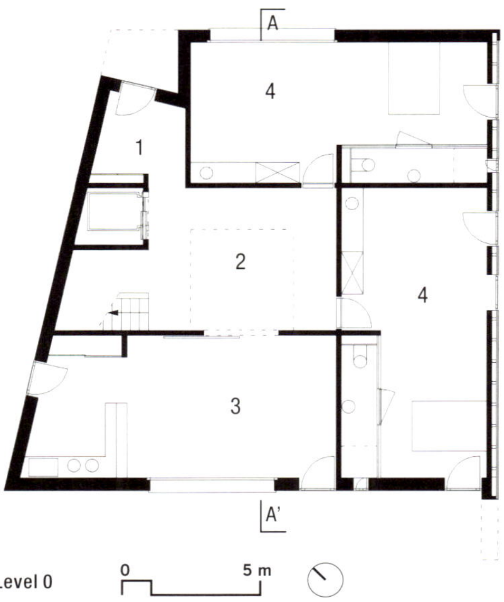

Level 0

Level 0, 1 & 2

1 entrance hall
2 main hall
3 communal living room
4 studio flat
5 void
6 bathroom
7 storage
8 duplex studio flat
9 fire place

Level 1

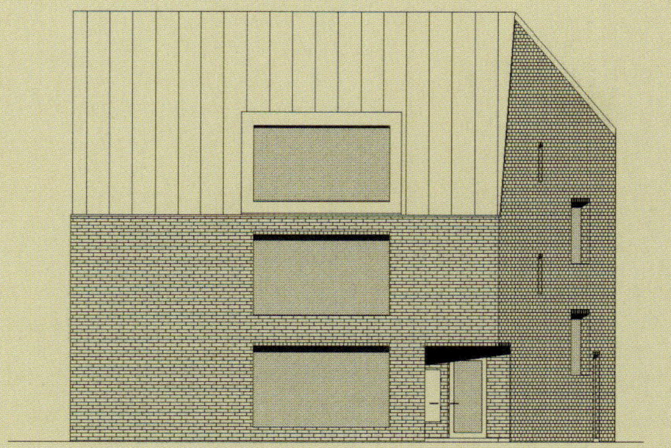
North facade

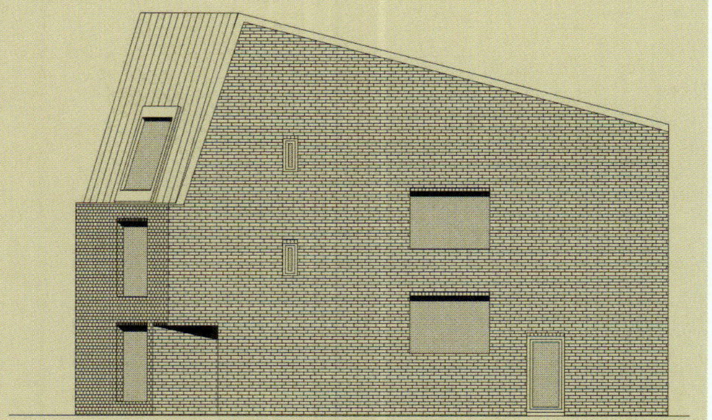
West facade

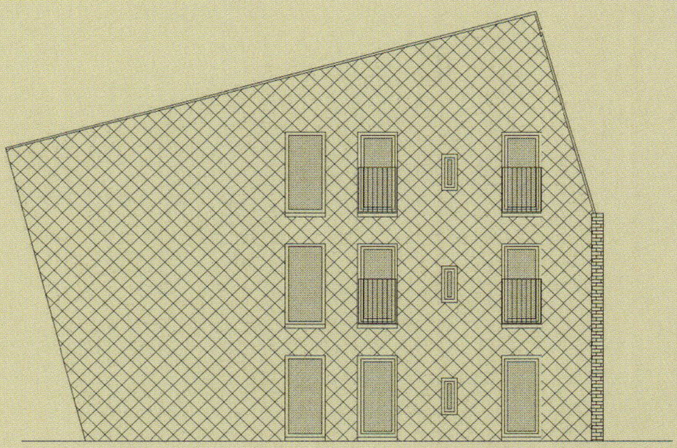
South facade

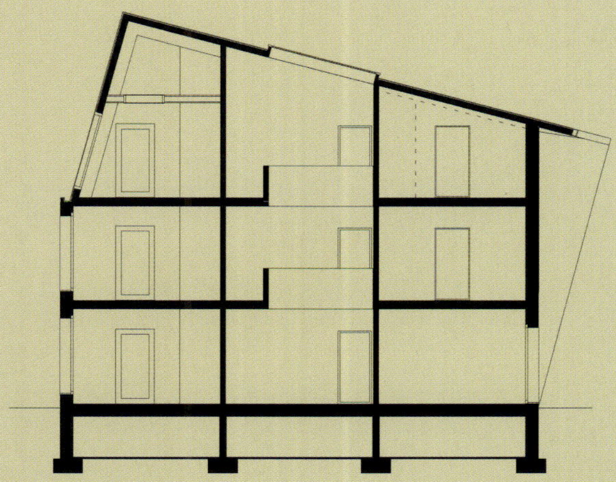
Section AA'

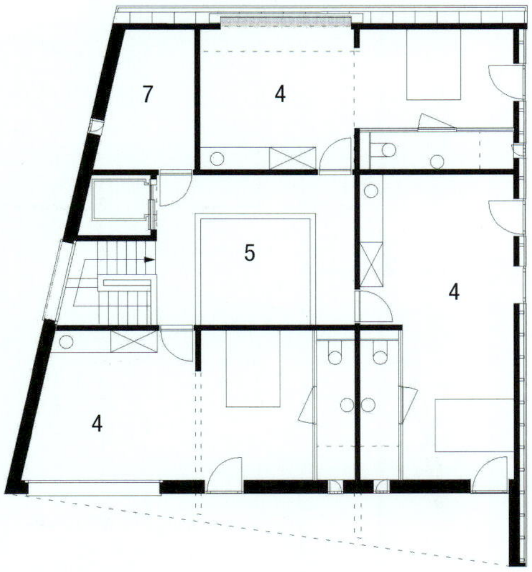

Level 2

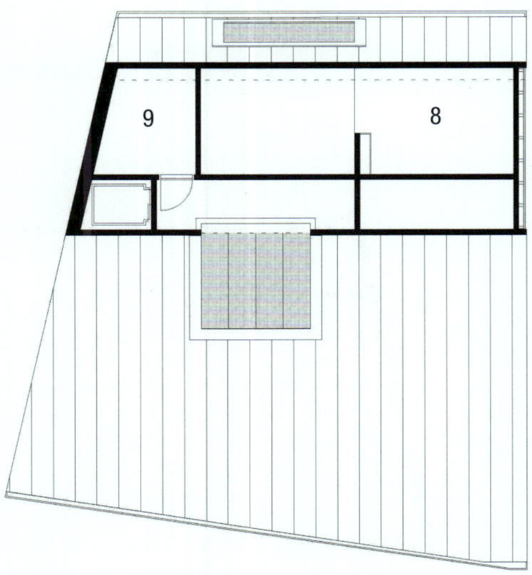

Level attic

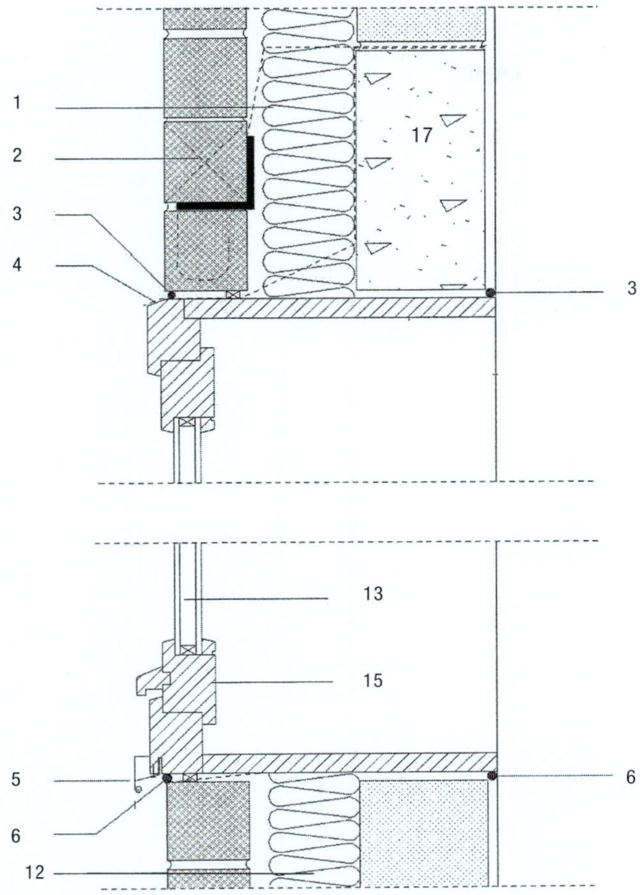

Window detail 1

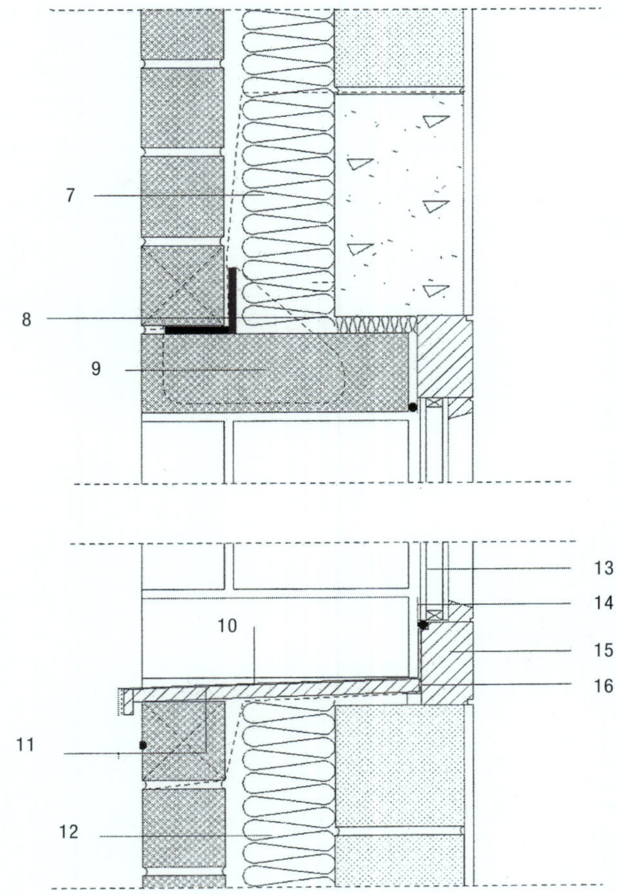

Window detail 2

1 PE foil flashing
2 open vertical joint brickwork
3 injected filling
4 folded zinc flashing
5 zinc flashing milled into frame
6 injected filling
7 PE foil flashing
8 L-section
9 suspension of strecher course on brackets
10 sill in folded zinc
11 plywood
12 cavity insulation, 10 cm
13 double glazing
14 aluminium L-section
15 wooden window
16 PE foil
17 reinforced concrete beam

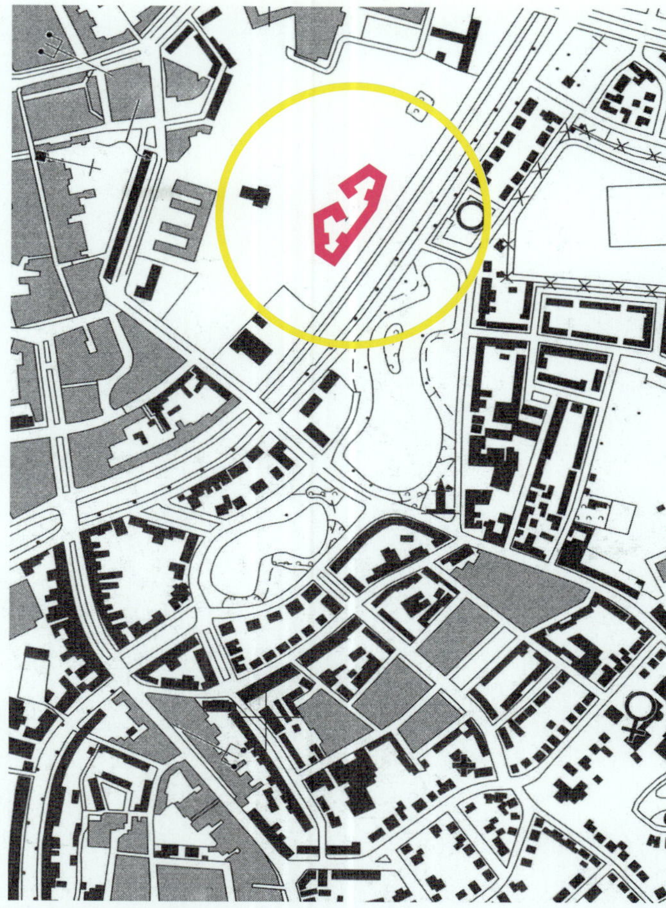

APARTMENT TOWERS ON THE CHASSÉ SITE

architect	**XAVEER DE GEYTER ARCHITECTS**
location	Chassé site, Breda (NL)

client	Chassé C.V. [Proper Stok Woningen I Rotterdam and Wilma BouwI Weert]
building brief	5 towerblocks with 137 luxury flats [13 floors], indoor parking [229 spaces] and inner garden
design	1996-1999
building	1999-2001
project-workers	Xaveer de Geyter I Ester Goris [project architects] Karolien De Schepper I Burton Hamfelt I Lieven De Boeck Lieve Van De Ginste I Oscar Juarros [†] I Arnaud Hendrickx I Freek Persyn
engineers	ABT Bouwkunde, Arnhem [architectural engineering] Snellen (NL) , Meulemans & van schaaik, Breda (NL) [stability] Inside Outside, Petra Blaisse, Amsterdam (NL) [landscape design]
contracted work	Wilma Bouw, Weert (NL)
area	33,420 sq. m.
building costs	18,562,180 EUR
building costs/sq. m.	555.42 EUR
project description	Els Vervloesem
photography	Karin Borghouts p.149 I Wim Ruigrok p.146 Hans Werleman p.147,148,152,153

146 APARTMENT TOWERS ON THE CHASSÉ SITE ▸ architect XAVEER DE GEYTER ARCHITECTS

In 1994 the city of Breda organised a competition for the Chassé site, a disused military domain in the historical centre of the city. The intention was to develop this domain, 'empty' but for a few barracks, for housing. Due to political disagreement about the selection, it took four years before the urban development plan by the Office for Metropolitan Architecture (OMA) was officially designated the winning design. The definitive urban development plan by OMA and Xaveer De Geyter (1998) is based on the campus model. This means that as much open space as possible was to be retained for a new park, while the housing density created had to be comparable to the centre of Breda. With reference to the campus model, a number of compact residential buildings had to be located in the park, with pronounced typological differentiation.

The urban development plan was worked out at the same time as the plan for the arrangement of the site and the draft designs for the buildings. This led to a remarkable density of 50 homes per hectare over the whole site, concentrated on only 28% of the area. Almost three quarters of the site was therefore available for the park, designed by West 8. In this way the sparse urban open space was no longer broken up into hundreds of individual lots and reduced to residual space, but was elevated to the role of binder, both literally and figuratively: for the buildings and for the users. The park functions as a collective garden for the residents and at the same time is an extra public space for visitors to and inhabitants of the city of Breda. The towers designed by Xaveer De Geyter Architects fit perfectly into this concept. They stand, five together, informally alongside the Chassé Singel on the east side of the site, each looking in a different direction. The parking ring-road that raises them up slightly above ground level encloses a sunken semi-public garden. The towers are situated so as to break away from the modernist way of arranging buildings in a fixed pattern. Homogeneity and dullness are replaced by heterogeneity and tension. Tension between distance and proximity. Tension between openness and the urban setting. Tension between looking and being looked at.

From the inside, the open glazed facade with its prefab V structure gives a broad view of the Chassé park, the greenery outside the city or the historical centre, depending on the orientation of the facades. At the same time, from the same window, you are confronted with the proximity of the other towers, the neighbours, whose facade is more closed from this angle. Outside too, walking around the towers, you experience the way the balance between openness and closedness changes at every step.

Sometimes you unexpectedly have a through-view, as for example of the water-tower on the adjacent land. Then the towers again coagulate into a monolithic mass. The creation

of semi-public spaces is also a bonus compared to the modernist principle. In the case of the towers the semi-public inner garden functions as a sort of communal reception room. This intermediate space is characterised by a certain ambiguity (how could it be otherwise?). On the one hand it forms the transition between public and private space, and on the other it offers the possibility of avoiding the public space.

The synchronous design of the masterplan, layout and architecture also led to a number of rules intended to optimise the connections with the existing urban fabric and the adjacent green area. The morphology of the existing large-scale and object-based buildings on the boundary of the site (including the Chassé Theatre and the Municipal Office) had to be incorporated into the new residential buildings. The intention was that the park should draw the green peripheral area towards the inner city. In this way, more than simply by the demolition of its enclosing wall, the Chassé site pulls not only itself but also the city and the peripheral area out of their isolation.

In the towers by Xaveer De Geyter Architects, the onus for communication with the surroundings is put on the composition of the facades. Although they are all made of identical materials, which are concrete, glass and white glazed bricks, each tower looks different. The facades facing the semi-public inner garden are clad in white glazed brick, which reflects the sunlight. In the other facades, large areas of glass with the V structure behind them alternate with a chessboard of black concrete panels and small windows. This varying pattern of open and closed facade elements is defined more by the direct surroundings than by the view and the orientation. Confrontations between the towers and the ring-road, the other towers and the neighbouring buildings define sharply delineated zones in the facades that should have been more closed. For example, the proximity of the *Brug*, a bridge-shaped housing block designed by Kollhoff, leads, in the tower opposite it, to a horizontal band of concrete panels and small windows in an otherwise fully-glazed facade. In this way the view in is blocked, while outside there arises a complex dialogue between the towers, the ring-road and Kollhoff's Brug.

It is clear that the interaction between the different design levels enables the views of density and context to be confirmed, reinforced or differentiated. But as far as the brief is concerned, there has been a major shift of emphasis. Whereas the local authority, with its programme of requirements for the master-plan, could still determine that a minimum of six hundred homes had to be provided, including at least one hundred rented social homes, the programme for De Geyter's towers was put in the hands of the free market. This means that there is now little to be found of the social mix

Situation plan

inherent in the master-plan. However, the result, 137 luxury flats for sale, is a commercial success. They were all sold in no time. And it was impossible to keep up with demand for the most expensive, the penthouses. Because a rational plan was used, it was possible to take account of this until six months before building started. This ultimately led to one tower with just one flat per floor, a larger block with four flats per floor and three blocks with a mix of one or two flats per floor. The social principle inherent to modernism was swapped for the principle of the highest bidder.

In the Netherlands it is no longer the government but the client and the market that play a fundamental part in housing construction. In the case of the towers this client was also the contractor. This had a powerful influence on the project. The choice of tunnel formwork and prefab concrete facade panels was for example no coincidence, but a direct consequence of the fact that the contractor owns several concrete companies. But even Dutch regulations impose certain restrictions. Each flat, for instance, had to have a certain standard percentage of outdoor space.

Yet Xaveer De Geyter Architects were in each case able to turn these limitations to their advantage. By providing sliding windows on two sides, the obligatory terrace can also be used as a separate indoor room or as an extension of the living area. At the same time this flexible arrangement makes it possible to make a relatively large percentage of the flat (up to 17% or 18 sq. m.) into 'terrace'. In the use of concrete too, an individual approach was sought that deviated from the standard solutions. The first example of this is the prefab V structures placed in the tunnel formwork. This meant that in addition to the end, one side of the tunnel could also be opened up to the maximum. The second and last example is the prefab concrete facade panels incorporating fragments of slate. Depending on the light incidence, the staccato rhythm of the glass and concrete changes into a tornado of illuminated silver pigments. Like giant freckles that come sensually to the surface in sunlight.

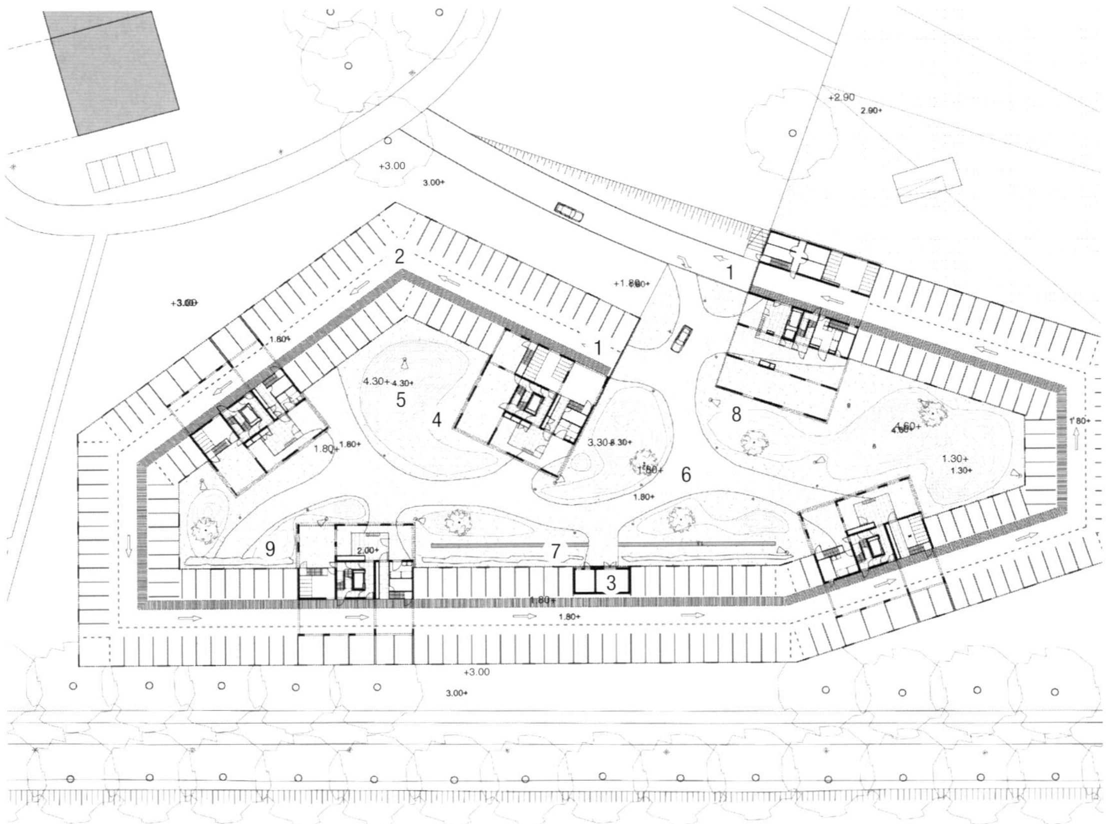

Positions - garage level

1 car park entrance/exit
2 225 parking spaces
3 substation
4 shells
5 grassy dunes
6 path
7 bench
8 *Pinus sylvestris*
9 bamboo

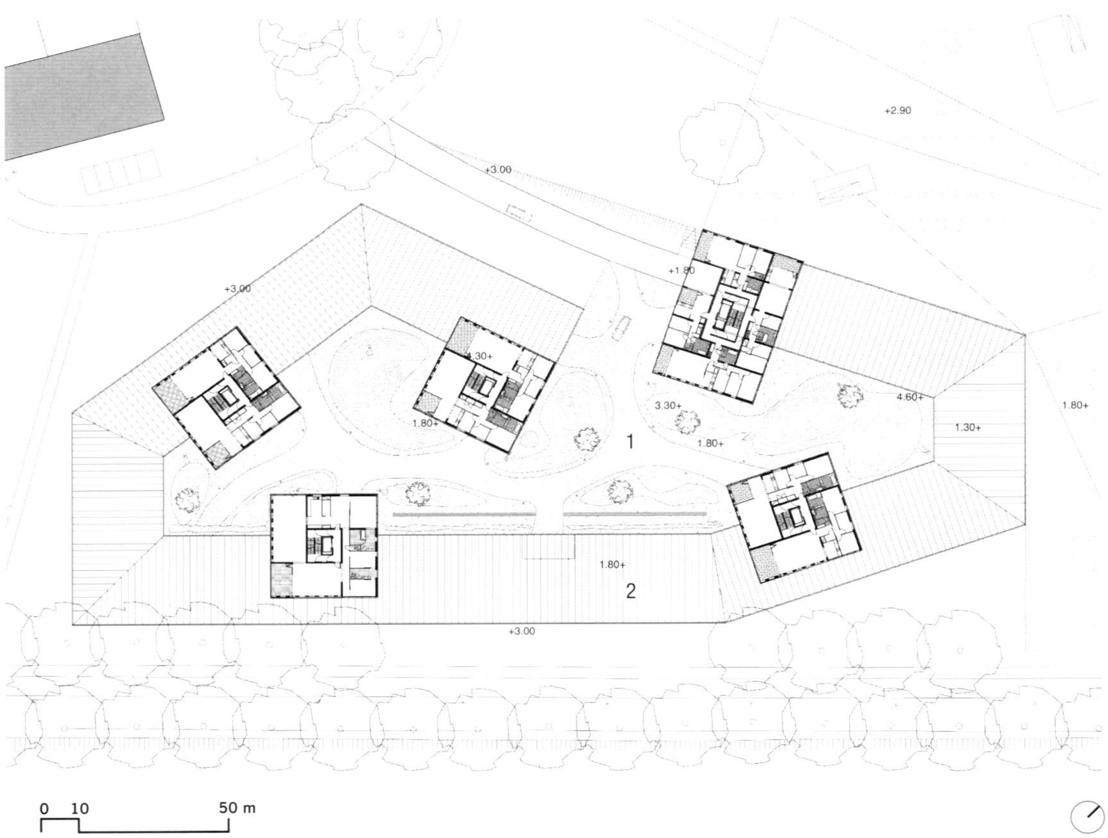

Positions - tower level

1 sunken inner garden
2 roof of car park

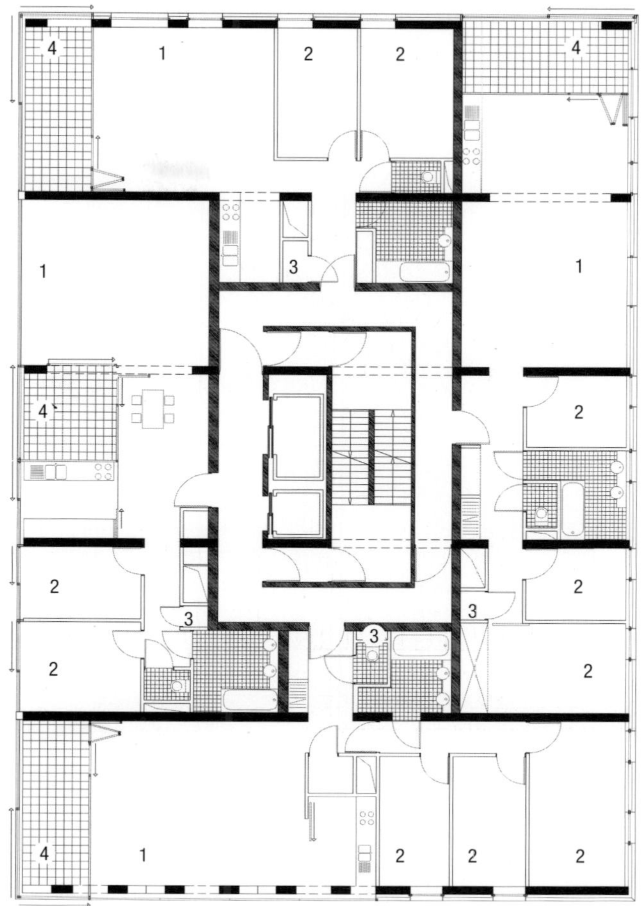

Typical-plan, rectangular tower: four flats per storey

1 living room
2 bedroom
3 storage
4 terrace

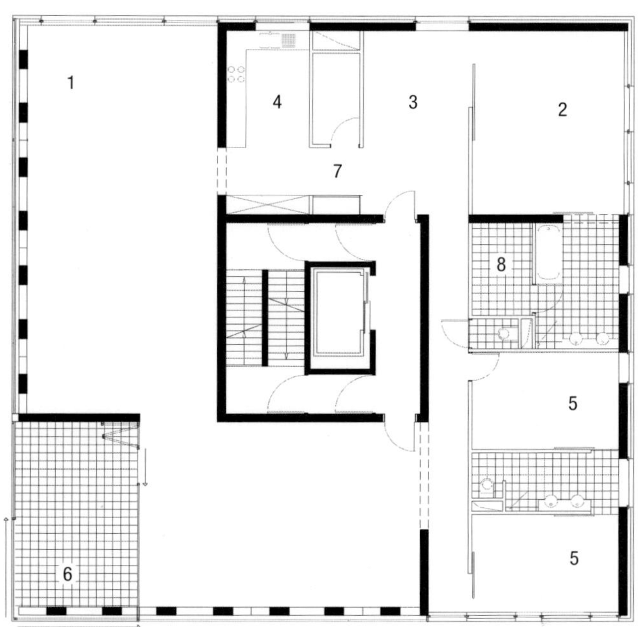

Typical-plan, square tower: one flat per storey

1 living room
2 master bedroom
3 workroom/library
4 storage
5 bedroom
6 terrace
7 service entrance
8 sauna

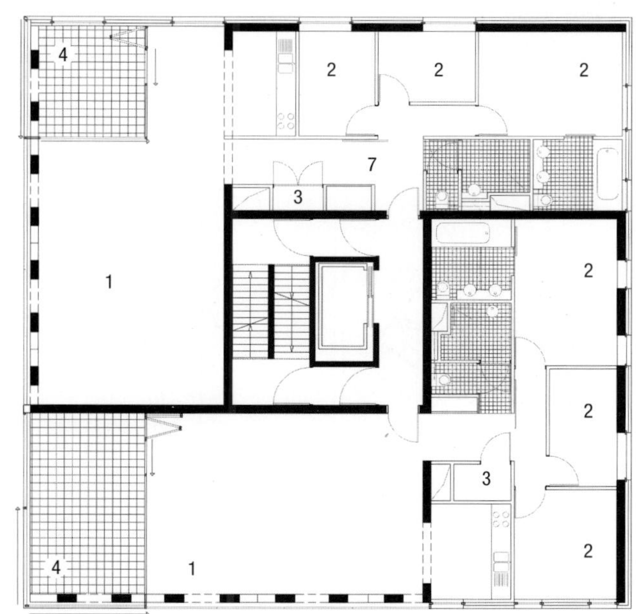

Typical-plan, square tower: two flats per storey

1 living room
2 bedroom
3 storage
4 terrace

I

2

ASPECTS OF DENSITY: EXTRAPOLATIONS FROM FOUR TOWN HOUSES

WILLIAM MANN

This article takes four town houses and a number of associated urban design projects as the basis for a discussion of the practical issues raised by the drive for greater density in Flanders. It is my contention that these projects, which demonstrate facets of an evolutionary, piecemeal approach to urban development, offer several valuable lessons in relation to questions of density: on the utility of house types which tolerate or support proximity; on the intimate relation between architecture and urban design in realising quality and quantity; and, in passing, on the relativity of density as a concept and the importance of a mixture of residential with other uses. These lessons may be of interest to neighbouring regions, but deserve particular consideration in Flanders, where it would be all too easy to overlook their local significance.

THE DENSITY QUESTION: THE SPECIFICITY OF FLANDERS

The ambition to build at higher densities in the regions of northwest Europe – Flanders, the Dutch Randstad, Southeast England – is driven by a number of factors: population growth, the tendency to smaller households, the decreasing supply of undeveloped land, and the ambition to manage urban growth in a more sustainable framework. In Flanders' neighbouring regions, the first of these issues – rapid population growth – dominates and distorts the agenda, to the point that the currency of debate is 'housing units' in their hundreds if not their thousands.(1) Flanders' situation is distinguished by less intense pressure from population growth, and by the relatively light market pressure on its cities. The relative absence of these pressures can either serve as an opportunity for the creation of exemplary solutions or as an excuse for complacency.

While the piecemeal tradition has kept Flanders free of large scale 'problem' developments in the past, it is not clear whether the administrative, commercial or design disciplines are in place to achieve even the modest housing expansion currently envisaged with a minimum of coherence. Is Flanders incapable of large scale urban expansion, or does it simply not need them? The everyday practice of Flemish development, with many levels of government and the relative dependence on private sector and individual actors, appears singularly resistant to urban design or strategic initiatives, with their requirement for decisiveness and political willpower.(2) This abdication threatens to place a burden of excessive expectation on architectural practice: to solve the challenges of city making without the full range of tools required for the job. In what follows, I have attempted to demonstrate the close interdependence of architectural and urban design disciplines in delivering both quantity and quality in urban areas.

3

4

AN 'EXHIBITION VILLAGE'

The VLABO (3) 'exhibition village' [*Kijkdorp*] at Londerzeel (illustration 3,4) is a very clear illustration of the possibilities and limitations of architecture as a tool for addressing the challenges of dense, or sustainable living. This project is underpinned by a praiseworthy but futile belief in typological experimentation: praiseworthy because the issues demand deviation from conventional practices and mentalities, futile because the 'types' are interpreted as freestanding objects, without a coherent urban plan to anchor them. (4) As such, the whole is less than the sum of its parts.

A number of architects (including BOB 361, Hugo Koch, Frank Delmulle and Hans Barbier) have tested their considerable ingenuity in sketching out permutations for the combination of houses (and, more successfully, on the design of the houses themselves): in staggered or straight rows, clustered, scattered on small plots. Yet the absence of a clear strategy for the public realm has led to considerable waste of space, as well as poorly defined linkages to the existing settlement. The whole appears to be dominated by a fear of proximity: difficult conditions, such as corners or back-to-backs are avoided. Despite the urban appearance of the architectural typologies used, all that has been achieved in terms of density is a distinctly suburban 30 units/ha. At face value, the four thoughtfully-conceived town houses in this year's selection distinguish themselves mostly through their inventive response to the specificities of their individual sites. Yet their handling of the generic issues around the proximity of urban living is also exemplary: how the privacy of the inhabitants is maintained in dense urban surroundings, the relation of living spaces to external spaces, the way orientation is managed to achieve sunlight, daylight and views. They are 'town houses' not so much in their location as in their compact character, which permits relations of proximity with other houses. We can characterise them as four distinct formal types: terrace house, patio house, shed and sawtooth-roofed factory; in the context of the Yearbook, let us consider them as parts of a paper *exhibition village*, representing the best of piecemeal Flemish production.

What is crucial in distinguishing the town houses from their equivalents in the real 'exhibition village' is that they are embedded in perimeter blocks which establish coherent and well defined public realms around them. The utility of these *types* lies in relation precisely to specific issues of the urban block: each type embodies a set of spatial and social relations extending from the public space to the interior, from the front to the back. At the risk of exaggerating the representativeness of the Londerzeel 'exhibition village', its fragmented quality contrasts with the consistent urban logic of the piecemeal examples, highlighting the Flemish strengths in 'evolutionary' practice as much as the weaknesses in relation to development from scratch. For rhetorical clarity, we can say that Flanders does 'evolutionary', and doesn't really know where to start with 'revolutionary'.

FOUR HOUSES

Nollet and Huyghe's house (illustration 5) in Assebroek, Bruges is part of a thin ribbon of urbanisation along the old highway to Ghent, with farmhouses and barns caught in a fabric of villas, terraces and workshops dating from the late nineteenth century onwards; outside this strip lie woods and water meadows of simple beauty. This is Flanders at its most unaffected and charming, with historical use and contemporary despoliation both lightly present. (5) [see plans 1, 12]

The plot is narrow and deep at 6 x 45 metres: typical terrace plot proportions. The house is on three floors, with rooms front and back divided by the stair. The narrow passage which runs from front to back at ground floor level is a fairly typical feature of semi-rural housing in Belgium: the entrance to the house is in its middle, as if combining front and back door. The displacement of the entry door from the front to the side creates a more severe, abstract character on the house front, reinforced by the blank wall at second floor level. Indeed, given the north orientation and the presence of a busy road, only the first floor office is opened up to the street: emphatically so, with a 4 metre wide picture window. The geometric purity of the street front is emphasised by the velvety sheen of the black-oiled bricks and the white-painted timber window frames. Its assured presence seems to lend a certain conviction to the surrounding ribbon development, uncertain of its urban status.

Terrace houses by definition draw their light and views at the front and back. The resolute privacy and relative blankness of the street front goes together with the extreme openness of the back of the house. This, in turn, is eased by both the depth (160 metres) and haphazard construction of the block, which mean that the house is barely overlooked from the rear, and by the south orientation of the living rooms and garden at the back of the house. However, even this strong rearwards orientation is given a balanced expression in the mix of screened and exposed views that the street front offers. The framed view of the office and deep view through to the garden give more in the way of variety to the street than the average, more open facade after the application of net-curtains – a selective application of Dutch-style living under the public gaze – as well as allowing for a modicum of passive surveillance.

The patio house is in essence an introverted house type, having its focus on, and drawing its light from, internal courts. In older examples, or more southerly countries, its street presence is often little more than a door in a blank wall. However, despite the dense surroundings of the Prinsenhof district of Ghent, and the small building plot, the *Leeuws-Croes house* (illustration 1, 2) by Marie-Jose Van Hee is engaging precisely in its openness to the street. [see plans 2, 13]

At 8 x 15 metres, the building plot is compact in the extreme (though it was in fact previously occupied by two workers' houses): crucially its width is sufficient to offer possibilities that terrace plots cannot. The site edges are built up on three sides, with a large warehouse volume, now converted to a theatre, on the site to the rear (until the late nineteenth century this was a large garden), and houses on both sides. The street is a mere 3.5 metres wide, which has the advantage that it receives only local traffic, however car-parking must be accommodated within the building plots. The three storey building accommodates two courts: on the street side a paved court, accommodating a car, at the rear a walled garden, with a narrow passage linking the two. These leave a house that is L-shaped in plan, with a small room at the front and a large one at the rear, and the stair in between. The diagrammatic simplicity of this layout contrasts with the dynamism and transparency of the rooms, achieved by the integration of the stair in the open interior and the disposition of windows, including internal and external corners.

The narrow passage linking the two courts is a telling detail: by consistently pulling the building away from the edge of the site, Van Hee allows light and sun to enter from the most unexpected angles. The benefits of this tactic are most evident in the first floor living room, which though only 6 by 3.5 metres has a feeling of great spaciousness. Full height glazing at the end reveals the brick party wall only one metre away, allowing in a slice of midday sun, while to the side, a horizontal window looks out to the garden, and the brick wall of the factory building behind. The light from these windows and the texture of sunlight on the garden walls animates the room. Opposite these, a view of surprising extent opens out: through the window that folds round the corner towards the stair, you see out over a rich patchwork of roofs and gardens, with in the distance the chimneys of Ghent's old industrial north.

The paradox of this house is that the highly enclosed and blank character of the site has permitted great openness and transparency, without compromising the sense of privacy from within. If a two storey brick wall at the rear seems on first consideration an unforgiving neighbour, it not only eliminates any question of overlooking, it helps define the garden as a room. As in the Nollet and Huyghe house, the office is placed on the street side, the least private if not necessarily the most public of rooms. The regular mullions provide a sensation of screening – there are no picture windows – while also

5

6

providing a rhythmic unity to the freely disposed window openings. A balanced contact between house and street has been achieved, where privacy is maintained but the street is overlooked, and animated by screened proximity and by shafts of sunlight.

The *De Vylder/ Hofkens* (illustration 6) *house* is part of an interior plot in the centre of Ghent, close to the church of St Michiel [see plans 3, 13]. It is one of a group of three houses in converted factory buildings, on the interior of an urban block formed by a variety of workers' and bourgeois houses. The number of developments on interior plots within urban blocks in Ghent are testament to its status as an early industrial city (indeed, extensive textile production chains were in place even before factory-centred production started). A survey of Ghent in 1800 shows 70 textile businesses in the centre of the city, mostly situated on the interior of blocks; and in 1826 there were already nearly 300 *beluiken* – groups of houses around a court or dead-end street on the interior of a block, accessed via a gate on the street.[6] At 22 x 11 metres the De Vylder/ Hofkens house has a generous footprint; however, the buildings line the perimeter of the plot, with a blank wall to the rear, conforming to the *beluik* type. The typical single sided

7

orientation of the *beluiken* is modified in the project by the creation of small patios and gardens at the ends of the houses. These give the houses different aspects, and more sunlight, and form private external spaces, the necessary complement to the grassed communal yard which the three houses face onto. The creation of a whitewashed light court only one metre deep at the north end of the De Vylder/ Hofkens house gives the adjacent rooms (bathroom and utility room) surprisingly generous light, but also increases the transparency of the house as a whole, diminishing its shed-like longditudinal emphasis.

The *Fonteyne studio house* (illustration 7), in a suburban allotment in Ostend, like the Nollet and Huyghe house, presents a relatively closed face to the street, and opens up to the rear. Its situation is different in two fundamental respects: the orientation of the rear is northwards, and the houses behind are only 30 metres distant. The design reflects the highly specific nature of the commission, to provide studio and guest accommodation for the main house behind, and although it is capable of use as an independent house, there is a degree of intimacy to the relation between main house and studio [see plans 4, 9].

The factory-like sawtooth roof permits a relatively deep construction of only one storey – the house dimensions are 8.8 x 12 metres – whose interior is handled in the manner of a loft, with blocks housing servant spaces defining a plan of primary rooms of varying sizes, the deceptive informality of the plan managing the transition from three rooms at the front to two at the rear. The interior is filled with cool north light, though the openness of the house allows through shafts of sunlight from the windows at the front. The fusion of single storey suburban house and metropolitan loft, a surprising meeting of opposites, is handled with self-evident calm.

TYPE AND ARCHETYPE

The idea of type in relation to buildings amounts to an acknowledgement that there are only so many solutions to typical plot structures and uses, and that these solutions mediate social patterns of use. (7) 'Type' is seen by some architects as limiting, by others as liberating, in its impersonality and restriction of creative freedom. The brief consideration I have given above to the way in which the architects of the four houses have interpreted type in relation to the specifics of their sites, and to the social conditions of their day, shows sufficiently the significant scope for patient ingenuity that is left to the architect. The architects' conception of these four houses reflects, however, a deeper awareness of the cultural history that is embodied in patterns of building and dwelling. The ability to make buildings which have an undemonstrative clarity to their organisation, which profit from the particularities of their situation, but which also possess a constructional language with wide resonances, testifies to the maturity of the architects' visions – all the more remarkable since three of the four are in their early thirties. More importantly, it also suggests that the idea of type offers access to deep-rooted social experiences, that they are able to tell us about the society and technologies we live with. (8)

Nollet and Huyghe's use of geometry is in many ways familiar, suggestive even of an architecture more concerned with abstract visual harmonies than the dense resonances of lived experience. However, their compositional tactics are also imbued with commonplaces of the Low Countries. In the street front of their house, the views offered to passers-by are both engaging and unaffected: taking the picture window of the office to the floor offers the interior as a mundane but intriguing tableau, while the perspective through the passage and corner window to the garden has a beguiling, intimate quality reminiscent of a painting by de Hooch.

Equally, the patchwork is a theme for both the building and its garden. The distinct black colouring of the house engenders tonal difference with its neighbours, discreetly drawing attention to the discontinuities of the urban fabric; the patchwork is reprised in the coloured glass balustrades on the rear elevation. The assertively geometric divisions of the garden, laid out as a series of parallel strips separated by hedges, moving from lawn through vegetable garden to chicken coop, echo the way the divisions of the land have been translated into an urban structure, the petrified agricultural framework which surrounds the house.

The mediterranean origins of the patio house type leave little explicit trace in Marie-Jose Van Hee's design: they register only in the house's surprising generosity and relaxed spatiality. On close examination, however, many of the house's qualities derive from Van Hee's assimilated knowledge of Roman and mediterranean houses, which the eight metre plot width has made it possible to deploy.

The garden plays a fundamental part in the life of the house, as is implicit in its the room-like proportions and dimensions, and explicit in the interlocked planning of house and external space. The direct relation between the dining room and the garden, reinforced by the large sliding door, is as typical of suburban as it is of Roman houses, though the enclosure of the garden give this relation an intimacy that recalls the latter. The play of layered transparency throughout the house, in the entry, where the rear garden can already be glimpsed, or in the living room where close and distant views are balanced with the sophistication of a house in Pompeii, all the more engaging for its unforced quality. For it is without doubt the naturalness of certain mediterranean propositions on privacy, gardens in town or views which give them a compelling relevance for contemporary urban houses. (9)

Where both Nollet & Huyghe and Van Hee engage with more archaic traditions of dwelling, Fonteyne's studio house engages with the recent but nonetheless distant past, that of industry. The imagery of Fonteyne's insertion into an area of undistinguished recent housing is understated, in part though the building's discreet volumetric difference from its neighbours. The sawtooth roof has long been assimilated to the language of artists' studios: distant echoes of both factory and loft are presented in domesticated form, both scale and materialisation removing any abrasive edges to the industrial associations.

Each of these houses seems to carry a small residual charge from the social evolutions which have influenced the structure of settlements: from agriculture to the town, from rural leisure to the city, from industry to leisure. Indeed, taken together, they seem to map the evolutions of the city through its successive expansions and contractions. Although not necessarily conscious, the evolutionary character that is fundamental to every city, and which is very much evident in Flanders' cities, seems to have left its mark on the conception of these houses.

The evolutions of the site are particularly evident in the house of De Vylder and Hofkens, where successive layers of urban development are presented as a composite, hybrid identity. The 'light touch' restoration re-presents industry with an archaic, humanising patina; the light courts give the factory shed the fragile aura of a ruin, emphasised by the tree growing around the column and through the beam in the entry court; the note of ruin is offset by the generous, unaffected liveability of the house and communal garden, counterbalancing melancholy with an unsentimental practicality. The grassed court is suggestive of the garden or pasture which preceded the industry, also witnessed by the magnificent trees in the garden behind; the greenhouse glazing overlays this with a note of industrialised agriculture. The mix of intuitive delicacy and commonsense in this intervention achieve what a more self-conscious project might not: a simultaneous presentation in one place of the different forces that have shaped this plot of land and its buildings over the long duration of the city.

FOUR URBAN PROJECTS

For all the qualities of individual houses, however typical the conditions, it is perhaps still difficult to extrapolate to wider questions of density and the planning of urban areas. It is, then, of particular interest that three of the above houses have served as 'prototypes' for medium scale urban housing projects: Nollet & Huyghe's 10 terrace houses in Brouwerstraat, Ghent (winning competition design, construction due to start in 2004), Marie-Josee Van Hee's 9 patio houses for Schaafstraat in Antwerp (competition entry), and noA.architects' 27 terrace houses for the Vetex factory site in Kortrijk (first ex aequo in competition). I will also discuss the recently completed housing complex 't Pandreitje in Bruges, containing 49 houses and 26 apartments.

The projects throw some light on practical issues of urban 'grain', a loose concept covering a multitude of interdependent issues relating to space and character, amongst them the complex interplay of block size, plot size, building type, uses and the spatial structure of the public realm. All four projects work within existing urban blocks of varying scale, and have had to bridge the gap between the individual plot and urban dimensions, reinterpreting the existing morphology to

8

contemporary expectations of domestic and public space. The question of public space raises issues for the architect which are not present in one-off houses. Instead of working within an existing street where the character is determined by other houses, and where, for example, a completely introverted house can be created without affecting the neighbourhood, the conception of the constituent houses is more closely interdependent with the idea for the public realm.

The *Ramen project by Nollet & Huyghe* (illustration 8), in which the construction of a large underground car park is the primary motivation, proposes the completion of the small perimeter block of only 90 x 55 metres with ten terrace houses on the narrow Brouwerstraat and an office and apartment building occupying the 'head' of the site on Ramen [see plans 5, 13]. A pedestrian route passes through the block behind the vehicle entrance, with a pedestrian entrance in the small public garden giving access to the vast below-ground public territory of the car park.

This level-headed urban strategy, which gives a respectable and appropriate density (63 dph), is raised to another level by a certain lyrical quality to the conception of the project. The ten houses are composed in a play of repetition and difference, with a continuous cornice level and flat facades, but with five house types designed by four different architects (Nollet and Huyghe have designed two different types themselves). The tension between individuality and commonality is expressed in the varying proportions, rhythms and degrees of openness of the street fronts, and in the lugubrious colour harmonies of three earth-toned brick types - green, grey and ochre.

However, the seductively reassuring image of an urban fabric restored with a known type cannot conceal the considerable ingenuity that has had to be expended on these houses in order to temper the inflexible orientation of the terrace house. Prior to the twentieth century, the orientation of houses in relation to the sun tended to be a secondary consideration to their location in the perimeter block. Continuity of the urban fabric is not fully compatible with good solar orientation – but, having discarded the means but not the aims of 'soleil, espace, verdure', how are we to weigh the virtues of urban continuity against the vices of a north facing living room, or the virtues of a sunny living area against the vices of urban fragmentation?

At Ramen, the south orientation of the street front and north facing garden are the exact opposite to the felicitous aspect of the Nollet & Huyghe house; equally, the three room deep plan of the houses, typical of nineteenth century terrace

9

houses, sets a number of further challenges. Three of the five house types are proposed with internal terraces on the second floor to light the depth of the house better; all except one are relatively open to the street; one is almost entirely symmetrical, offering identical accommodation to front and back, as if unable to decide between sun and privacy. In the context of ongoing density discussions, it will be interesting to see how far the explorations at Ramen – perhaps these are worthy of the description 'typological experiments' – convince as perspectives on the renewal of this house type.

In her competition *project for Schaafstraat in Antwerp* (illustration 9), in the area just to the north of the Central Station, Van Hee utilised the small plot depth of the patio house to effect a change in the public space of the area [see plans 8, 14]. Taking a typical plot size of 8 x 16 metres (almost identical to Leeuws-Croes house in Ghent, therefore), she proposed a block of nine patio houses, composed of one row of six houses on a north-south orientation, and a second row of three houses on an east-west orientation, along with two apartments. Her scheme takes advantage of the fact that the disposition of rooms in patio houses is more tolerant of rotation and reversal than in a terrace house, permitting a close back-to-back arrangement; equally, the far smaller plot depth makes corners a much less problematic condition than in a terrace house perimeter block. Thus in a relatively small depth a four-sided block can be created, with inhabited street frontage on all sides.

The gain of this compactness is in this case that the existing perimeter block could be shortened, and a second, smaller block created, with a small public space in between, onto which the new Design Centre 'de Winkelhaak' would face. This act of cutting the head off the existing block has a specific logic here, creating a pedestrian link between the covered market to the west and the shopping street to the east. By working against the prevailing grain of narrow, deep terrace plots, and replacing a row of north-facing houses, dwellings of a very different stamp are inserted into the area, and a worthwhile addition to the existing public realm network is proposed.

Van Hee uses the slightly tapering geometry of the block to create small differences between the houses. The shifting of volumes within the plans betrays an anxiety to avoid repetition that is perhaps disproportionate to the small number of houses, but offers a way of ensuring difference between similar houses within a unified architectural language. The public space, inflected by the rhythm of tall doorways, and overlooked from the raised half-level from living rooms and kitchens (the half-level is a typical tactic of nineteenth century middle-class houses to achieve distance from the street), suggests a balance of neighbourhood intimacy and urban anonymity.

This project offers two concrete insights into the vicissitudes of 'urban architecture'. The proposals make sense in part because they are conceived in the context of a wider set of interventions, billed by the city of Antwerp as 'Stationsomgeving: een integrale aanpak', which include the new square and underground car park at Sint-Jansplein, and the Permeke centre on the De Coninckplein, as well as the Design Centre; the wider framework for this renewal project is the (controversial) project for the city's ring boulevard and the new high speed line from Brussels to Amsterdam, stopping at Antwerp Central Station. However, it was exactly this wider framework of infrastructure and acupuncture which encouraged Van Hee to step outside the limits of the competition site, and propose moving the building line by a metre on one side, and purchasing an adjacent site for creation of the public space. It is difficult to call on the procedural tools of urbanism, in the form of changing land ownership or compulsory purchase, in an architectural competition, without scaring the horses: it appears that in this case these considerations played a role in deterring the jury from this scheme.

The cocktail of high expectations without strategic back-up is also evident in the inventive but flawed project for *'t Pandreitje in Bruges* (illustration 10) [see plans 7, 11]. The policy tensions between the desire to attract young 'city-leavers' back to the city, and the ambition to achieve high densities generated a near impossible task, of high density, house-based construction. If we may reasonably take the 72 units/ ha which could be achieved by repeating the house Pluimstraat as an indication of where the maximum density achievable with single family houses may lie – and for all its undoubted charm I would repeat the description 'compact' that I used earlier – the 91 units/ ha that were to be achieved at 't Pandreitje were unlikely to be compatible with generous single family houses for 'city leavers'.

Perhaps in deference to Bruges' predominant single family houses, probably in relation to the target market, too, the development consists of 62 'houses', based on a 10 x 10 metre module, of which 80% are one family houses, with the remainder divided into two apartments each. At the level of the houses, the compactness of the plots is in too many places expressed in an uncomfortably attenuated feel: with dwellings spread over four floors, the houses retain little of the 'garden-centred' feel that is the patio house's main asset as a type.

At the urban level, the shallow block which was a virtue in the situation of Schaafstraat, Antwerp, is here less clearly positive, in the context of an urban block 280 x 100 metres. The blocks of back-to-back patio houses create five cross-streets: there are nine 'clusters' of houses on the site in all. The one example where the cross street connects to an existing narrow street, therefore offering a link between Garenmarkt and the

Astrid Park, links the development discreetly (elegantly, even) into the existing urban fabric; the remainder are the result of the project's internal 'grain', and run into dead-ends against the garden walls of the properties to the rear. The internal network they form is neither fully integrated with the wider network of public space, nor clearly demarcated from it.

In the majority of sites, it seems necessary, or even useful, to accept the distinction between the exterior and interior of the block. This is an archetypal feature of the perimeter block, which in the larger blocks of the city edge was often a separate plot - a yard or a garden, a place of productive work. With industrialisation of work these plots were taken into increasingly intensive use, for factories and also housing. The urban blocks on the outer edge of Kortrijk are at up to 300 x 150 metres unusually large, and perhaps for this reason proved viable as industrial locations for longer than was the case in central Ghent. The closure or departure of these industries to the city periphery has led to a number of projects to build housing on the interior of the block.

Although the studio house by An Fonteyne was designed for a terrace site on the periphery of Oostende, the proposal by noA.architects (An Fonteyne, Jitse van den Berg, Phillippe Viérin) uses it as a prototype for houses on the interior of a *block in Kortrijk, vacated by the Vetex textile factory* [see plans 6, 10] (illustration 11, 12). The site was a sea of sawtooth roofs lapping up to the edge of the back gardens of the houses which form the exterior block, although due to their apparently poor condition the decision was taken prior to the competition to clear the interior of the block, with the exception of the large cubic factory building at the centre.

As in the original factory complex, the project seeks to build up the spatial structure of the interior of the block from the repetition of a single dominant orientation, building up a repetitive grain that echoes the rhythm of the demolished factory roofs. The blocks are aligned, according to the basis of the type, on a consistent northerly orientation (in this case north-east-southwest), with the living area of the houses alternating between front and back. Although the brief allowed for relatively large areas of public space and communal facilities, which have subsequently proved to be unattainable, the type itself appears capable of higher densities.

The generous space and informal arrangement of the studio house appear plausible as urban family houses, though the adoption of the factory 'grain' gives a dominance of northlight that is perhaps hard to justify. Possibly the most engaging aspect of the scheme is the way in which an identity is established for a series of houses. As in the studio house, the blocks which house servant spaces are brought to the glazed facades forming a strong but varied rhythm. The gentle angling of front and rear elevations interacts with the roof profile to create rising and falling rooflines. The shifting reflections, forced perspectives and modulating rhythms which these would generate suggest a recognition of difference and individuality within the composition, without emphasising the individual unit.

PUTTING DENSITY IN PERSPECTIVE

The projects discussed above illustrate some of the complex challenges of urban renewal which face Flemish cities. Here, density is far from being the primary issue: density is a means

10

to an end, and not a goal in itself, and little is served simply by building more densely, or higher, in cities or in the countryside. The goal of more sustainable development which underpins the Flanders Spatial Structure Plan depends among other things on radical reduction of construction in rural areas, and increased use of public transport. With wealthier inhabitants and businesses having left the city for the comforts and conveniences of the periphery, achieving these aims will depend on the quality of accommodation realised and the resulting character of the urban areas. Excessive densities, or public spaces without the population or services to support them will not contribute to the process. Significant urban design interventions may be necessary, perhaps like Eduard Bru's proposals for Poblenou in Barcelona, where new streets cut through the Eixampe blocks look to open up the under-utilised interiors for higher density and more mixed development. Is such a radical 'piecemeal' approach conceivable in Flanders? Whatever, the perimeter block seems to be the vehicle of this evolution *par excellence*.

With the current Flemish demographic situation, there seems little excuse for an obsession with quantity, or in particular the easily quantified housing unit. For it is also productive that business or even cultural uses are integrated in the urban fabric, where they benefit from public transport accessibility. The suitability of the interior of perimeter blocks for uses other than housing is demonstrated by a number of projects in the current selection. The former factory building behind the Leeuws-Croes house is now in use as a theatre; the administrative centre in Kortrijk by noA.architects makes effective use of the interior of a city centre block for offices; while the university lecture hall in Antwerp by Driesen-Meersman-Thomaes excavates a public space for the students from within a perimeter block of housing, and underneath the lecture hall itself. The construction of the premises for the student organisation as the last of the row of terrace houses before the lecture theatre block is more than just a contextual gesture, it is a recognition of the important overlap between institutional and domestic realms.

The renewal of inner cities requires much decrease as well as increase in density. It is worth making the point that although Marie-Jose Van Hee's Schaafstraat project stands as an example of medium-density, low-rise residential construction it represents a de-intensification of the city from its current density, halving of the number of houses on the site. 23 houses would make way for nine houses and two apartments, mirroring the transformation of the Leeuws-Croes House,

11

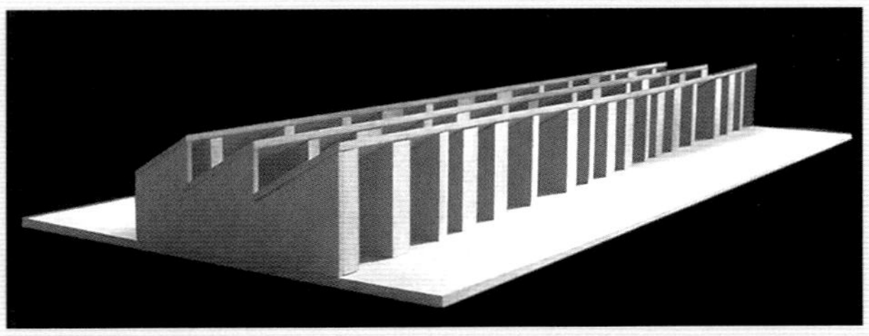

12

Ghent, where two houses have been replaced by one. Equally, in the case of the De Vylder/ Hofkens house, any talk of intensification is highly relative: the three houses are slight in relation to both the 11 apartments which a developer proposed for this same site, and the one hundred employees who worked in this factory one hundred years ago. The need for dense de-intensification is the simple product of the situation that unattractively high densities and wastefully low densities are still both very much present throughout Flanders.

The projects discussed in this article illustrate that town houses occupy an important place in the density spectrum between apartment buildings and suburban houses – all the more important as plots for the latter get progressively smaller, and the fear of proximity becomes more and more untenable. However, the effective use of urban house types depends on an urban design framework where the 'difficult' conditions of corners, backs and interior plots are acknowledged and economically answered.

It is not just the house type, but above all the way that adjacencies are handled, that leads to quantitative and qualitative gains. This is true in urban areas but also in the many half-urban, half-rural areas of Flanders, where urban typologies have long been used and appropriated. Indeed, it is possible to say that much of Flanders is in an explicitly evolutionary condition – is in a state of perpetual *becoming* – in transition from a state of wild nature (there is little of this left) to an urban state, with most of the region in a multitude of hybrid conditions between the two.

The policy of 'inbreiding' – the intensification of existing settlements – requires a reading of the existing urban grain, and of its relation to contemporary social practice, of considerable subtlety. Finding appropriate and affordable proportions between new housing, employment sites, collective services and public space is essential to the short- and long-term success of such interventions.

Is it unrealistic to think that such careful consideration be brought to bear on a mass of small and medium scale projects? Possibly: but *if* Flemish 'evolutionary' practice can be stepped up to a new scale and a new quality – a radical 'piecemeal' practice – the failure to manage development at a larger scale might be seen not so much as a shortcoming but as a blessing. Such a path would take Flemish action on density away from those pursued in neighbouring regions. But ingrained though some of the habits may be, this is no easy option: it may seem paradoxical, but harnessing the power of piecemeal development will require much urban design intervention and political will.

Illustrations

1. Leeuws-Croes House, Gent, Marie-José Van Hee © Peter Lorré.
2. Aerial view , Ghent, © NGi.
3. Aerial view , Kijkdorp Londerzeel © Ondersteunend Centrum GIS Vlaanderen.
4. VLABO-kijkdorp, Londerzeel, © William Mann.
5. Nollet/Huyghe House, Bruges, © Karin Borghouts.
6. De Vylder/Hofkens House, Ghent, © Jan Kempenaers.
7. Fonteyne Studio House, Ostend, An Fonteyne en Jitse van den Berg © Karin Borghouts.
8. Project Ramen, Ghent Tomas Nollet and Hilde Huyghe architects.
9. Sketch Schaafstraat, Antwerp, Marie-José Van Hee.
10. Housing complex 't Pandreitje, Bruges Haverhals - Heylen architects.

11. 12. noA.architects, Housing complex Vetexsite, Kortrijk.

Footnotes

1. 800,000 new houses planned in NL 1995 - 2005; 2,000,000 new houses planned in Southeast England 1996 - 2016; 400,000 new houses planned in Flanders 1995 - 2010. Past experience of such numerically obsessed expansions in Britain suggests little scope for optimism; and, although planned in many cases with considerable care and skill, urban expansion in the Netherlands has taken place at a breathless pace that the social impact will take time to assess.

2. There are, of course, cities where some discreet and sophisticated urban design practice has been carried out in recent years, amongst them Leuven, Eeklo, Kortrijk.

3. VLABO: 'Vlaanderen Bouwt', a not for profit organisation which in partnership with local government and contractors seeks to stimulate the construction of 'good, characterful and affordable houses' ['degelijke, karaktervolle en betaalbare woningen']. www.vlaanderenbouwt.be. The exhibition village *Kijkdorp Kruishoeve* at St. Jozef Londerzeel consists of 92 houses for sale, and was developed in partnership with Intercommunale Haviland and the local authority.

4. It is a larger scale use of the approach which in an earlier version, at Aalbeke, was described as the 'cacophonous climax' of Flemish housing praxis, a 'microcosm of the Belgian chaos...supposed [through the quality of the architecture] to deliver a *reductio ad absurdum*, by generating a high quality, coherent housing project'. Bruno De Meulder, Jan Schreurs, Annabel Cock, Bruno Notteboom, 'Patching up the Belgian Urban Landscape', in *OASE 52*, p 109. [Sleutelen aan het Belgische stadslandschap]

5. It is worth pointing out that this strip varies between one and three blocks deep, beside accessible areas of countyside. This is fundamentally different to the typical *lintbebouwing* or strip development, where construction one plot deep bleeds off into the countryside, creating large areas of inaccessible open land.

6. Roger Moreau, *Archiefbeelden Gent, Deel V: Beluiken, Poortjes en Cités*, p 8. See also: Robert Duplessis, *Transitions to Capitalism in Early Modern Europe*.

7. Adrian Forty summarises the concepts of type and typology developed in Italy in the 1950s and 60s as follows: 'Typology was a means of describing the relationship between buildings and the city of which they formed part, and thereby showing how individual buildings were manifestations of the collective and historical processes of urban development; it was a way of showing that an 'architectural event' was not just four walls and a roof, but something that existed only as part of the general urban phenomenon, considered both spatially, socially and historically.' in Forty, *Words and Buildings: A Vocabulary of Modern Architecture*, p. 308

8. I take this to be one implication of the following passage by Alan Colquhoun: 'Just as language always pre-exists a group or individual speaker, the system of architecture pre-exists a particular period or architect. It is precisely through the persistence of earlier forms that the system can convey meaning. These forms, or *types*, interact with the tasks presented to architecture, in any moment in history, to form the entire system'. Colquhoun, 'Typology and Design Method' in Forty, *Words and Buildings: A Vocabulary of Modern Architecture*.

9. The sophisticated spatiality of Roman houses of the Imperial period was the result of the attempt to incorporate the features of large country villas in often impossibly compact urban sites: this suggests interesting echoes between the problems the Romans experienced in relation to speculation and density, and those of our own time.

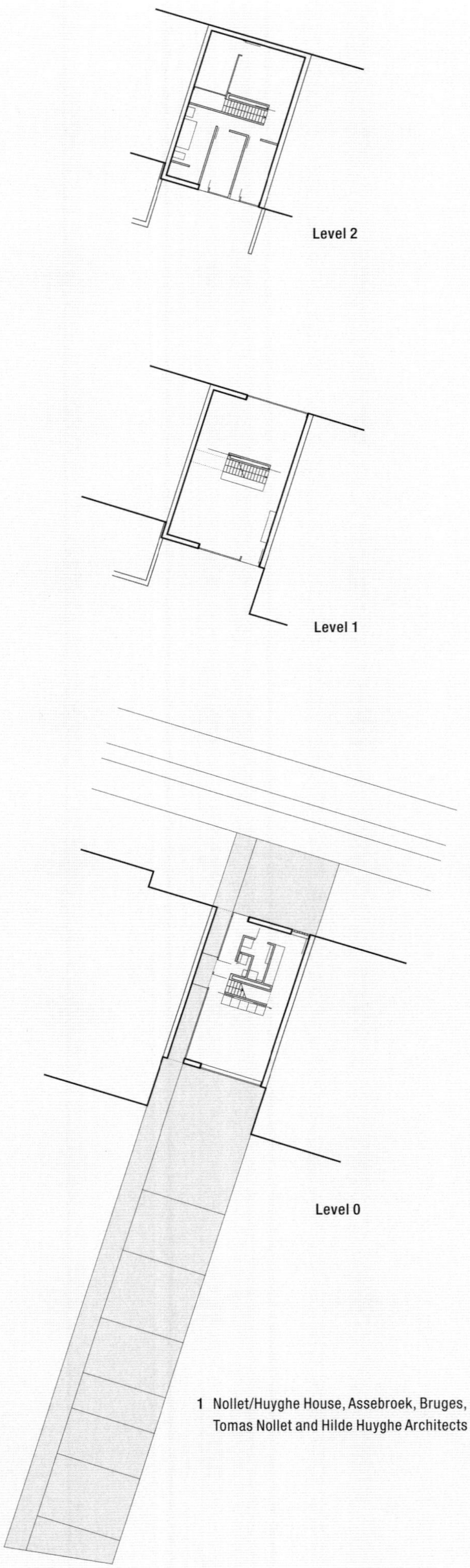

1 Nollet/Huyghe House, Assebroek, Bruges, Tomas Nollet and Hilde Huyghe Architects

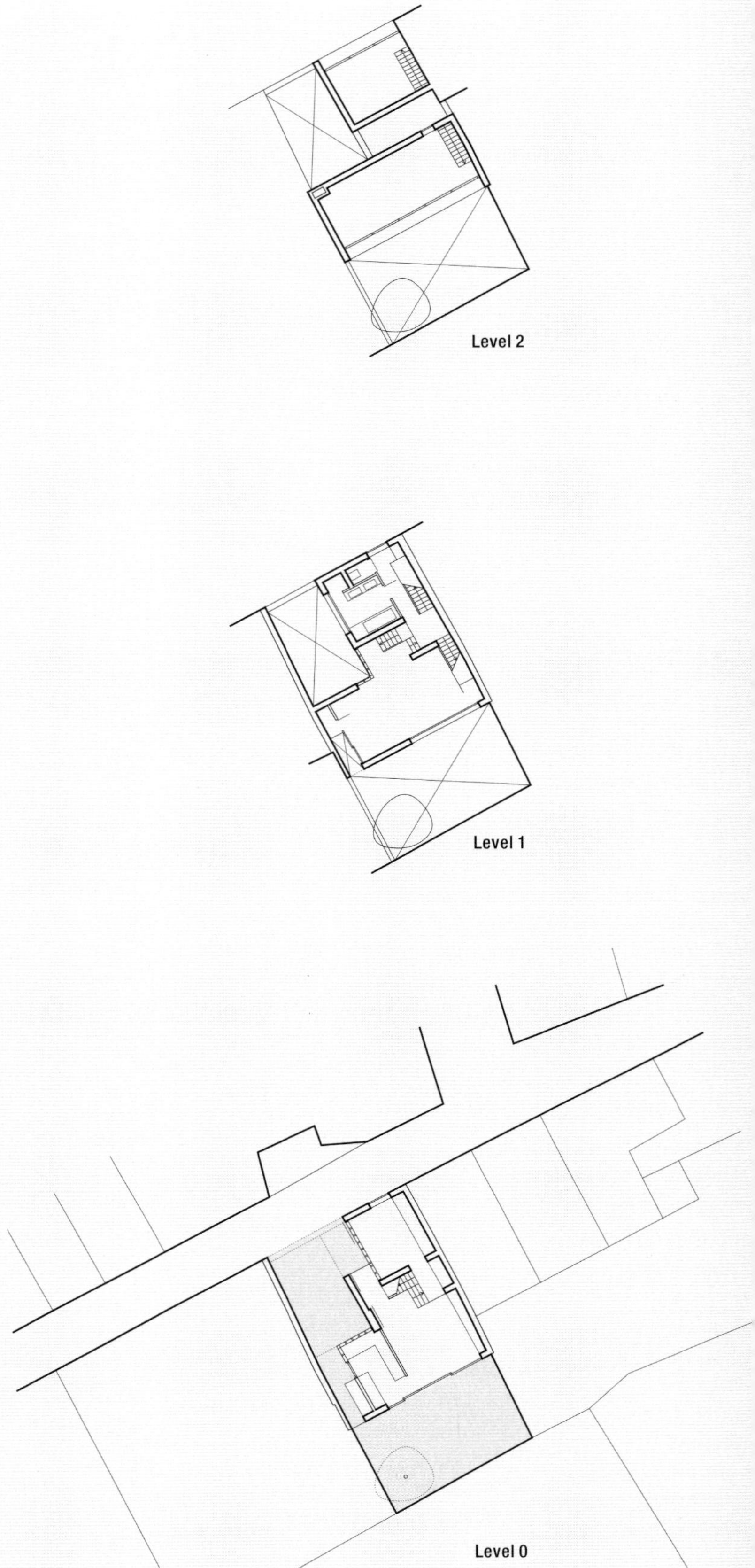

2 Leeuws-Croes House, Pluimstraat, Ghent, Marie-José Van Hee

All plans drawn by Witherford Watson Mann Architects (Nina Scholz) on the basis of information provided by the architects and on the basis of the topographical maps of the National Geographic Institute, Brussels.

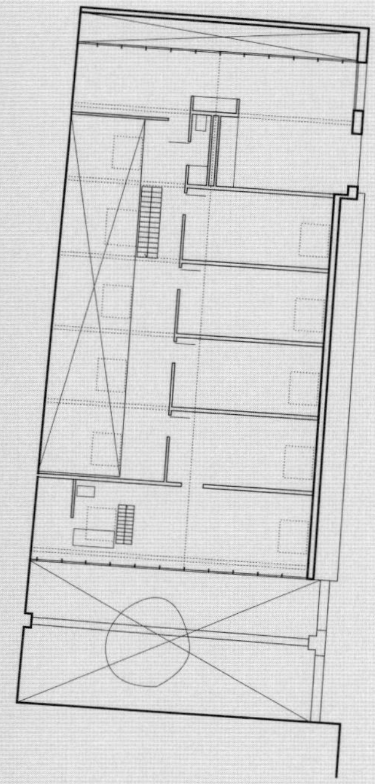

Level 1

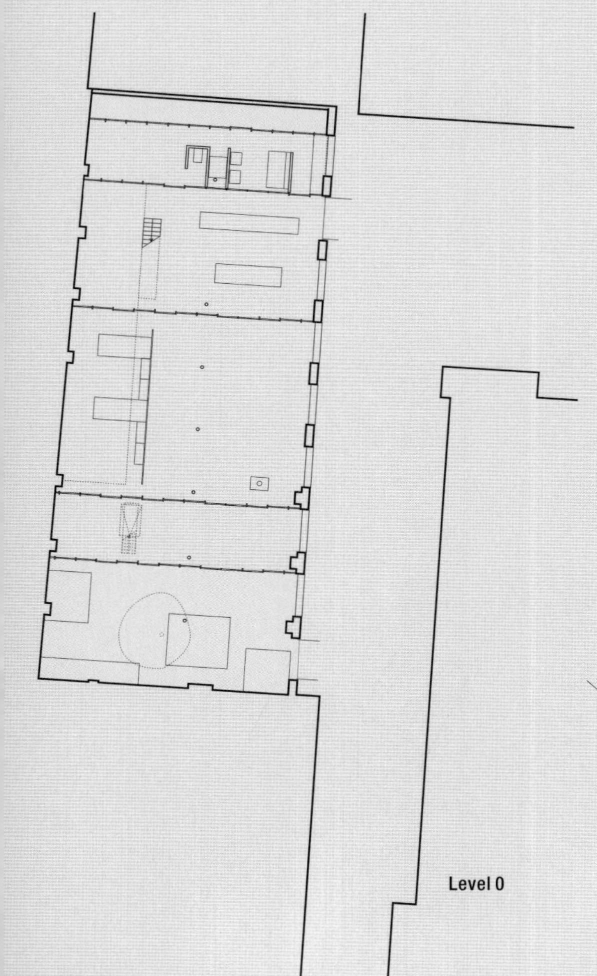

Level 0

3 DVH House,
Schouwvegersstraat, Ghent,
Jan De Vylder and Trice Hofkens

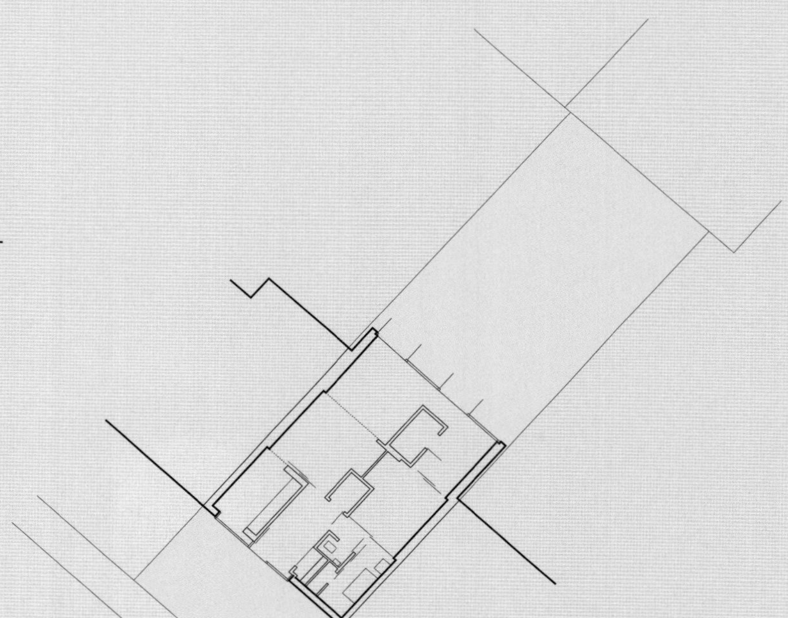

Level 0

4 Fonteyne Studio house,
Melkerijstraat, Ostend,
An Fonteyne and Jitse van den Berg

5 Project Ramen, Ghent:
parking 240 cars and 10 terraced houses,
5 apartments,
Urban plan by Tomas Nollet
and Hilde Huyghe Architects

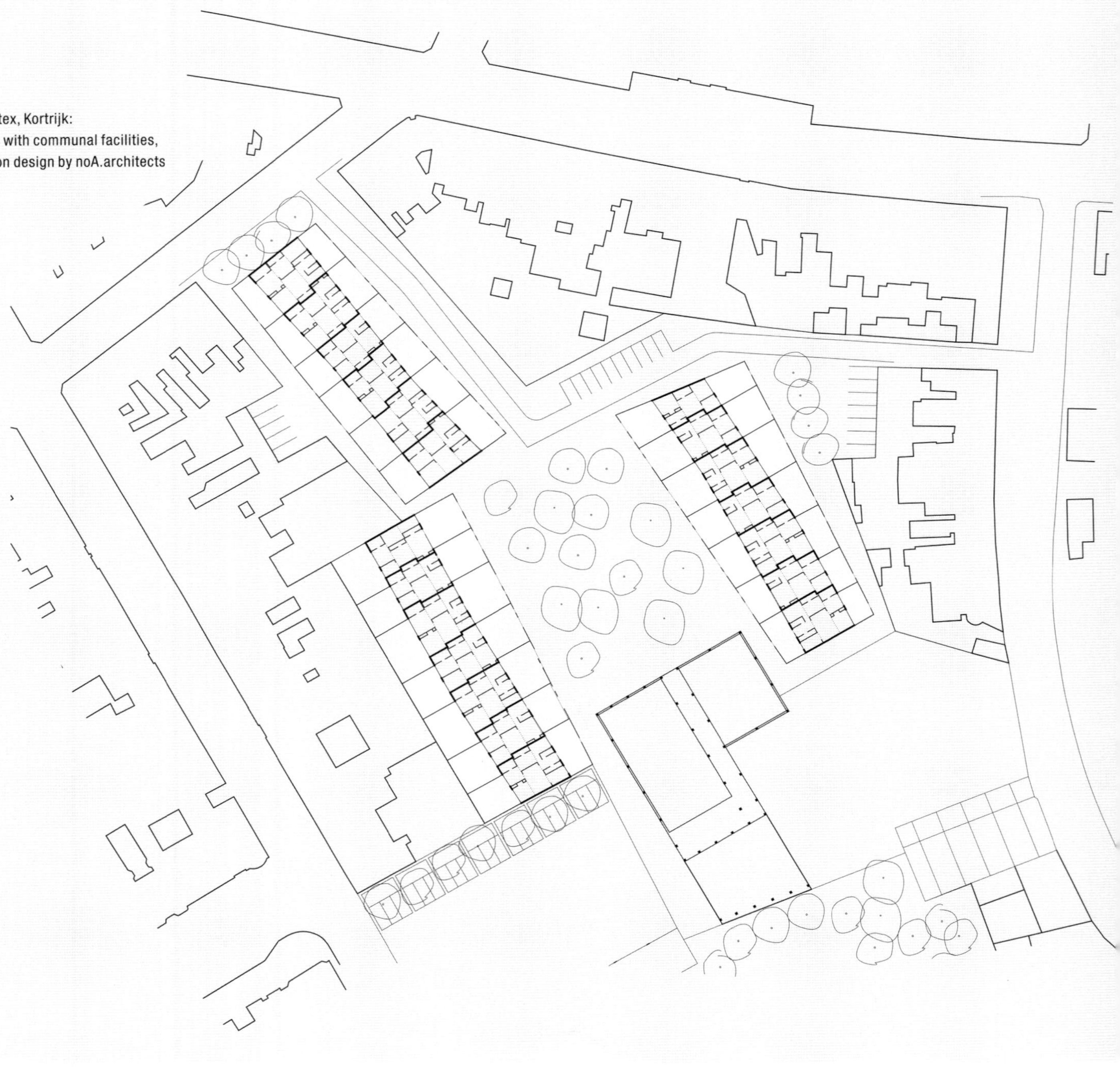

6 Project Vetex, Kortrijk:
27 houses with communal facilities,
competition design by noA.architects

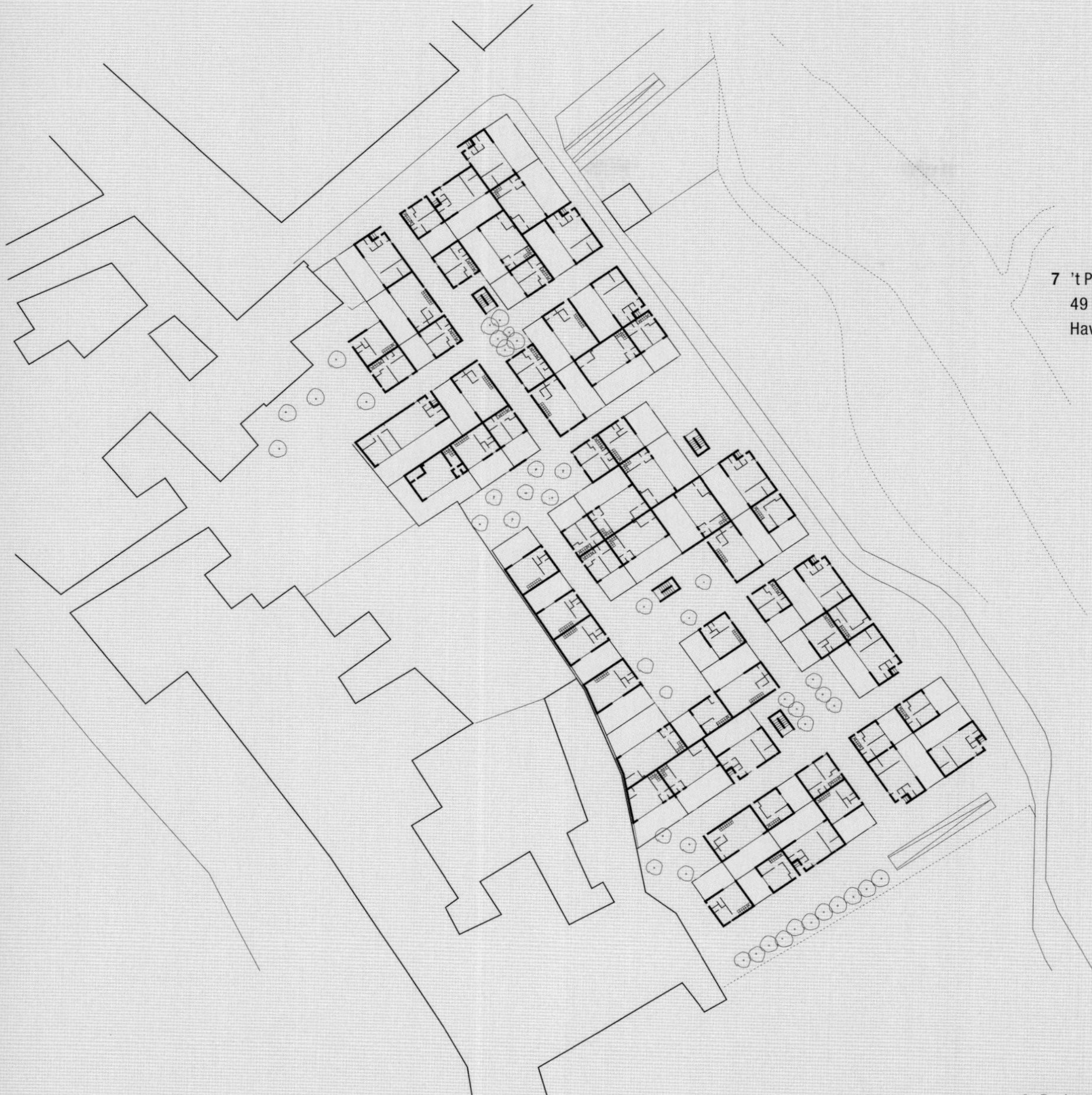

7 't Pandreitje, Bruges:
49 houses 26 apartments,
Haverhals-Heylen Architects

8 Project Schaafstraat, Antwerp:
9 patiohouses, 2 apartments,
competition design by Marie-José Van Hee

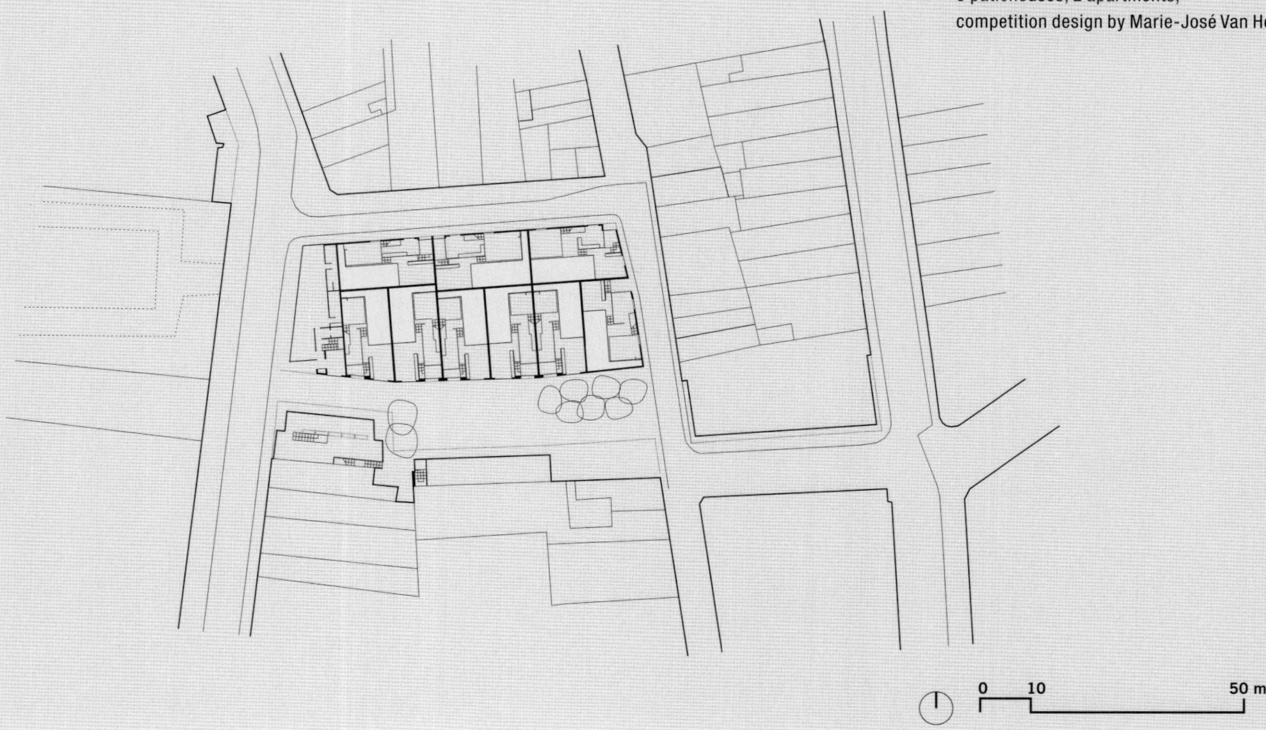

9 Stene, Oostende,
with indication of studio house Fonteyne

10 Brugge,
with indication of 't Pandreitje

11 Kortrijk,
with indication of project Vetex

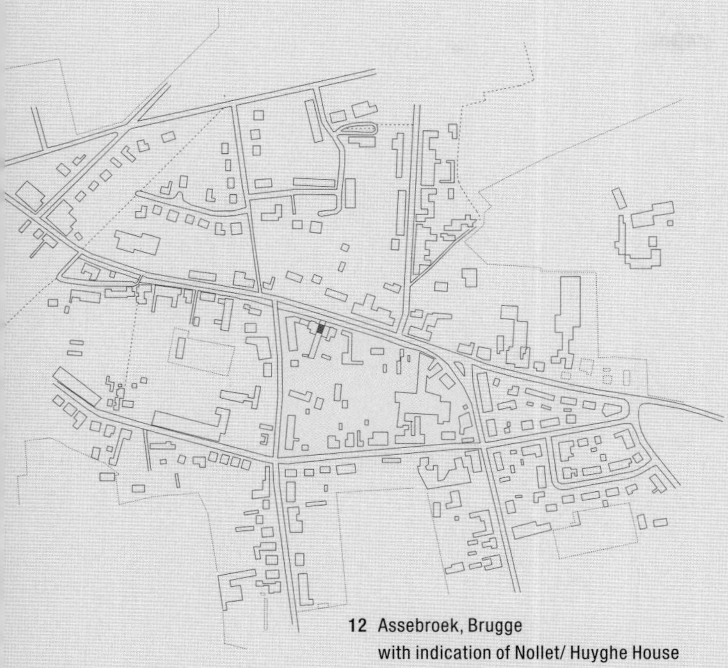

12 Assebroek, Brugge
with indication of Nollet/ Huyghe House

14 Antwerpen,
with indication of project Schaafstraat

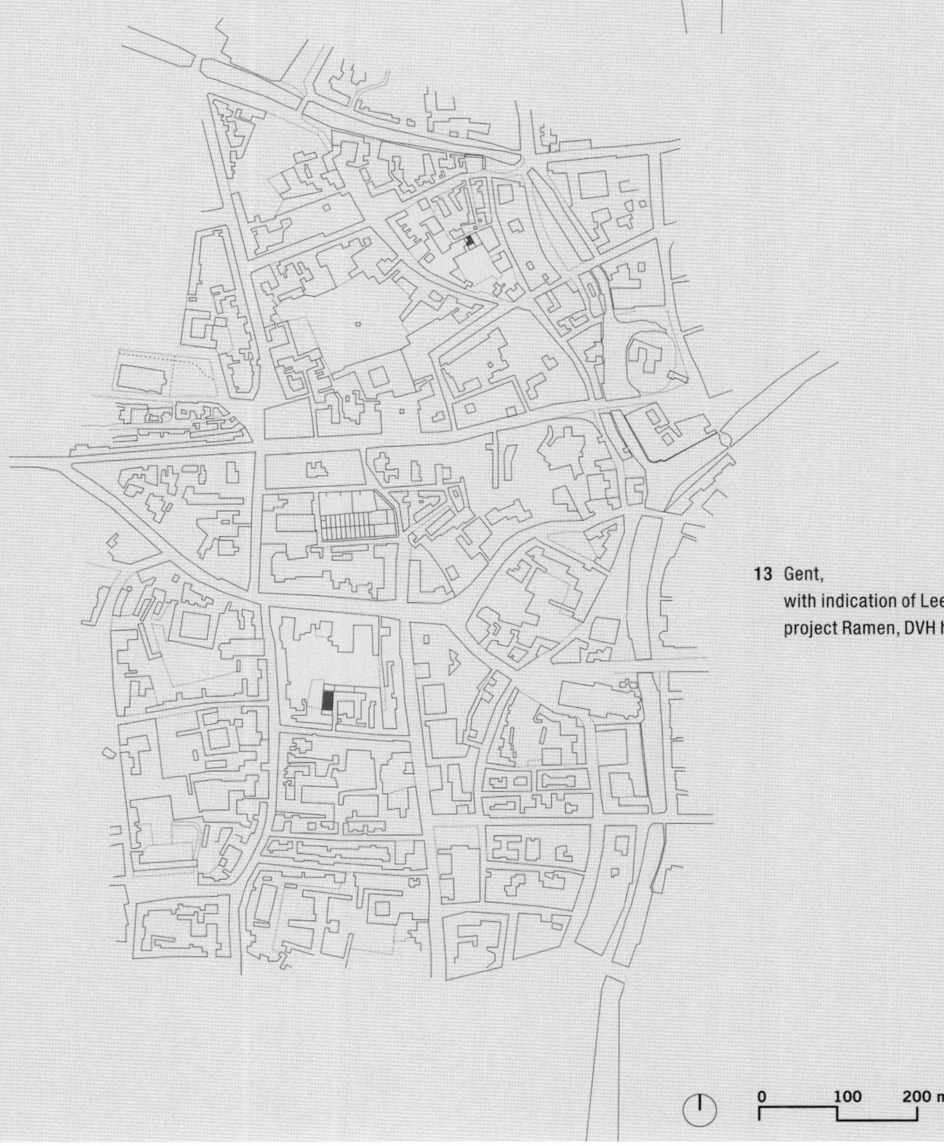

13 Gent,
with indication of Leeuws-Croes house,
project Ramen, DVH house

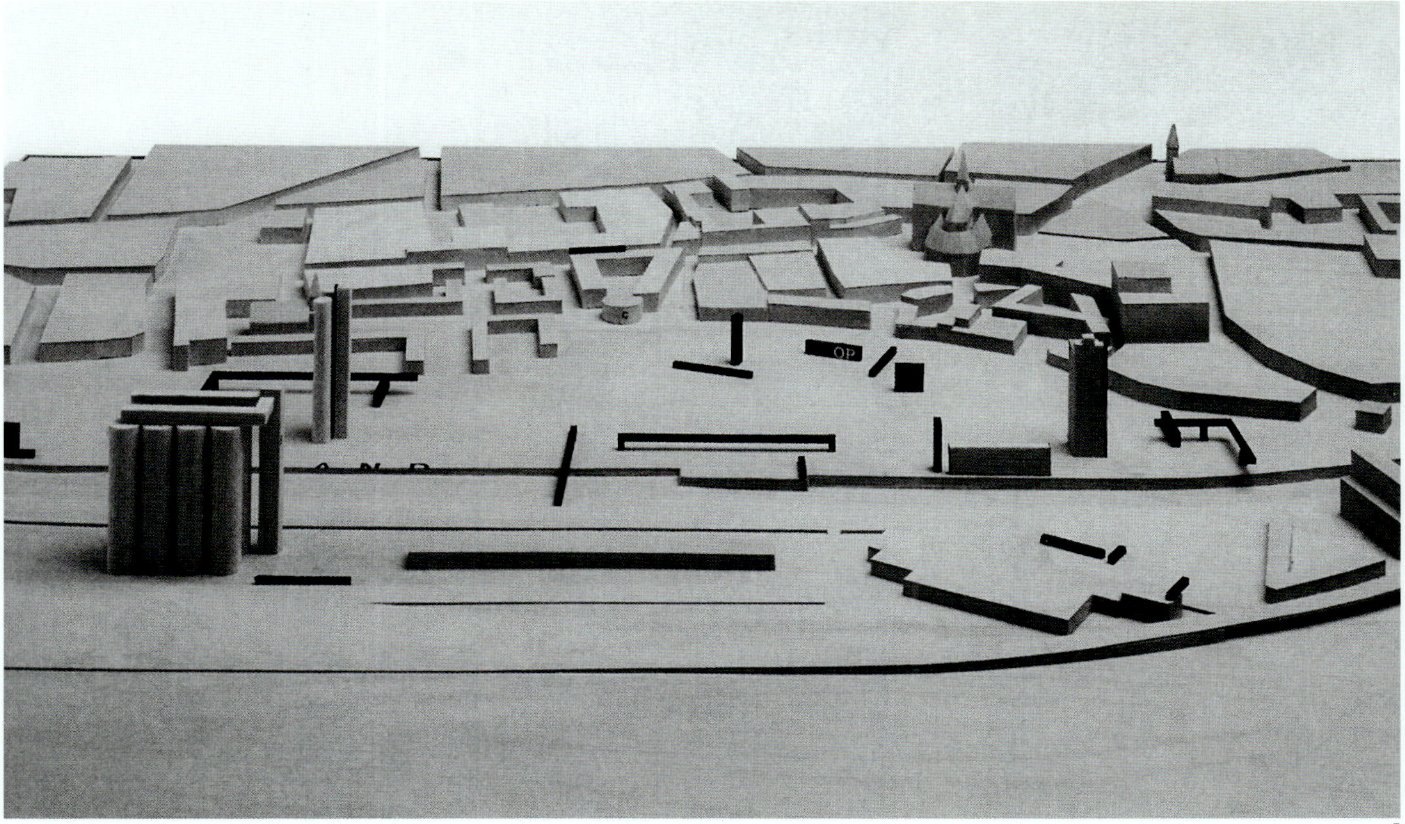

I

'UNE RECHERCHE PATIENTE'

Tom Avermaete

ARCHITECTURAL DESIGN AS A FORM OF RESEARCH (INTO THE CITY)

In architecture, there is a fundamental need to research. Design is a research activity. (Tim Stonor)

1. RESEARCH BY DESIGN

Research by Design, design-based research and research-based design, are the phrases currently creating a furore in international architectural debate. At first sight both phrases seem to be tautologous. After all, ideally every architectural design displays an exploratory or investigative attitude and all research includes by definition the design of a hypothesis or concept.

However, in recent years there has been a notable interest specifically in the research potential of architectural design. In the context of competitions and educational and research assignments, such internationally renowned architectural firms as OMA, MVRDV, Greg Lynn and CHORA have been explicitly putting design forward as a form of research. (1) This new interest in design-based research goes together with a flood of new forms of depiction. Koolhaas' diagrams, MVRDV's datascapes and CHORA's models have in recent years become real trade marks of design-based research.

The international academic world is interested too. After all, the phrase 'design-based research' describes in a nutshell the position of architectural education: at the intersection of the design nature of project-based education and the scientific aspects of research. In recent years schools of architecture and universities have in fact made an active contribution to the debate on design-based research. The research qualities of architectural design have been discussed in lectures, seminars and colloquia. (2)

In the wake of Dutch and international developments, design-based research has gradually acquired a place for itself in Flanders. At universities and polytechnics, students are challenged to see the design not just as a prelude to a building or urban district but as an instrument for the exploration of the contemporary urban condition. Studio Open City, established in 1992 with the aim of allowing students from various schools and universities to work together on similar themes, plays an important part in this. (3) By means of colloquia, debates and presentations, this organisation opens up to view and discussion the design-based research that takes place in the academic setting.

Design-based research is also steadily winning ground in Flemish architectural practice. Luc Deleu's designs for cities such as Brussels and Barcelona are research projects which, by means of utopian interventions, magnify and thereby points out the characteristics and potential of various urban places. In the

2

3

early nineties Christian Kieckens entered into collaboration with the artist Peter Downsbrough to investigate an industrial site in Aalst by means of a minimal design. In recent years De Geyter architects' book *After-Sprawl* and projects by 51N4E, Bruno De Meulder, Monarch, Citymine(d) (4) and Bunkerhotel (5) have presented themselves as forms of design-based research.

2. DESIGN AND RESEARCH

This great interest in design-based research leads one to suspect that it is entirely new; that today's architectural design is allotted a character or a role it has never before had. But is this right? Or is it rather a rephrasing of a characteristic of design that always has been extremely important?

The answer to this question is complex. After all, the question of the research role of design is not a recent one. As early as 1920 Le Corbusier had already considered it one of the most important issues in contemporary architecture. He sought an answer in his famous magazine *L'Esprit Nouveau*, under the motto 'The spirit that dominates the work of this journal is one that welcomes all scientific study'.(6) In the mid-sixties the American architect Christopher Alexander also sought a decisive answer. In his *Notes on the Synthesis of Form* he tried to interpret the scientific character of design by comparing it to a system of coherent requirements that could be mathematically analysed, unravelled and solved. (7) Alexander looked for the research aspect of design in direct comparisons with scientific research. The value of architectonic thinking was measured against the gauge of conventional science. In the seventies and eighties the interest in the research potential of architectural design ebbed away. The postmodern architectural debate was characterised mainly by self-criticism and self-reflection and much less by a research attitude.

The question of the research dimensions of design is now topical once again. The basis of this is not the similarity between architectonic and scientific thinking but rather the specific nature of design. In his 1962 book *La pensée sauvage*, Claude Lévi-Strauss proposed considering scientific and design-based thinking as 'two parallel approaches to reality'.(8) This suggestion is a striking illustration of the main concern in today's design-based research. It examines whether an architectural design can represent a knowledge of its own and can generate its own insights. It verifies whether design can be an approach to reality, deserving of a position on a level with other scientific approaches to the built environment. In short, it asks aloud what role design can play in research into built space.

In recent decades Flemish architects have offered possible answers to these questions through their projects. In fact it seems they have formulated answers on the basis of a particular point of view. Whereas in international architectural debate design-based research became known mainly as a result of attractive methods of analysis and representation, in Flanders it seems the strategic position of design was most important. In other words, it seems as if the research dimension of architectural design was directly linked to the way it was employed in a particular framework or context. To illustrate this interpretation, I shall examine several exemplary approaches to design-based research in Flanders. (9)

Urbanism under discussion: De Onaangepaste Stad [The Unadapted City]

This meta-project by Luc Deleu and TOP Office provides the first significant illustration of my proposition. In this project, Deleu uses architectural design to examine the implications of the theoretical framework of contemporary urban planning (illustrations 2, 3). (10) The basis for this is the *Atlas of Urban Facilities* on which Deleu's firm has been working since 1995. This collection of maps examines 'what sort of facilities a city actually needs to present itself as a contemporary metropolis'. (11) Maps are developed, *ex abstracto*, that link the number of inhabitants in a city to a particular sort of service or a well-defined number of collective amenities. The quantitative insights into the scale and complexity of the city thus acquired are then used in a design. In his architectural designs for The Unadapted City, Deleu examines the qualitative – spatial and formal – implications of his theoretical assumptions. Regardless of any contextual concerns, he examines the relationship between quantitative reflection and spatial implications. As several of the models in The Unadapted City make clear, this

4

results in large, often linear urban structures in which only the services and amenities are determined in advance. Deleu assumes that every other part of The Unadapted City can be filled in at will. Any relation between form and function is indeterminate from the start.

The research quality of Deleu's strategy only comes fully to the fore in the concrete projections of the The Unadapted City onto several actual urban sites. It is here that the strength of The Unadapted City lies. Like the city of *New Babylon* devised by the Dutch artist Constant, it is able to bend to the lines of force of the existing urban landscape and can enter into connection with it at strategic points. The models of The Unadapted City display linear structures set down in existing areas of the city by means of vertical legs. These legs contain staircases and lifts to link the two by means of existing streets and squares. In combination with the indeterminate character of the DOS, these links with the existing urban fabric have a very suggestive effect. Deleu's models suggest images of surprising urban scenarios or new developments, but at the same time tell us about the characteristics and potential of existing areas of the city.

Deleu employed his principles of The Unadapted City as a research instrument for competitions. In his competition design for the Museum Aan de Stroom (MAS, 1999), the towers of the VIP part of The Unadapted City were projected onto the northern part of Antwerp. The confrontation between the theoretical model and the existing city not only illustrated the impact of The Unadapted City but also provided an insight into the complex, layered and often contradictory characteristics of the existing area. For instance, in the design for the MAS, the limited scale and the fine grain of the existing urban fabric – mainly from the nineteenth century – is made explicitly clear. The confrontation between the architectural design and the urban site exposes the individual nature of the urban fabric; it forms an 'indirect demonstration'. Deleu made similar use of the architectural project in competitions for social housing in Wevelgem and Meulestede Noord in Ghent.

Exploring concrete spatial potential: Christian Kieckens and 51N4E

We find a second example of the research nature of architectural design in the strategy Christian Kieckens proposed in his 1996 study *Densities*.[12] Whereas in Deleu's case the design was used in theoretical research, in Kieckens' case a real and concrete urban situation is the focus. He concentrates on the industrial area along the intersection of the River Dender and the railways on the eastern fringe of Aalst. This area originally housed several small-scale industrial activities that were relatively well connected to the town. The withdrawal of most industrial activity from the town centre and the vigorous expansion of one single factory have transformed the area into an alien zone; a heterotopia in the urban fabric. Industry and town have a tense relationship. The area does not appear to contain any margin for expansion at all for either the factory or the town.

Kieckens' study is intended to break this deadlock by looking for the area's potential. The premise is that the area as a whole will be given neither to the town nor to industry, but that the tense relationship between the two is sustained. Together with the artist Peter Downsborough, Kieckens carefully analysed the spatial characteristics of the area. On the basis of photos and models they examined what the remaining industrial buildings' potential for and impact on the town might be. They checked where possibilities for link-ups to the nearby urban fabric of residential areas might be found (illustrations 1, 4).

This photographic and model-based analysis was supplemented by what can be described as a minimal architectural design. Kieckens and Downsborough do not propose any new buildings, only basic elements. On the site – and sometimes in the neighbouring urban fabric too – rectangular elements were introduced, reminiscent of the geometric sculptures of Richard Serra. They do not indicate the position of buildings, nor of urban ensembles, but suggest new spatial relations between the elements themselves and between the site and the town. In their minimal architectural design they examine the concrete spatial potential of the site, in both urban design and architectonic terms.

We encounter a related use of architectural design in the project for the Lamot site in Mechelen, by architects 51N4E firm. It focuses on an area on the edge of the town centre. In 2001,when the old Lamot factory was already half demolished, the town council conceived the idea of using it to house a museum that would form part of a wider axis of cultural institutions. The ideas competiton organised for this was explicit in requesting scenarios that would pull together Mechelen town council's museum policy in terms of both programme and space (illustrations 5, 6). 51N4E interpreted this brief on

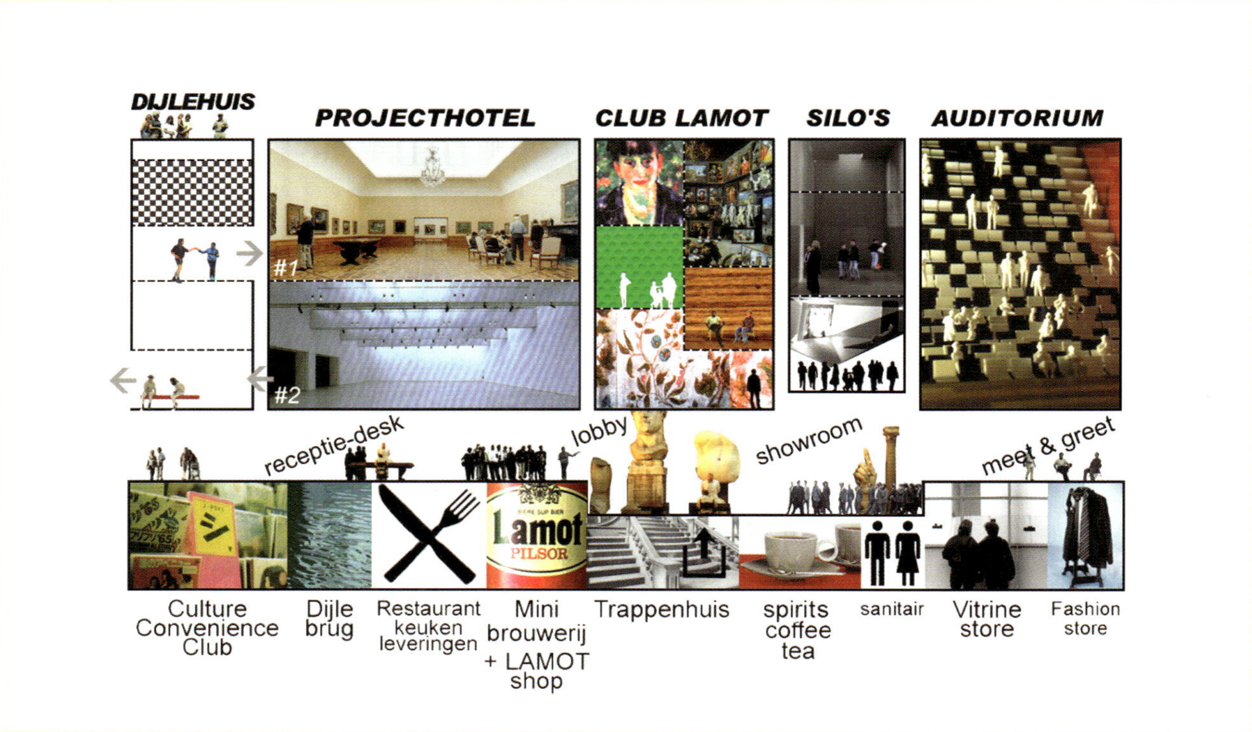

5

6

the basis of the project's specific spatial location between the town centre and the periphery. The developments in the periphery have always fuelled the prosperity of the town centre. The range of services and culture in the town centre have always exerted a strong attraction on the periphery. This mutual relationship is not only a social or economic link. It is also a concrete spatial cohesion of roads, locations and places, that involve the town centre and the periphery with one another. However, this relationship now seems to have disappeared.

The proposal put forward by 51N4E does not involve fitting a brief and a built form to one another, but rather the exploration of the concrete spatial potential of a site and the architectural characteristics of a building by means of an architectural design. In this case the design examines the capacities of the Lamot site – as a pivotal point between the periphery and the town centre – to bring about new relationships and introduce new connections into the urban fabric. An important part in this is played not only by the location of the Lamot site in the urban landscape of the town, but also by the concrete spatial characteristics of the old brewery building. The industrial structure of the brewery is as it were an *objet trouvé*, a naked concrete skeleton onto which associations and dreams can be projected. On the basis of diagrams, collages and models, 51N4E shows that within this structure it is possible to experiment with a mixture of spaces and programmes, so that new relationships will in their turn arise between the centre and the periphery.

In 51N4E's proposal, the architectural design is an integral part of the analysis of the town. It is a special sort of analysis, however. At its heart lie not so much general statements about the town but rather an examination and indication of the concrete potential of a part of the town. Each new configuration of spaces and programmes introduces new links between the outskirts and the town centre. In short, 51N4E employs the design to study the concrete spatial potential of an area and make its importance clear.

The problematisation of assumptions and premises: *After Sprawl*

In the research into the contemporary city Xaveer De Geyter Architects carried out under the title *After Sprawl*, a second element was added to the testing of concrete spatial potential. De Geyter explicitly deploys design to study, problematise and complement prevailing assumptions and premises regarding contemporary urban space. Two approaches are examined. The first is the body of theoretical concepts that has been developed for suburban space since the fifties. De Geyter questions such concepts as sprawl and nebula because, in good Western tradition, they conceive of built space as positive and empty space as negative. The second frame of reference is the Flanders Spatial Structure Plan (RSV) from 1996 (illustrations 7, 8). The RSV was the first clear and unambiguous planning instrument in Belgian history, and lays down limits for the development of space in Flanders. De Geyter's study is intended to complement the RSV's general top-down approach. To this end it takes as its starting point the concrete spatial potential of the spaces between buildings, villages and towns. In the margins of the built space, De Geyter locates new, concrete architectural changes that complement or break up the structure of the built space and thereby introduce new articulations.

The 'Overlay' sub-design, for instance, examines whether the open space might play a structuring role in the most central area of the Flemish 'diamond': that between the cities of Antwerp and Brussels. De Geyter superimposes an orthogonal grid of dykes – negative and open spaces – on the existing situation and asks himself what scenarios for the development of the urban space this makes possible. 'In the zones between the dykes, certain programmes will very specifically seek out the qualities of these enclosed areas, while other programmes will withdraw from these areas in order to settle along the dykes. As a structure, the dyke system is so normative that one can expect a thinning of the intermediate areas and condensation around the dykes,' says De Geyter. He thereby demonstrates that the concrete spatial operation represented by the dykes exposes several forms of urban logic which can probably not be uncovered by means of other research methods.

8

7

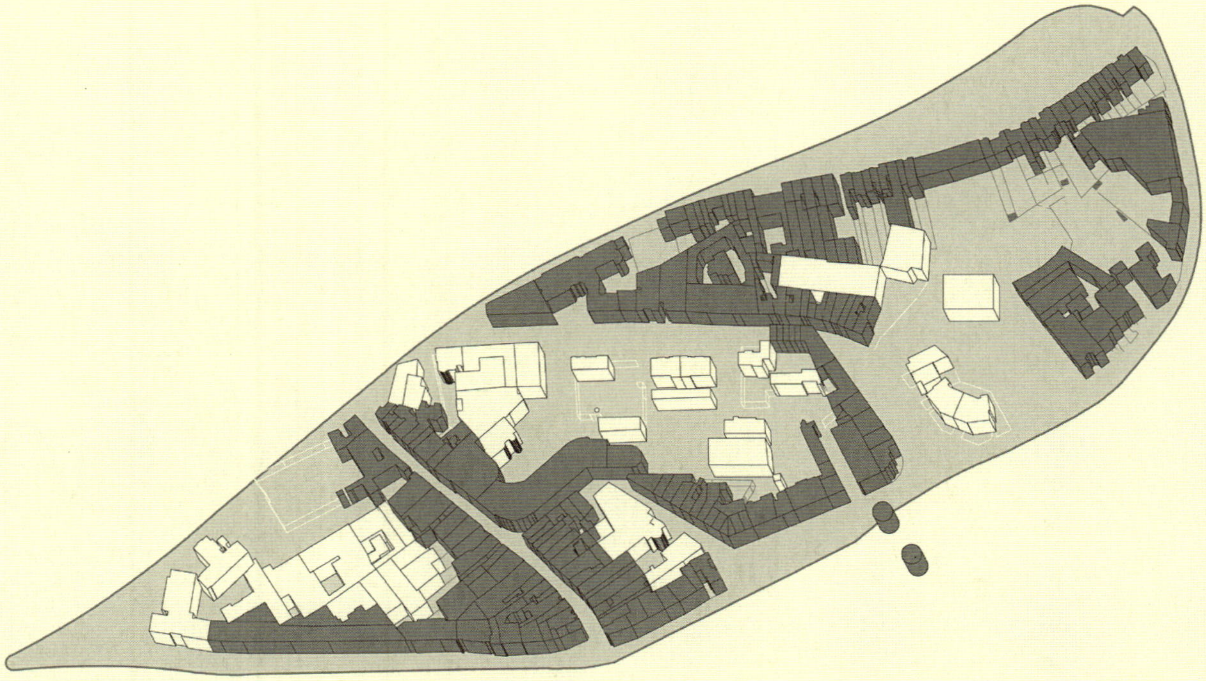

9

10

Design as an integrating framework: Buda island, Kortrijk

A completely different research aspect of architectural design is employed in the project that Bruno De Meulder developed for the Buda island in Kortrijk in 2003.[13] Buda Island is an area between two arms of the River Leie on the fringe of the town (illustration 10). The straightening of the river, in part a consequence of greater tonnages in inland shipping, has in Kortrijk long been seen as the perfect opportunity to tinker with the town itself. The plans for the Leie Valley, Jacques Wirtz' green plan and the municipal network of cycle paths had from various angles already hinted at the potential of these infrastructural works. On top of this first series of plans came the report by the sociologist Rudi Laermans, which recognised Buda island as a major site for the development of cultural infrastructure in Kortrijk.

De Meulder's approach does not reject this prior history. In fact, the existing plans and statements are explicitly taken as the basis for an examination of the site. Each plan and statement is considered as an interesting contributing view of a complex urban area. De Meulder wonders what concrete role Buda island can play in the various plans and, more especially, how the different views can be combined. The strategy he developed to cope with this is based on the integrating capacities of the architectural design. After all, every architectural design has the power to unite varied parameters. Architecture can bring together a variety of elements in synthesis, contradiction and ambivalence. It is precisely this capacity that De Meulder employs to examine Buda island. Several teams of young designers were asked to devise projects that endorse the various plans. Projects that give shape to the earlier plans and thereby translate them into concrete spatial operations.

The result is a number of interesting urban figures such as the Buda beach on the banks of the Leie, a succession of outdoor rooms and the concept of the paperclip. Each of these figures unites several earlier visions and plans. Each one also makes statements on the individual characteristics of the various locations on Buda island. The design concept of the paperclip, for example, tells about the morphology of the island (illustration 9). It makes it clear that the area is structured by large street blocks whose edges are dense and finely-meshed but which inside are actually large and open. The figure of the Buda beach clarifies the strategic spatial position of the island. It emphasises its location at the separation of two arms of the river and along several green axes. Each figure is the synthesis of previous plans and visions, an analysis of the place and a starting point for future developments.

3. RESEARCH-BASED DESIGN: A STRATEGIC DEFINITION

The examples given here do not demonstrate that every architectural design is by definition a form of research. They make it clear that the 'research' aspect is not a characteristic of design itself, but depends rather on the way an architectural design is used for a specific problem. In recent years, the research character of the design has in Flanders been defined as a strategic property, a characteristic that depends on the strategic implementation of the architectural design in a given context. This context may be the theory of urban planning (Deleu), a spatial structure plan (De Geyter) or the various plans and visions developed for a particular urban area (De Meulder). By carefully positioning an architectural design in these contexts, it can fulfil a research function.

In this way the design takes the place of an hypothesis in empirical research. It embodies a particular assumption about these contexts, which is verified by the confrontation with reality. However, two characteristics of architectural design distinguish design-based research from other research into the city. First of all there is the concrete spatial dimension. An architectural design does not deal in abstract figures, zones or regulations, but in the concrete articulation of built space. The hypotheses in design-based research are not noncommittal or theoretical statements, but rather ambiguous changes in the built space. This concrete spatial nature makes the hypotheses of design-based research easily imaginable and gives them an exceptional range. Another characteristic is their ability to integrate. An architectural design has the quality of being able to bring together a variety of elements or parameters from the built environment in a single spatial figure. Moreover, a design can unite different – sometimes even contradictory – elements in figures of synthesis, dialogue or ambivalence. In other words, the hypotheses of design-based research do not have to be rectilinear assumptions, but can also include complexity and contradiction.

It is precisely these characteristics of a design that break down the traditional pattern of empirical research and offer interesting alternatives to current research into contemporary urban space. Design-based research can occupy a specific position in the broader field of urban research. After all it does not follow a process of extensive inventorisation, analysis and evaluation of statistical facts, or the drawing up and testing of a programme. In fact the order is rather the reverse: design-based research is the starting point for the formulation of programmes and objectives and for carrying out base analysis and market research. It is evident that a spatial design can fulfil a function where empirical urban research falls short: research into the as yet unknown possibilities of urban areas or locations.

The strategies mentioned, by Deleu, Kieckens, 51N4E, De Geyter and De Meulder, make the potential of this sort of use of the architectural design very clear. They show that design-based research can play an important part in the broader research into urban space.

4. THE STATUS AND IMPORTANCE OF DESIGN-BASED RESEARCH

Design-based research currently occupies a marginal position in the Flemish architectural world. Recognition is limited in the academic world because, as a scientific activity, design still occupies a disputed position. For graduation projects and research for a Ph.D., the design is usually supplemented by a written component in order to guarantee the scientific status of the work. In the everyday practice of Flemish architects there is often just as little space for design-based research. Strict deadlines, economic restrictions and result-minded clients are a hindrance to design-based research. Lastly, the uncertain finality of design-based research means there is a lack of clarity about the applicability of its results. This has major implications for financing by the customary funds, institutions and subsidy systems.

Yet design-based research is of crucial importance in the Flemish context. In the first place because it takes a spatial approach to the urban context. This concrete spatial approach seems to be perfectly geared to examining the complex and often contradictory characteristics of the Flemish nebular city.

What is more, design-based research is the perfect instrument for studying the major impulse given by the Flanders Spatial Structure Plan (Ruimtelijk Structuurplan Vlaanderen) in concrete spatial terms, as De Geyter's work illustrates. Design-based research is just as important in the field of urban renewal. Here too there is a need to allow the concrete spatial qualities to play a greater part, to study and indicate the true spatial potential of particular areas.

Design-based research offers another advantage. If we view the form of the built environment as a matter not only for specialists, but also for the various groups whose daily practice is involved in it, design-based research is one step ahead of sociological, geographical and economic research. As I have previously stated, design-based architectural research differs from other sorts of urban research because of its spatial nature. The hypothesis is not a theoretical or abstract premise, but a proposal for a concrete spatial change: redesigning the spaces in an existing building to create possibilities for new functions, restructuring an urban area so that new connections are formed in a city, and so on. It is precisely this concrete spatiality that is the strength of design-based research. The realistic spatial images and concepts with which it works guarantee broad accessibility. They allow a large number of people to form an image for themselves of the premises of the research, to express their ideas about it and thus become involved or be able to participate. In this way design-based research can make an essential contribution to greater general involvement in the transformation of the everyday environment.

Lastly, the importance of design-based research must also be situated in the context of contemporary building in Flanders. The logic of rapid production, which applies to other areas of society too, is nowadays also often a determining factor in the growth of the built environment. Design-based research can offer a counterbalance. After all, by definition it provides plenty of space for the reflective, investigative and questioning nature of design. It creates time to explore, deepen or problematise the design brief. As early as 1960, Le Corbusier described architectural design as *une recherche patiente*. Faced with present-day building production, Le Corbusier's statement acquires a strikingly critical tone. It suggests that the built environment should not be a matter of hasty solutions, but rather the result of well considered and patient questioning.

5. CONCLUSION: BEYOND THE STUDY OF THE CITY

The projects discussed here illustrate how well design-based research is suited to the urban condition in Flanders. After all, design in the Flemish nebular city hardly ever implies the creation of something completely new, but rather what the Viennese architect Hermann Czech described as *Umbau*: change, transformation or conversion.(14) By means of this concept, Czech wanted to make it clear that architectural design always amounts to changing the urban fabric. This fabric may be very taut (historical city centres) or with a widely-spaced mesh (periphery), but is always a close interplay between landscape, infrastructural and built articulation on several scales. Designing, says Czech, necessarily means the careful shifting of threads, the redefinition of their content or the initiation of new connections. Czech's statement seems to be eminently applicable to the situation in Flanders. In this sort of *Umbau* situation, design-based research can play an important role. After all, it is not intended to provide generally applicable knowledge, but makes statements on concrete places and specific problems. By repeatedly studying urban space by means of designs, a detailed knowledge is generated concerning the design activity, and also concerning the built urban environment. Every design adds something to this knowledge, refining it or thoroughly adjusting it. By means of such meticulous study one creates a basis for design decisions that are both well-founded and innovative. If we want to take a high-quality approach to the urban fabric of Flanders, there is a consequent constant need for design-based research.

However, the role played by design-based research need not remain limited to the analysis of a city. An architectural design may just as well be given an important part to play in other fields. In the years to come, Flanders will be facing major challenges in the form of collective housing. The development of new housing types in villages and towns against the background of the Flanders Spatial Structure Plan is also a constant challenge. In addition there are many neighbourhoods and buildings from the sixties and seventies that no longer meet present housing requirements and are therefore due for urgent restructuring. Another field that has lost much ground in recent years and will have to be given a great boost in the years to come is that of school buildings. This means both the thorough renovation of existing stock and the development of contemporary types of school.

The tremendous challenges in these fields must be tackled with due consideration. The research potential of the architectural design can to this end be employed to the full. After all, design-based research can in these areas too put incisive questions by offering both concrete spatial proposals and innovative prospects. It is therefore a matter of urgency that social housing companies, local authorities and private clients create contexts and frameworks in which design-based research can take place.

Illustrations

1. Christian Kieckens and Peter Downsbrough, Densities, 1996, model, wood, collaborator: Robert Prewett, photo: Reiner Lautwein.

2. Luc Deleu, De Onaangepaste Stad [The Unadapted City], model, photo: Luc Deleu.

3. Luc Deleu, De Onaangepaste Stad [The Unadapted City], section.

4. Christian Kieckens and Peter Downsbrough, Densities, 1996, interventions by Peter Downsbrough, (adhesive tape and transfer letters on colour photo by Christian Kieckens).

5. Aerial view citycenter Mechelen, 51N4E.

6. 51N4E, concept Lamot-site, Mechelen.

7. Xaveer De Geyter Architecten, After-sprawl, project overlay.

8. Xaveer De Geyter Architecten, After-sprawl, project overlay.

9. Workshop under the direction of Bruno De Meulder, design Buda-eiland, paperclip, Kortrijk.

10. Workshop under the direction of Bruno De Meulder, design Buda-eiland, global view Kortrijk

Footnotes

1. On one single occasion this even led to the establishment of a new research department such as OMA/AMO. While OMA remains concerned with building projects, AMO concentrates entirely on research and is concerned with questions regarding organisation, identity, culture and programme

2. Examples of this academic interest can be found in the results of the international Research by Design Conference, which was held in the Faculty of Architecture at the Technical University of Delft from 1st to 3rd November 2000. For this see Marieke Ouwerkerk & Jurgen Rosemann (eds.), *Research by Design. Proceedings A, International Conference*, Delft, Delft University Press, December 2001. For an introduction to recent design-based research see Harm Tilman, 'Architectuur als wetenschap. Onderzoekpraktijken van Ronald Wall and Duzan Doepel, Marlies Rohmer en Tarra' in *De Architect*, July/August 2003, pp. 30-39.

3. Bruno De Meulder, Alexander D'Hooghe, Jan Mannaerts (red), *A Moving City*, Studio Open City, Brussels 1998

4. City Mine(d) is an organisation set up in 1997 with the aim of supporting, initiating and/or producing projects of a socio-cultural nature, mainly in public space, at places and in neighbourhoods characterised by typical metropolitan problems such as poverty, exclusion, lack of identity, etc. See *http://www.citymined.org*

5. The *Bunkerhotel npo* is a platform for design-based research focusing on the development of instruments for practical use, design and development strategies in cooperation with various social actors (academics, authorities, private sector, etc.). With an emphasis on the definition of relevant spatial problems.
See *http://www.geocities.com/bunker_hotel/index.htm*

6. Le Corbusier, 'Domaine de L'Esprit Nouveau' in *L'Esprit Nouveau*, no. 1, 1925.

7. Alexander, Christopher, *Notes on the Synthesis of Form*, Cambridge (Mass.), Harvard University Press, 1964.

8. Levi Strauss, *La Pensée sauvage*, 1962, [*The Savage Mind*], University of Chicago Press, 1966, p.27-28.

9. The intention here is not so much a complete picture of design-based research in Flanders, rather the indication of a number of positions that illustrate the strategic applicability of the design as a research instrument.

10. Deleu Luc, *Urbi et orbi : De Onaangepaste Stad*, Ghent, Ludion, 2002.

11. Interview with Luc Deleu in: *FFI Letter, nr.1*, 1999, p.8.

12. Christian Kieckens, Peter Downsbrough & Raymond Balau, *Densities*, Imschoot, Ghent, 1996.

13. The project for Buda island is described in the fifth volume of the FASCIKEL series published by Anno '02. For another discussion of this project see Linda Boudry, Peter Cabus & Eric Corijn, *De eeuw van de stad. Over stadsrepublieken en rastersteden*, Brussels, Urban Policy Project, Department of Home Affairs, Ministry of the Flemish Community, 2003.

14. Hermann Czech, 'Der Umbau' in *Zur Abwechslung. Ausgewählte Schriften zur Architektur*, Löcker Verlag, Vienna, 1996, pp. 125-127.

UNIVERSITY OF ANTWERP (UFSIA) - RECTOR DHANIS AUDITORIUM

architect	**DMT - ARCHITECTS**
location	Kleine Kauwenberg 14-22 / Vekestraat 37, 2000 Antwerp

client	UFSIA vzw
design - building	1998-2002
project-workers	Jan Thomaes I Laila Landtmeters I Adinda Van Geystelen I Jan Goderis
engineers	Projectmanagement: Starke Dierkstra (B) I Stability: Constructor (B)) Technical installations: Stockman (B) I Acoustics: Daidalos (B) Technical support: Bureau Bouwtechniek voor architectuur (B) Art interventions: Perry Roberts (UK) and Aglaia Konrad (A) Landscape design: Eric Dhont (B) I Scale model : Luc Bogaerts (B)
contracted work	General contractor: Ilegems (B) I Interior: Vooruitzicht Interieur (B) Electricity: EDF (B) I HVAC: Keysers (B) I Plumbing: Zsapinszky (B) Elevators: Thierry (B) I Audio-video: CD Acoustics (B) I Kitchen: Furka (B) Landscaping: Proost (B)
area	11,200 m^2
building costs	9,000,000 EUR (excl. VAT and fees) Architecture and stability: 5,500,000 EUR Technical installations and audio/video: 3,000,000 EUR Furnishing and signalisation: 395,000 EUR Art interventions: 100,000 EUR Landscaping: 5,000 EUR
building costs/sq. m	803.57 EUR/sq. m.
project description	Sven Sterken
photography	Sarah Blee p.184,185,188 I Kristien Daem p.183,190 André Nullens p.189 I Stefan Vandermeulen p.182

UNIVERSITY OF ANTWERP (UFSIA) - RECTOR DHANIS AUDITORIUM ▸ architect DMT-ARCHITECTS

Universities account for some of the oldest buildings in the centres of several European cities; these urban campuses grew up organically with the surrounding urban fabric. In Leuven this even led to a small network of covered passages and semi-public inner squares that function parallel to the public domain. A similar network is also developing in Antwerp where this large auditorium and learning facilities for its Economics and Law students stands in the immediate vicinity of the existing university buildings in the city centre.

Since this was a project managed by the university itself, it was able to choose its architects and involve them from the very beginning in translating the brief into an actual building project. A number of major urban planning considerations had to be taken into account. The accommodation had to be built in the fragmented area within the bounds of a block between Kleine Kauwenberg and Vekestraat, which had previously been filled by a sports hall and several university classrooms. The complex to be built also had to connect well with the other, nearby buildings on the urban campus. Whereas the historical university buildings had generated an urban entity, the challenge now was the reverse, to make an architectural entity from a residual urban space. For this reason the brief was broken up into four independent elements; the student house forms an autonomous volume along Klein Kauwenberg, with, alongside it, the block that contains two small auditoria (each 100 seats) and four classrooms (each 50 seats). On the other side of the block (Vekestraat) another small office building has been erected whose form and volume is entirely in keeping with the existing houses in the terrace. The auditorium is the only element that is actually in the interior of the block. So the various parts of the programme function like houses in the city, each with its own address, whereby the coherence between the different buildings is suggested by using the same type of dark brick for all of them except the auditorium.

The block containing the small auditoria along Kleine Kauwenberg is raised on piers of exposed concrete in order to allow fire engines to drive onto the site. The entrance to the underground car park is also located here. Despite the great openness this creates, the closed nature of the block is assured by means of gates and cycle racks along the street side. They soften the visual contact between the street and the interior of the block. The angle between the volume containing the classrooms and the student house creates a wedge-shaped opening as a continuation of the alleyway opposite; this forms a passage from this inner square to the buildings of the Faculty of Literature and Philosophy a short distance away. In the reverse direction, this opening directs the gaze clearly towards the auditorium, the centre of this spatial composition. The small office building in Vekestraat is also raised off the ground; beneath it lies the exit from the car park. This

opening also ensures a connection with the nearby Agora building, which houses several student amenities. By opening up the block at three strategic places, the new complex is fully incorporated into the network of the urban campus.

The auditorium, with its 700 seats, is conceived as a huge concrete shell supported by tapering concrete columns and surrounded by a glass curtain wall. It is set against a large blank wall, as far as possible from the adjoining buildings. This location leaves two open spaces within the block: one that follows the uneven outlines of the existing lots and another, rectangular, space that is more static.

The latter seems to refer to the enclosed courtyards of the sixteenth-century Hof van Liere a short distance away, but lacks the intimacy and acoustic screening to be able to function as a true inner garden. The foyer of the auditorium, which is actually the space left between the projecting concrete shell and the glass curtain wall, is conceived as an extension of the outdoor space; the cobblestones run on inside under the curtain wall, the effect of which is reinforced by the glass, which reaches down to the ground, and by the street furniture which is repeated inside. The transparency of the curtain wall means that the whole inside of the block is involved in the social goings-on in the foyer; the foyer is thus the heart of the whole design. However, the

1 forecourt:
- cobblestones, diam. 8 cm
- double-layer seal
- filter cloth
- stabiliser

2 gutter:
- grill over gutter
- gutter element, H. 15 cm, B. 13 cm

3 glass curtain wall

4 courtyard
- cobblestones, diam. 4 cm
- bed of mortar
- filling around floor heating
- PVC foil
- insulation, injected PUR
- cellular concrete filling

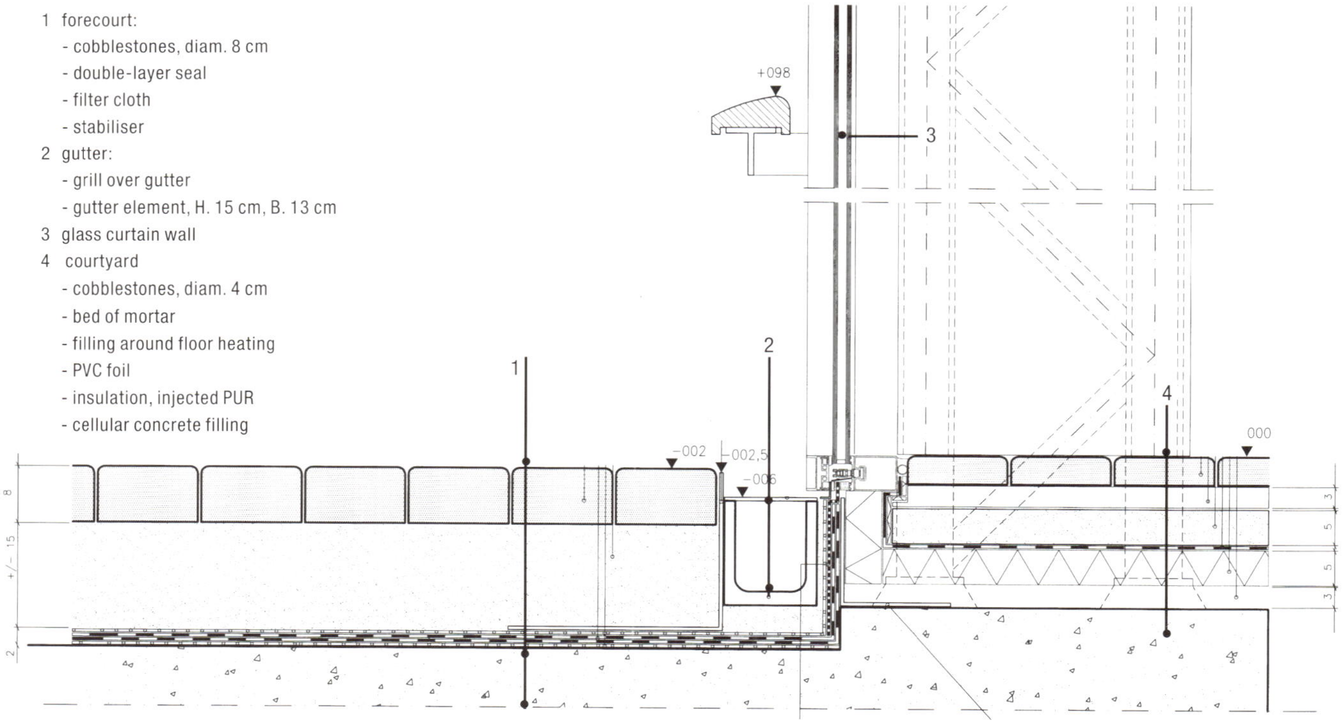

Vertical section through facade between courtyard and forecourt

play of views and perspectives is at no point obtrusive; the architects have been scrupulously respectful of the neighbours' privacy. On the first floor, a narrow, heavy steel tube connects the foyer to the block with the smaller auditoria and the classrooms; but this element contrasts rather awkwardly with the elegant spatiality of the rest of the design.

The remaining circulation zones are generously proportioned, which means they are potential social spaces in which encounters with fellow students and informal contacts with lecturers can take place. The large balcony is conceived as an outdoor room; from here one can survey the entire area inside the block. By contrast, in the classrooms everything has been done to create a serene and stimulating learning environment; it is all light, air and colour. Daylight is able to enter the two small auditoria through broad slits in the ceiling, while the four classrooms have large windows that open onto the street.

For the design of the interiors, the architects collaborated with the artist and colour specialist Perry Roberts; he designed a rich range of pastel colours inspired by the variety of colours now revealed on the back walls of the surrounding buildings. The walls of the classrooms and the smaller auditoria were done in greys. This gives free rein to the varied range of colours of the furniture – in the smaller auditoria all the tables are painted a different colour. The spatiality of the large auditorium is also defined entirely by light and colour. Just as in the smaller auditoria, daylight is able to enter through slits in the ceiling. The colour strategy is the reverse, however: the furniture is here in greys while the walls are done as large, light coloured surfaces.

This use of colour seems to help the walls of the auditorium lose their mass. Perry achieves a similar effect with some of the partition walls on the inner area; in this way he blurs their precise outlines. This treatment summarises the strategy of the project well. By stretching boundaries into transitional zones and transforming residual spaces into usable areas, the architects have succeeded in turning a silted-up inner area into a structuring element in the urban fabric. In this way the new university complex is able to give a new impulse to the unity of habitation, work and study in the city.

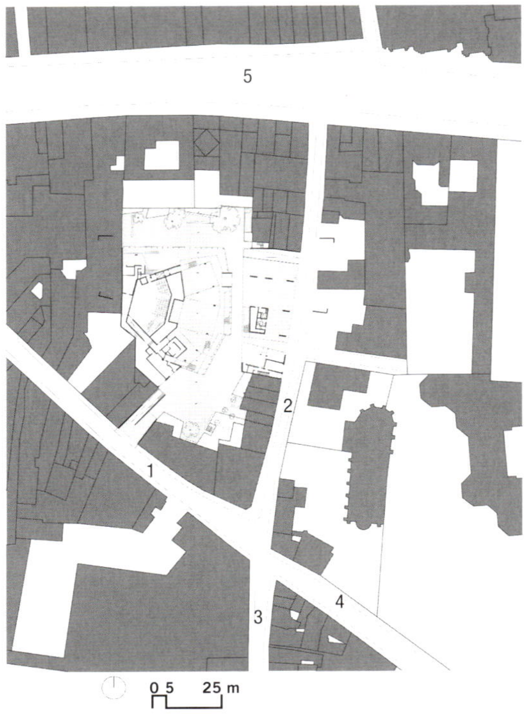

Situation plan
1 Vekestraat
2 Kleine Kauwenberg
3 Grote Kauwenberg
4 Lange Winkelstraat
5 Paardenmarkt

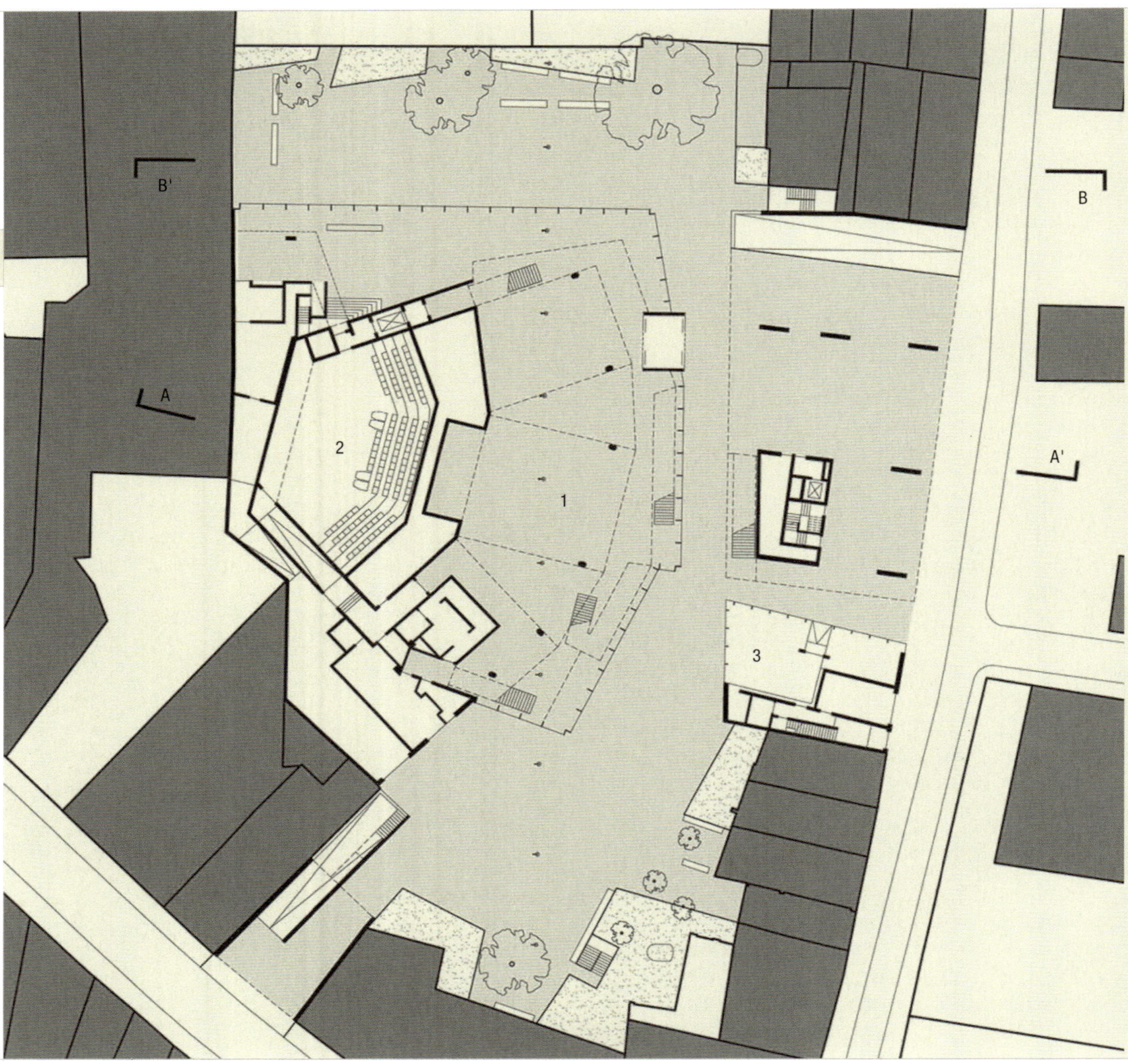

Level 0
1 foyer
2 auditorium, 700 seats
3 Unifac student house

Facade Vekestraat

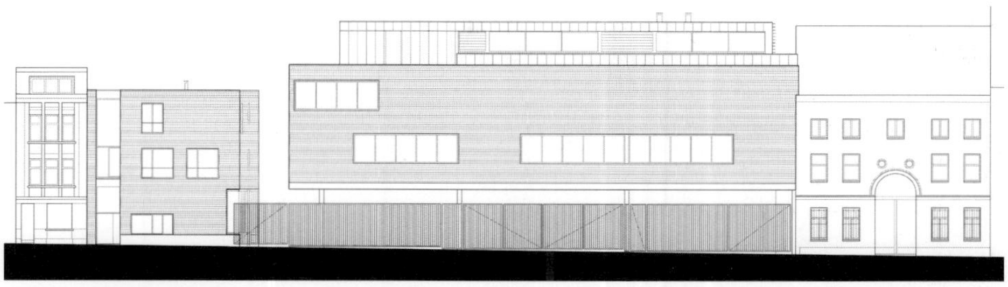

Facade Kleine Kauwenberg

Level 2

1 auditorium, 700 seats
2 Unifac student house
3 classrooms
4 offices
5 small auditoriums

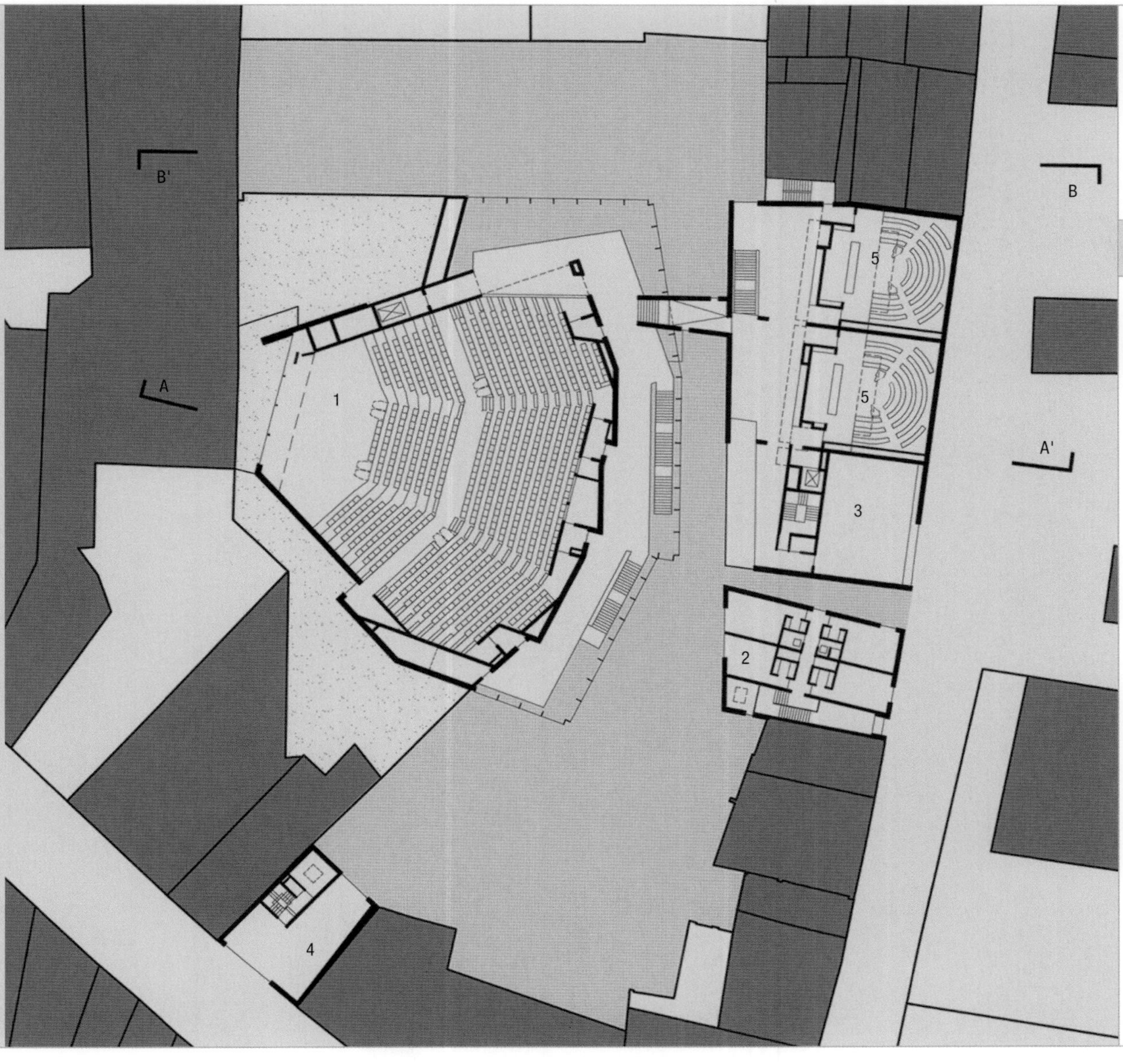

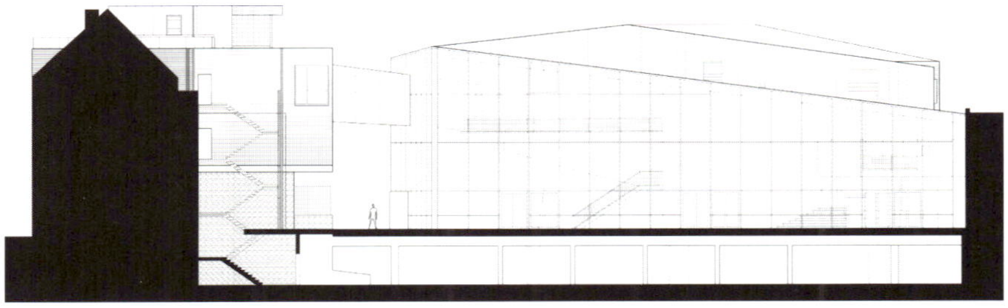

Section BB'

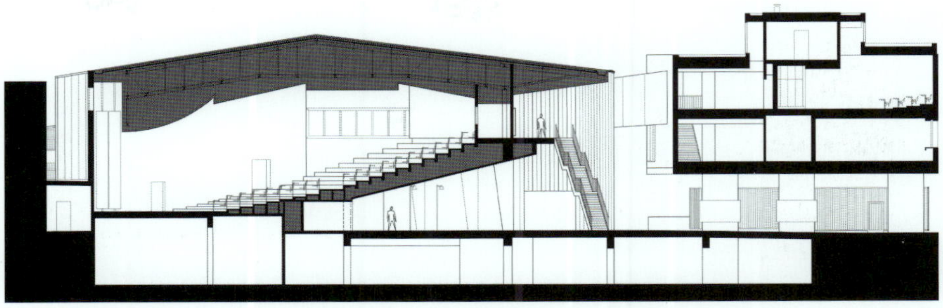

Section AA'

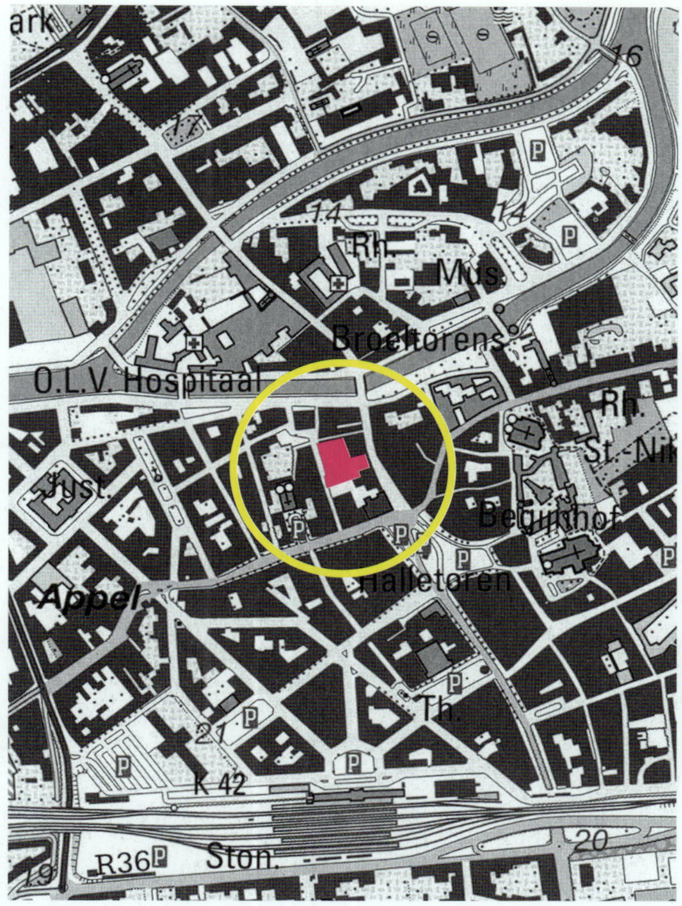

TOWN HALL

architect **noA.ARCHITECTS**

location Grote Markt 54, 8500 Kortrijk

client	Kortrijk town council - Facility Department, headed by the municipal architect and director Jean-Pierre Vanacker coordinator Mathieu Desmet
design - building	2002-2003
project-workers	Danny Dezutter I Bart Dehaene I Gert Somers counters in association with Thomas Nachtergaele Interieur garden in association with Philippe Haven and Chantal Viérin Landscape architects
engineers	Technical installations: Ingenium, Bruges Data/telephony and renovation of tower facade: Kortrijk town council Facility Department Stability: VK engineering, Bruges I Safety coordination: BTB, Ronse
contracted work	Structural work, finishing and fixed furnishings: Verstraete nv, Rumbeke Electricity: Rojolux, Pittem I HVAC: Stallo Industrie, Kalken Sanitation: Vandorpe, Kortrijk I Telephony: Nextiraone, Zaventem Data: Sella Corporation, Londerzeel I Detection and access control: Korelec, Kortrijk Paintwork: Jodecor, Kortrijk I Lifts: Thyssen, Brussel Tables and sofas: Surplus bvba, Gent I Cupboards: Must nv, Brussel Chairs: Artiv, Gent I Mobile cabinets: Bruynzeel nv, Brussel Garden: Dewulf Gebr. bvba, Boezinge
area	2,866 sq.m. (ground floor)
volume	8,800 cubic m. (ground floor)
building costs	3,260,000 EUR
building costs/sq. m	1,137.47 EUR/sq.m.
project description	Caroline Goossens
photography	Karin Borghouts p.196,197 I Paul d'Haese p.195,199,201 Stefan Vandermeulen p. 194

 TOWN HALL ▸ architect **noA.ARCHITECTS**

When Kortrijk town council acquired this former bank building, the most important argument in favour of its purchase was its location: immediately behind the town hall, flanked by three streets and in the middle of a couple of important roads crossing the inner-city. The starting signal was immediately given for the council's latent plans to transform the unwieldy municipal administration, spread over several offices, into an efficient central service-providing machine.

There remained only one problem: the budget available was almost entirely used up by the purchase of the building itself. Since it was not an option to take on the existing furniture and fittings for the ambitious management staff, there was some powerful lobbying for extra money. In the end, the town council organised an open architectural competition, in which the extremely tight conversion budget (3,375,000 Eur) was perhaps the main challenge. The trio of Brussels architects called noA won the competition with a proposal that provided the council with an exceptionally practicable framework for its restructuring plans but at the same time left every avenue open for the future.

Despite its location in the centre of Kortrijk, the former bank branch has hardly any presence in its surroundings. It hides like a blind mastodon in an enclosed block and turns its back on the adjoining streets. Even at the point where it rises five storeys above street level and becomes a small office block, the volume still does not transcend its anonymity but continues to play a secondary role in the shadow of the town hall. The interior of the ground floor was in keeping with this: shimmering under fluorescent light, packed full, pale and frankly unpleasant. These aspects were in total opposition to the ambitions of the council's management staff, which was aiming for transparency, customer-friendliness and efficiency.

So the whole ground floor was stripped, down to the bare structure. What appeared – a concrete grid construction with fine formwork patterns – was not only materially considerably more pure but also displayed an imposing spatiality that suggested breadth.It was decided to retain this 'bare structure effect'. The exposed concrete now frames the open-plan office in which 100 members of staff work in six departments, each with its own colour. In order to let daylight penetrate deep into the extensive ground floor, two outer facades were given large windows and the roof was opened up in six strategic places. Standard greenhouses were put up over these openings, giving a surprising spatiality to the rigidly delineated angle of view from inside.

They present a view of the 'tower', the five office floors above the entrance area that house the less public-oriented municipal departments. The staff that work in the tower are

in their turn treated to a slightly surreal sight: a green roof – the roof garden will be laid out in the second stage – with six empty greenhouses in a rhythmic pattern, brightly lit at dusk. However unattractive it may have been, the given situation nevertheless formed the starting point for the design of the conversion. The architects accepted the given context and set to work on it. Their changes were guided mainly by a pragmatic agenda: the best possible functioning of the official machine and its provision of services to the public.

They did not therefore opt for a flashy exterior, but concentrated on the experience of the interior. Even the large picture windows, because they look out onto a narrow residential alleyway, draw the street inward rather than projecting the interior outward. In their explanatory notes, the architects repeatedly illustrate this approach by interpreting their changes from the inside out. Where and in what way they put a window into the facade was determined by where natural light was needed on the inside.

In fact very little has changed in the old bank building: it remains an open interior space with zones for public contact and with open work spaces. But the modification is more than a contemporary upgrading of the interior. As a result of the dismantling, the open plan and the introduction of natural light, the architects forced the rigid, unequivocal inner block into the future, whatever it may bring. The building's location in commercial heart of the town was the most important reason for the architects concentrating mainly on the ground floor. They came up with the idea of a covered service market, an idea that fitted in perfectly with the more customer-oriented approach the council had in mind. Following the example of the open shop platforms that latch onto the pedestrian streets in the centre of metropolises, various services fan out over the whole floor in colourful, small-scale 'shop-in-shop' units.

Three entrances on two axes ensure the flow in and through the building by a public that is not necessarily looking for the municipal services, but may be simply walking through or using it as a place to meet. Is this administrative centre a link that is not to be missed on the recreational shopping or walking route through Kortrijk town centre? In reality the town centre is as good as dead during the week and, as yet, visitors seem to be seeping into the new service centre only of necessity.

Even though the ideal of administration tailor-made for the consumer naturally illustrates well how market-based thinking transcends purely commercial concerns. Kortrijk, which for years has been trying to present itself as a dynamic Flemish design town, possibly took this image job slightly too seriously. The dream of the management staff and architects, which combines the clean desk principle – no personal workspaces and central file management –

with an open structure of authority – the management of each department works among its staff – appears for the moment to be beyond its reach. Here and there one still notices a cuddly mascot, and framed photos and calendars still decorate many a desk. Paper trays are obstinately considered indispensable and some officials forget to store their files away systematically before they leave.

Some things have now been put right by regularly referring playfully to the 'Manifesto of Neatness', that was drawn up by the management and architects. But there are also assets that aid its day-to-day functioning. For instance, the circulation plays a crucial part. In order to ensure immediate orientation in the large open hall, each department appears in a different colour. The principle here was that the expected permanent flow of public would where necessary be channelled and filtered in a way that combined customer-friendliness with efficiency: from quick-service counter through info desk to consultation room.

Up to now however, this flow has not turned out to be so permanent and the pattern of visitors shows many dips but also some unpredictable peaks. The spatial changes made by noA, however logical and no-nonsense they may be, never claim total control over this sort of situation. In this way the user becomes a fundamental ingredient in the experience of the building.

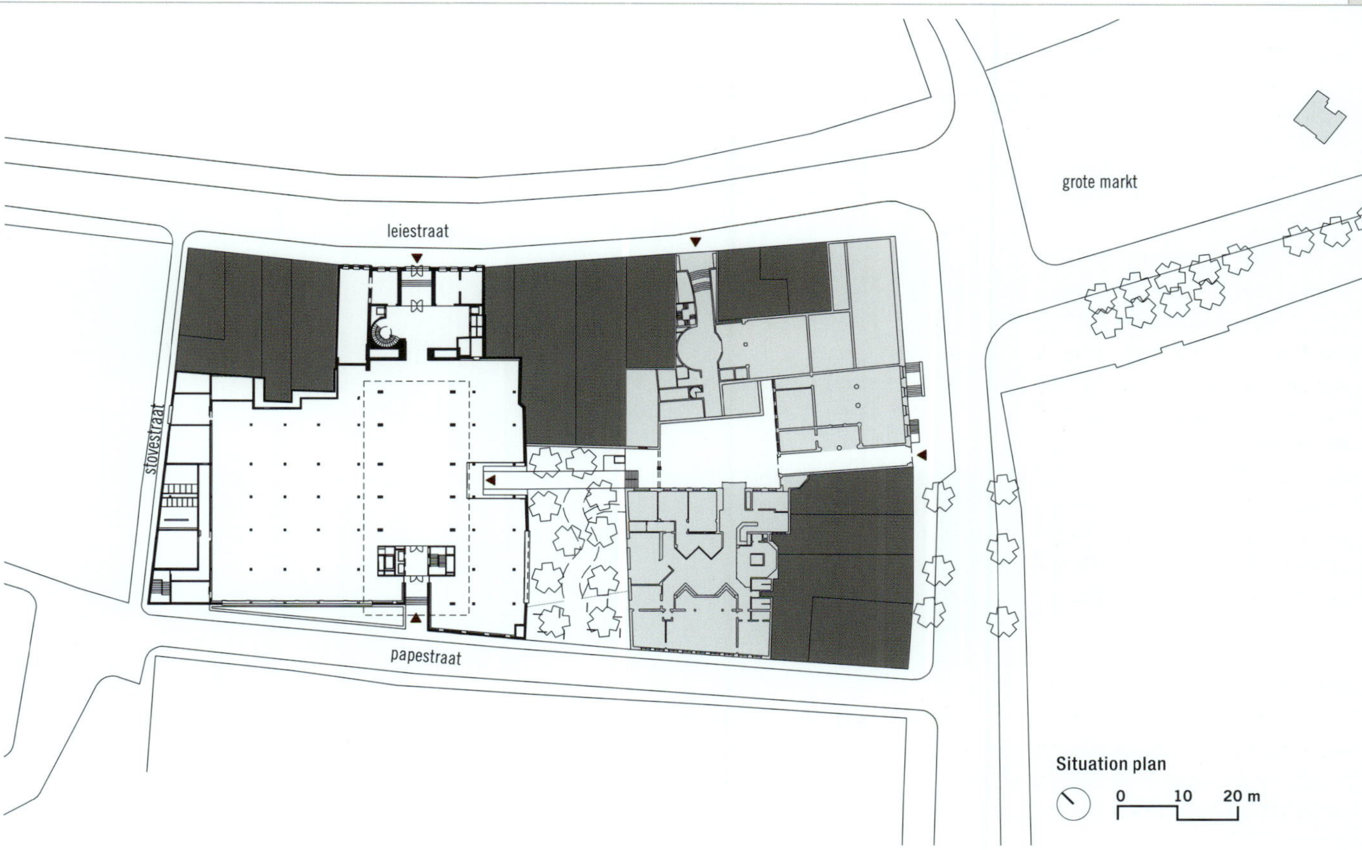

Situation plan

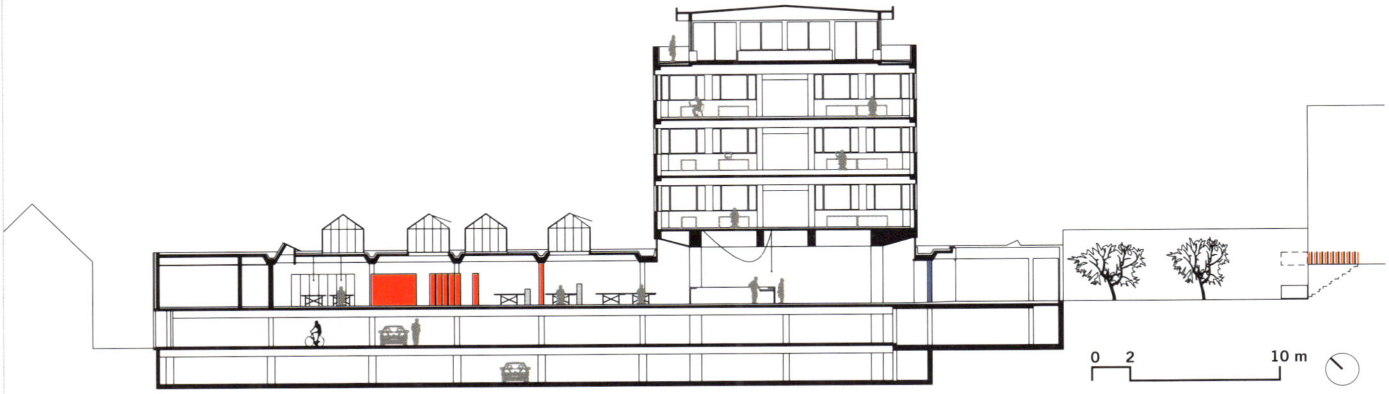

Section AA'

Level 0

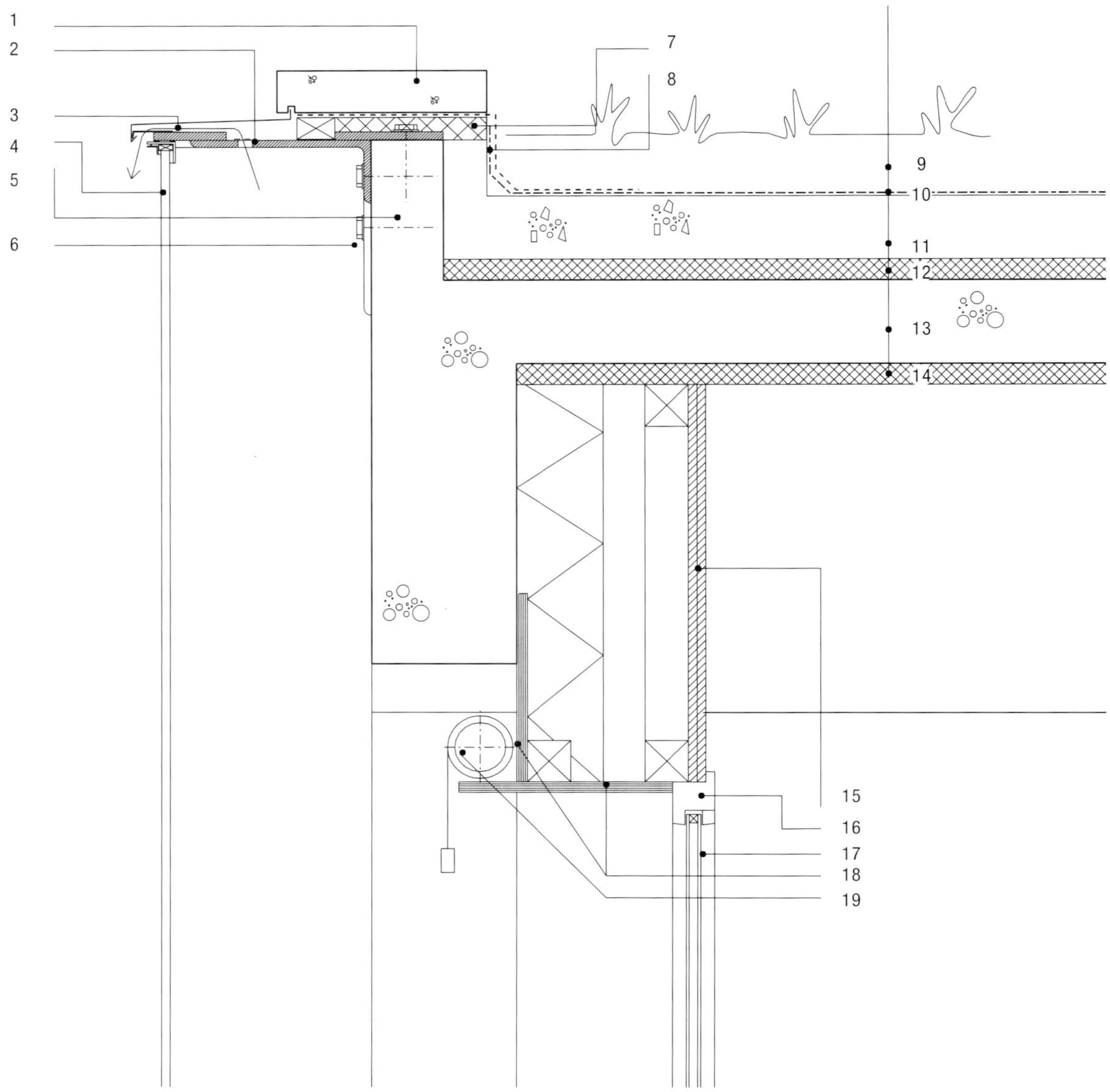

Detail: vertical section through glass curtain wall - joint with roof

1 concrete coping (reused)
2 steel L-section - ventiltion holes, 30 mm diameter, 150 mm centre to centre (covered with insect mesh)
3 aluminium flashing
4 glass curtain wall
5 existing concrete structure
6 steel in cantilever post settlement joint
7 insulation to be repaired
8 new waterproof flashing
9 green roof
10 existing waterproofing
11 mass concrete to falls
12 insulation, 3 cm
13 concrete slab
14 existing woodwool cement slab
15 plasterboard (2 x 12,5 mm)
16 wooden window frame
17 double glazing
18 plywood lining
19 vertical sunshade on roller

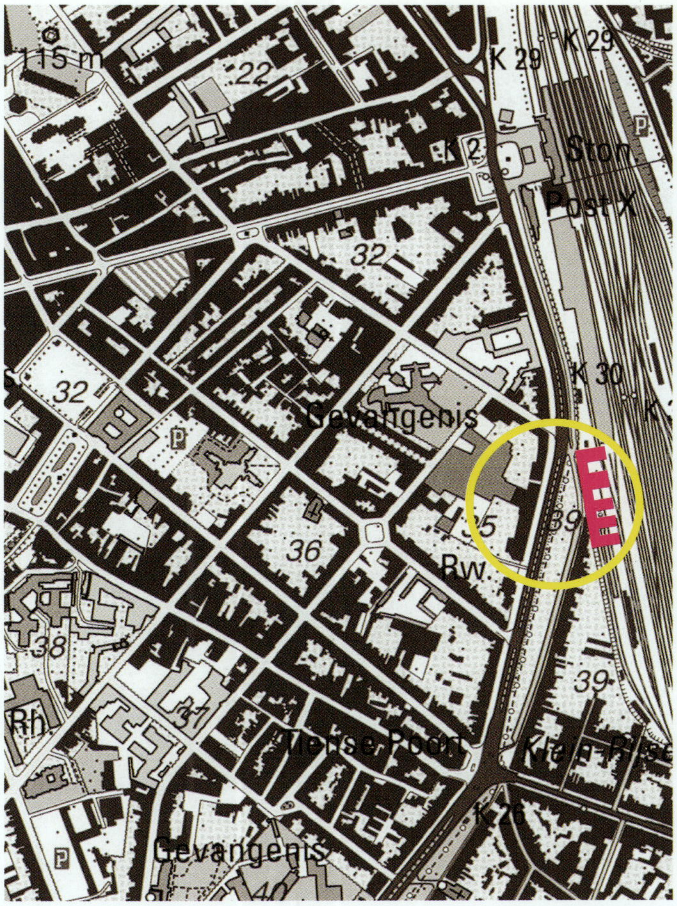

PROVINCIAL ADMINISTRATION BUILDING

architect **GONÇALO BYRNE ARQUITECTOS / WIT ARCHITECTENVENNOOTSCHAP**

location Provincieplein 1, 3010 Leuven

client	Province of Flemish Brabant
design	[TV Ontwerpteam Provinciehuis Vlaams-Brabant]: architecture – stability – technical installations Gonçalo Byrne Arquitectos LDA, Lissabon WIT architectenvennootschap, Outgaarden Bureau voor Architectuur en Stabiliteit, Dirk Jaspaert, Leuven Nv Partners, Ghent
design - building	1998-2003
engineers	engineers were part of the design team
contracted work	Developer-client: Tijdelijke Vereniging Artesia Banking Corporation nv and TV Ondernemingen Maurice Delens nv I Antwerpse Bouwwerken nv I Van Rymenant nv
area	29,321 sq. m.
volume	119,541 cubic. m.
building costs/sq. m	1,080.42 EUR/sq. m.
project description	Sven Sterken
photography	André Nullens p.204, 205, 206, 207 I Stefan Vandermeulen p.208

 PROVINCIAL ADMINISTRATION BUILDING ▸ architect **GONÇALO BYRNE ARQUITECTOS / WIT ARCHITECTENVENNOOTSCHAP**

After the Province of Brabant was divided into its Flemish and Walloon parts in 1989, a solution had to be found for accommodating the provincial administrative departments. The idea of building something new provided an opportunity to put the fundamental elements of the Flanders Spatial Structure Plan into practice, achieving condensation by locating active centres in the existing urban setting.

It was also quite natural that the building should be integrated into the urban design for the station zone in Leuven, which Projectteam Stadsontwerp of Marcel Smets drew up in 1992. In this way a project took shape which not only had to reflect the ambitions and the dynamism of the new Province of Vlaams-Brabant, but was also to be an example of the Flemish government's new architectural policy.

In autumn 1997 an international architectural competition was organised. It was a combination of a public and a limited competition: the candidates were asked first to propose a team and a vision of the brief; on this basis five architects were asked to draw up a design. Account had to be taken of the preconditions set by the urban design. The building had to consist of a rectangular tower and a low rear building. The tower had to form a visual landmark. It lies on the intersection of the railway and the Tiensevest, and thereby marks the boundary of the office zone that stretches as far as the station. By contrast, the lower building had to adapt to the scale of the residential area behind it. Although (or perhaps precisely because) the architects' freedom was thereby kept very much within bounds, the competition yielded five high-quality entries, from which that by the association of Byrne Arquitectos and WIT Architectural Partners was unanimously chosen. It did after all respond most fully to the range of requirements and also looked as if it would survive the construction stage more or less unscathed. In fact the plans were hardly modified at all, and the set budget of 30 million Eur was adhered to.

The building is conceived as a rhythmical sequence of indoor and outdoor spaces connected by a long, broad indoor street parallel to the Tiensevest. Seen from the station, the office block, the large council chamber, the auditorium, the multifunctional space and the staff restaurant succeed one another, separated by spacious patios. All these elements are set on a common plinth that runs under the forecourt. This makes the forecourt an integral part of the building. The substantial difference in level between the Tiensevest and the railway cutting (7 metres) allows the plinth to be buried in the ground; it comprises two storeys, on the lower of which there are large archives and a car park for 188 cars. The other storey is occupied by logistical functions such as a post office, refrigeration room for the restaurant, workshops, etc.) and 47 visitors' parking spaces. All the places where people

work receive daylight. Whereas the layered and patterned structure can be clearly observed in the facade facing the railway cutting, the building presents itself to the city as a single continuous entity. The tower and the rear building seem to merge into one another, an effect that is reinforced by the seamless transition of the bluestone facade cladding between the two elements.

When one enters the building the mass of the tower is at no time tangible or visible. The forecourt simply runs under the tower and there becomes the reception area. It then links up with the indoor street in an almost equally natural way. The indoor street is on two levels: on the lower, ground floor level it is a public corridor, while on the second level it is only accessible to staff. The offices of the governor, the deputies, the provincial registrar and their staff are all here. By means of a system of 'lock gates' they have direct access to the public rooms. Despite the almost graphic clarity of the plan, the spatial effect of the indoor street – and by extension that of the entire building – is surprisingly varied, but without the need for any subtle trickery.

For example, the patios are used to their utmost; they are conceived as outdoor rooms, three of whose walls are entirely in glass. The indoor street and the public rooms thereby make a very light and airy impression. The fourth wall of the patios is only hinted at; they are after all open on the railway side. But a strip of pre-tensioned concrete slabs ensures visual continuity in the facade along the railway cutting. This gives rise to a clever visual effect seen from the public corridor, one that is reminiscent of a long horizontal window *(fenêtre-en-longueur)*. The low-hanging concrete screen frames the railway landscape in such a way that all that remains is the silent and abstract movement of the passing trains.

The public rooms are fitted and furnished in a simple and multifunctional fashion, one of the most striking elements being the abundant use of wood for the floors and ceilings. Most of the fixed furniture is also in varnished wood. The same restraint characterises the offices.

They are arranged in two strips along the facades of the tower, with a third strip in the middle for circulation, fire stairs and sanitary facilities. Each floor in the tower is fitted out differently. The concept was in fact formed in consultation with the users-to-be. A module of 1.8 x 1.8 m was used, with an area of 10 sq. m. (3 modules) per function (work, meetings, reception).

Flexibility and durability were the chief criteria; in order to save space and energy, for example, flat computer screens were used everywhere, while the furniture is sectional and extendable. The compact plan of the tower means all work-

places enjoy plenty of daylight. In addition, they almost all have a splendid view of the city centre and the unceasing arrival and departure of trains. On the south side, the windows even extend from floor to ceiling, in order to make maximum use of the winter sun; automatic sunblinds provide the necessary screening. The intensity of the electric lighting in the offices is geared to the amount of daylight coming in. In addition, each employee has their own desk-lamp so they can adjust the light to suit themselves.

The less well-lit zone in the middle of the tower is kept open as much as possible. This indefinable space is used in several ways: as a meeting space, a place to consult professional journals and for the photocopier. Just as in the public corridor downstairs, the natural way the users fill in these 'empty' spaces reveals the effectiveness of this architecture. After all, in its well-considered simplicity, it is an invitation to informal use of the space. By working with the elementary principles of mass, void and light, Byrne provides a powerful but inconspicuous spatial matrix that connects seamlessly with the city.

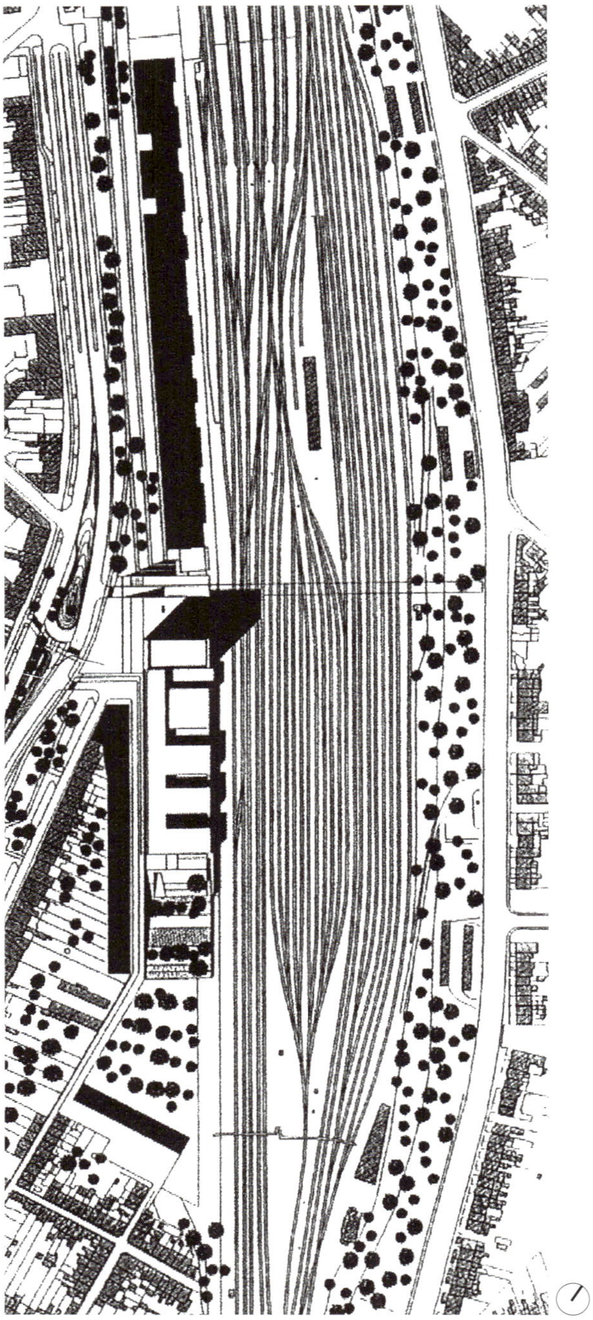

Section AA'

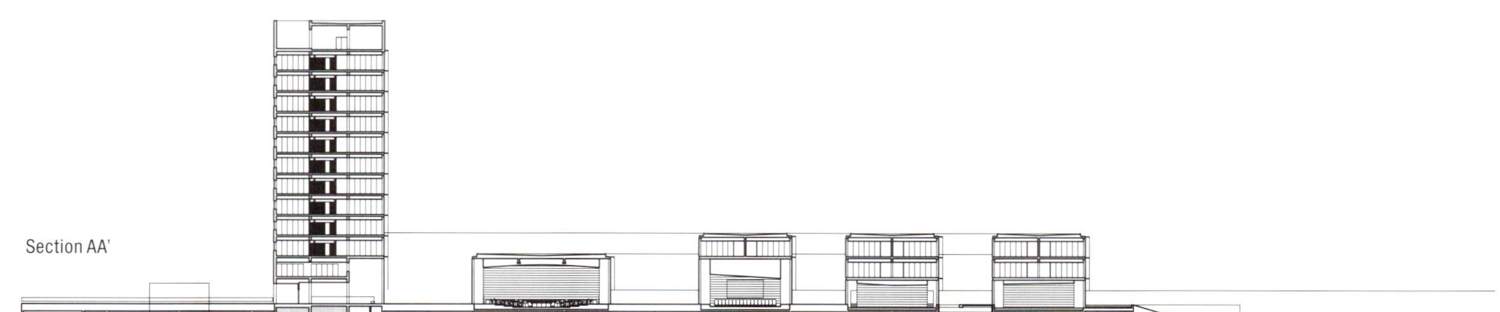

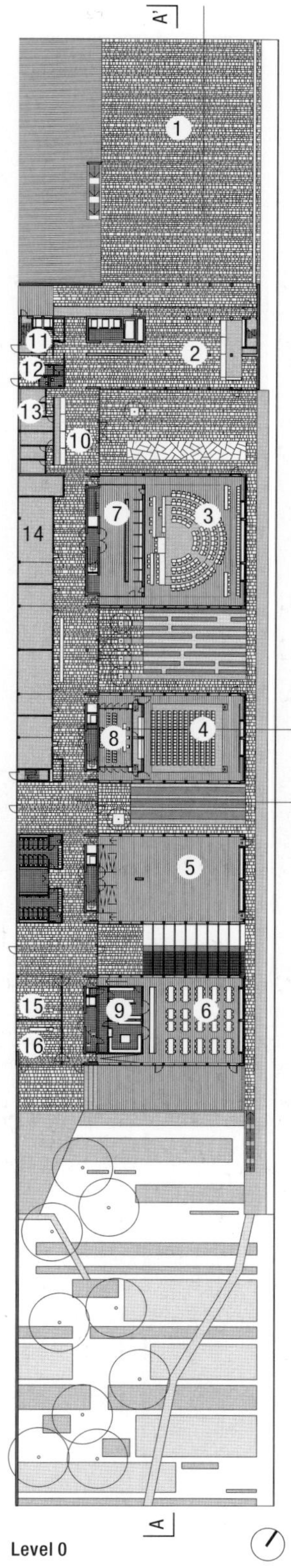

Level 0

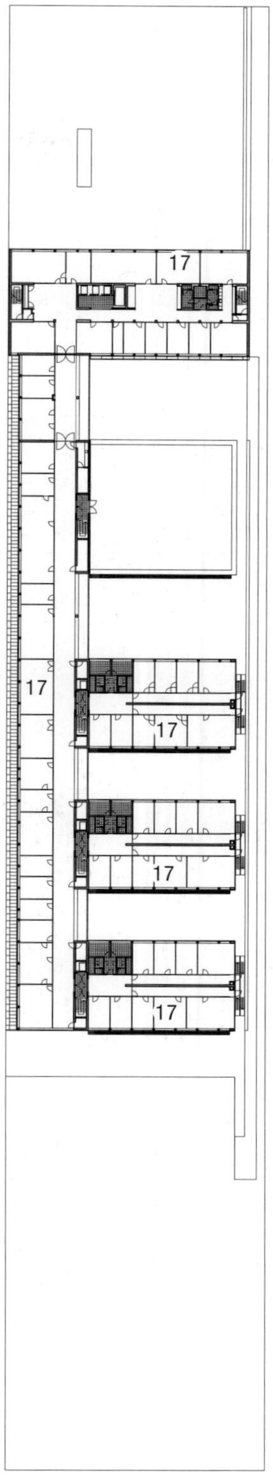

Level 2

1 forecourt
2 entrance hall
3 council chamber
4 auditorium
5 multipurpose hall
6 restaurant
7 foyer
8 press room
9 kitchen
10 indoor street
11 control room
12 First Aid room
13 visitor centre
14 meeting rooms
15 coffee corner
16 visitor restaurant
17 offices

AMBROGIO

THE EDITORS AND THE AUTHORS

Architecture and urbanism

Maarten Delbeke
01 MACKEN & MACKEN – 5 HUIZEN / 5 HOUSES
Vlaams Architectuurinstituut / A16, 80 p.
ISBN 90-807787-1-0
Nederlands en Engels

Tijl Vanmeirhaeghe
02 FLC – FUTURE CONFLICTS
Vlaams Architectuurinstituut / A16, 80 p.
ISBN 90-807787-3-7
Nederlands en Engels

Saskia Kloosterboer, Bruno Notteboom, Katrien Vandermarliere (red.)
ACHTERGROND #01 BEDRIJFSGEBOUWEN
Vlaams Architectuurinstituut, Antwerpen, 64 p.
ISBN 90-807787-2-9

Xaveer de Geyter Architecten
AFTER-SPRAWL – ONDERZOEK NAAR DE HEDENDAAGSE STAD / AFTER-SPRAWL – RESEARCH FOR THE CONTEMPORARY CITY
deSingel Internationaal Kunstcentrum / NAi-uitgevers, Antwerpen - Rotterdam, 256 p.
ISBN 90-5662-264-1 (N), ISBN 90-5662-265-X (E)

Lieven De Cauter, Michiel Dehaene (red.)
AGENDA 2003 / WERKBOEK – HET KLEINE LEXICON VAN HET VLAAMSE (ARCHITECTUUR-)LANDSCHAP VAN ACHTERKEUKEN TOT ZONEVREEMD
deSingel Internationaal Kunstcentrum, Antwerpen ism. Vlaams Bouwmeester en Vlaams Architectuurinstituut
ISBN 90-75591-13-6

Iwan Strauven
ALFRED HARDY 1900-1965
Ghent University Architectural and Engineering Press, Gent, 80 p.
ISBN 90-7671414-2

Christiaan Leysen
ANTWERPEN - ONVOLTOOIDE STAD
Lannoo, Tielt, 180 p.
ISBN 90-209-5341-9

Hardwin De Wever, Ellen Lambrechts (red.)
ANTWERPEN – SPOOR NOORD – EEN STEDELIJK PARK IN ZICHT
Ludion, Gent-Amsterdam / Stad Antwerpen, 128 p.
ISBN 90-5544-483-9 (N), 90-5544-484-7 (E)

Tom Avermaete, Stefan Devoldere, Liesbeth Silverans
ARCHITECTUUR LEUVEN 1999-2002
Stichting Stad en Architectuur vzw, Leuven, 40 p.

OSA+ (KULeuven), Bruno De Meulder, Oswald Devisch
ATLAS ZUIDELIJK WEST-VLAANDEREN FASCIKEL 3 - WEVELGEM
Anno'02 vzw, Kortrijk, 111 p.

Hubert-Jan Henket, Hilde Heynen (red.)
BACK FROM UTOPIA – THE CHALLENGE OF THE MODERN MOVEMENT
010 Publishers, Rotterdam, 411 p.
ISBN 90-6450-483-0

Koen Van Synghel, Marc Dubois, Jan Thomaes, e.a.
BATAILLE & IBENS - PROJECTEN EN OBJECTEN 1968-2003
Ludion, Gent-Amsterdam, 176 p.
ISBN 90-5544-441-3 (N), 90-5544-442-1 (F)

BELGIUM NEW ARCHITECTURE 2
Prisme Editions, Brussel, 264 p.
ISBN 296-00103-53
Nederlands, Engels en Frans

Vlaams Architectuurinstituut (red.)
DAG VAN DE ARCHITECTUUR - PROGRAMMABROCHURE
Vlaams Architectuurinstituut, Antwerpen

Wim Cuyvers, Marc De Blieck
E-403
Yves Gevaert, Brussel, 208 p.
ISBN 2-930128-20-8

Geert Bekaert, Ronny De Meyer
EEN REIS NAAR JAPAN. MET TOEVAL ALS NORM
Ghent University Architectural and Engineering Press, Gent
ISBN 90-76714-09-6
Nederlands en Engels

Dirk Van de Vijver, Krista De Jonge
INGENIEURS EN ARCHITECTEN OP DE DREMPEL VAN EEN NIEUWE TIJD (1750 – 1830)
Leuven University Press, Leuven, 224 p.
ISBN 90-58673146

Hilde Heynen, David Vanderburgh (red.)
INSIDE DENSITY – INTERNATIONAL COLLOQUIUM ON ARCHITECTURE AND CITIES # 1
La Lettre volée, Brussel, 192 p.
ISBN 2-87317-202-9
Engels en Frans

HET PROVINCIEHUIS / ARCHITECTUUR EN KUNSTINTEGRATIE
Provincie Vlaams-Brabant, Leuven, 75 p.

Steven Jacobs
HORROR VACUI: FOTOGRAFIE VAN DE LEGE STAD
Ghent Urban Studies Team (GUST), Gent, 90 p.
ISBN 90-77302-01-8
Nederlands en Engels

Max Borka, Koenraad Janssens
JO CREPAIN ARCHITECT '73-'03
Stichting Kunstboek, Oostkamp, 352 p.
ISBN 90-5856-114-3

Marc Dubois
LENS°ASS ARCHITECTEN
Lannoo, Tielt, 176 p.
ISBN 90-209-5452-0

Kristiaan Borret, André Loeckx, William Mann
MARIE-JOSÉ VAN HEE – ARCHITECT
Ludion, Gent-Amsterdam, 128 p.
ISBN 90-5544-424-3

Dirk Lauwaert, Linda Loppa, Kristiaan Borret, e.a.
MODEMUSEUM ANTWERPEN
Ludion, Gent-Amsterdam, 192 p.
ISBN 90-5544-423-5

Marc Dubois
NIEUWE ARCHITECTUUR IN BRUGGE
Stichting Kunstboek, Oostkamp, 84 p.
ISBN 90-5856-068-6

Ghent Urban Studies Team (GUST) (red.)
POST EX SUB DIS : URBAN FRAGMENTATIONS AND CONSTRUCTIONS
010 Publishers, Rotterdam, 312 p.
ISBN 90-6540-478-4

Anne Van Loo (red.)
REPERTORIUM VAN DE ARCHITECTUUR IN BELGIË VAN 1830 TOT HEDEN
Mercatorfonds, Antwerpen, 608 p.
ISBN 90-6153-526-3 (N), 90-6153-527-1 (F)

Evert Lagrou, Marc Dubois
STATIONS & STEDEN/EUROSTATION 10 JAREN ONDERWEG
Eurostation Brussel, 256 p.

Hera Van Sande
TOYO ITO BUILDS THE BRUGES 2002 PAVILLION
Stichting Kunstboek, Oostkamp
ISBN 90-5856-076-X

Marcel Smets (red.)
TUSSEN STAD EN SPOOR - DE STATIONSOMGEVING VAN LEUVEN
Ludion, Gent-Amsterdam, 192 p.
ISBN 90-5544-390-5 (NL), ISBN 90-5544-391-3 (E)

Luc Deleu
URBI ET ORBI
Ludion, Gent-Amsterdam, 160 p.
ISBN 90-5544-425-1

Jan Amelynck, Stefan Devoldere, Yves Schoonjans, e.a.
VICTOR BROOS – DE KRACHT VAN HET ALLEDAAGSE
Stichting Stad & Architectuur vzw, Leuven, 84 p.

Marc Dubois
WONING/HOUSE GASTON EYSSELINCK 1930-1931
Stichting Kunstboek, Oostkamp, 48 p.
ISBN 9058561232,
Nederlands en Engels

Policy

Kristiaan Borret, Maarten Delbeke, Dirk Janssen, André Loeckx, e.a. (red.)
JAARBOEK ARCHITECTUUR VLAANDEREN 00/01 ANALES DE L'ARCHITECTURE EN FLANDRE / FLANDERS ARCHITECTURAL YEARBOOK
Ministerie van de Vlaamse Gemeenschap, Departement Welzijn, Volksgezondheid en Cultuur, Administratie Cultuur, Afdeling Beeldende Kunst en Musea, Brussel, 294 p.
ISBN 90-403-0145-X

Vlaams Bouwmeester i.s.m. Nederlands Rijksbouwmeester
MEESTERPROEF VLAANDEREN - NEDERLAND 2001
Vlaams Bouwmeester, Brussel, 255 p.
ISBN 90-403-0144-1

bOb Van Reeth, Willem Van Den Hoof, Katrien Laenen (red.)
MEESTERPROEF VOOR JONGE KUNSTENAARS
Vlaams Bouwmeester, Brussel, 93 p.
ISBN 90-403-0153-0

Mark Santens, Dirk Somers, Saskia Kloosterboer (red.)
JONGE ARCHITECTEN IN EUROPA – SEMINARIE ANTWERPEN (B) 2002 / JEUNES ARCHITECTES EN EUROPE – SÉMINAIRE ANVERS (B) 2002 / YOUNG ARCHITECTS IN EUROPE – SEMINAR ANTWERP (B) 2002
Ministerie van de Vlaamse Gemeenschap – Team Vlaams Bouwmeester, Brussel, 32 p.
ISBN 90-403-0148-4 (N), ISBN 90-403-0150-6 (F), ISBN 90-403-0149-2 (E)

Team Vlaams Bouwmeester
KUNST - WERK: WERK MAKEN BIJ VLAAMSE OVERHEIDSPROJECTEN
Ministerie van de Vlaamse Gemeenschap – Team Vlaams Bouwmeester, Brussel
D/2003/3241/063

Dominique Thirion - Team Vlaams Bouwmeester
OPEN VENSTER 01 - OPEN VENSTER 02
Ministerie van de Vlaamse Gemeenschap – Team Vlaams Bouwmeester, Brussel
ISBN 90-403-0175-1 + DVD

Linda Boudry, Peter Cabus, Eric Corijn, e.a.
DE EEUW VAN DE STAD. OVER STADSREPUBLIEKEN EN RASTERSTEDEN (VOORSTUDIES – WITBOEK)
Project stedenbeleid – administratie Binnenlandse aangelegenheden – Ministerie van de Vlaamse Gemeenschap, Brussel, 716 p.
ISBN 90-403-0189-1

Ministerie van de Vlaamse Gemeenschap, AROHM ism. CIBE, Architectuur als Buur vzw
DICHTER WONEN
Ministerie van de Vlaamse Gemeenschap, Brussel
D/2002/3241/057

Conservation of monuments and historic buildings

Michelangelo Meerten,
Greta Verbeurgt, Bart van der Herten
BUITEN-SPORIG BRUSSEL: 50 JAAR NOORD-ZUIDVERBINDING
Lanno, Tielt, 96 p.
ISBN 90-209-4870-9

Ruth Eaton
DE IDEALE STAD – UTOPIA EN DE (NIET) GEBOUWDE OMGEVING
Mercatorfonds, Antwerpen, 256 p.
ISBN 90-6153-473-9

Daan Anthuenis, Birgit De Vries
GEBOUWEN SPREKEN. WAT DE HAAN OP DE TOREN JE KAN VERTELLEN
Clavis, Hasselt, 64 p.
ISBN 90-6822-967-2

Michiel Heirman, Linda Van Santvoort
GIDS VOOR ARCHITECTUUR
Lannoo, Tielt, 103 p.
ISBN 90-209-4152-6

Livia Snauwaert, Luc Devliegher
GIDS VOOR ARCHITECTUUR IN BRUGGE
Lannoo, Tielt, 383 p.
ISBN 90-209-4711-7

Dirk Laporte, Livia Snauwaert
GIDS VOOR ARCHITECTUUR IN GENT
Lannoo, Tielt, 480 p.
ISBN 90-209-5212-9

Marjan Buyle, Marcel M. Celis, e.a.
M & L CAHIER 7: DE BEELDENTAAL VAN SYMBOLEN
Ministerie van de Vlaamse Gemeenschap, Afdeling Monumenten en Landschappen

Anne Brumagne, Marjan Buyle, Marcel M. Celis, e.a.
SYMBOLEN. OPEN MONUMENTENDAG VLAANDEREN 2002
Stichting Kunstboek ism. Erfgoed Vlaanderen, 80 p.
ISBN 90-5856-065-1

Heiner Borggrefe, Peter Fuhring, Barbara Uppenkamp, e.a.
TUSSEN STADSPALEIZEN EN LUCHTKASTELEN HANS VREDEMAN DE VRIES EN DE RENAISSANCE
Ludion, Gent-Amsterdam, 400 p.
ISBN 90-5544-419-7

Landscape architecture

Peter Fuhring, Ursula Härting, Krista De Jonge, e.a.
DE WERELD IS EEN TUIN. HANS VREDEMAN DE VRIES EN DE TUINKUNST VAN DE RENAISSANCE
Ludion, Gent-Amsterdam, 144 p.
ISBN 90-5544-420-0

Patrick Taylor, Marco Valdivia
THE WIRTZ GARDENS
Wirtz International n.v., 612 p.
ISBN 9076704368

Penelope Hill
TUINEN VAN HEDEN – VERNIEUWENDE TUINARCHITECTUUR IN EUROPA
Mercatorfonds, Antwerpen, 264 p.
ISBN 90-6153-495-X (N), 90-6153-494-1 (F)

Flemish architecture in important foreign professional journals

ABITARE

- *Belgio/Belgium: Projects for the future – New architecture – Landscape, nr. 428, maggio/may 2003.*

ARCA

- *Filippo Beltrami Gadola, Una scatola magica (architecten: Samyn & Partners), in Arca, nr. 171, juni 2002, p. 26/31.*
- *Stefano Pavarini, Espressionismo organico [Antwerp Court House] (architecten: Richard Rogers Partnership), in Arca, nr. 172, juli 2002, pp. 26/31.*
- *Maurizio Vitta, Agora: dreams and visions – Lab[au], in Arca, nr. 176, December 2002, pp. 38/49.*
- *Damiano Rizzini, Ambiente e trasparenza [Espace Christian Dotremont] (architecten: Samyn & Partners), in Arca nr. 177, januari 2003, pp. 64/69.*
- *Mario Antonio Arnaboldi, Tra avignone eponte Vecchio [Copiapo Bridge, Chile] (architecten: Samyn & Partners), in Arca nr. 181, mei 2003, pp. 64/67.*

ARCHIS

- *Wim Cuyvers, -Ing-society, in Archis #1, 2002, pp. 80/81.*
- *Koen Van Synghel, Sturm der Ruhe. What is architecture? Openingstentoonstelling in Architekturzentrum Wien, in Archis #1, 2002, pp. 102/103.*
- *Arthur Wortmann, Van deur tot dorp en verder. Patrick Vonck in Alsemberg, in Archis #2, 2002, pp. 82/89.*
- *Wim Cuyvers, La douce France, in Archis #2, 2002, pp. 38/40.*
- *De agenda van Katrien Vandermarliere, in Archis #2, 2002, p. 120.*
- *Wim Cuyvers, Sarajevo Revisited, in Archis #3, 2002, pp. 54/56.*
- *Kristiaan Borret en Pieter T'Jonck, Stad, stad, stad. Werkelijkheid en ideologie van het Leuvense kunstcentrum Stuk, in Archis #5, 2002, pp. 50-68.*
- *Ole Bouman, Euroferno – architecture for the European nation, in Archis #1, 2003, pp. 64/73.*
- *Bert de Muynck, Intrigues in Brussels – the future history of the European Quarter, Archis #1, 2003, pp. 74/87.*
- *Jacob Voorthuis, Window on the city: Boymans Van Beuningen extension (architects: Robbrecht & Daem), in Archis #5, 2003, pp. 104/107.*

DE ARCHITECT

- *Peter Swinnen, Tussen huisvrouw en courtisane. Colloquium 'Architecture, Gender & Domesticity in Leuven, in de Architect, januari 2002, p. 12.*
- *Dominique Pieters, Doos-in-doos uitgekleed. Aula Magna van Samyn and Partners in Louvain-la-Neuve, in de Architect, januari 2002, pp. 62/65.*
- *Marc Dubois, Gebouwen voor de industrie. Architectuurprijs Provincie West-Vlaanderen, in de Architect, maart 2002, pp. 15/16.*
- *Marc Martens, Poëtisch engagement. De 'onaangepaste stad' van Luc Deleu en T.O.P. office, in de Architect, maart 2002, p. 16.*
- *Dominique Pieters, Vermoeiende beproeving in deSingel. Tentoonstelling 'Honderd huizen voor honderd architecten', in de Architect, maart 2002, pp. 16/17.*
- *Janny Rodermond, Jonge architecten verkennen Europees werkterrein, in de Architect, maart 2002, p. 17.*
- *Dominique Pieters, Zo klaar als een klontje. Belgosuc kantoren van CCP-architecten in Beernem, in de Architect, maart 2002, pp. 76/79.*
- *Janny Rodermond en Harm Tilman, Op zoek naar een juist begrepen identiteit. Gewest Vlaanderen wil eigen cultuur internationaal positioneren, in de Architect, maart 2002, pp. 30/37. met o.m. 51N4E (Lamot TM, Mechelen), SmaR (project voor Europese sociale ruimte)*
- *Dominique Pieters, Janny Rodermond en Harm Tilman, Potsierlijk maar geweldig. Jonge architecten onderzoeken potenties Vlaanderen, in de Architect, maart 2002, pp. 38/47.*
- *René Erven, Promotiecentrum in historisch interieur. Verbouwing Vleeshuis in Gent door Coussée & Goris Architecten, in de Architect, maart 2002, pp. 94/97.*
- *Janny Rodermond, Jonge architecten positioneren zich. Discussie jonge architecten in Europa, in de Architect, april 2002, p. 15.*
- *Marcel Smets, Yorgos Simeoforidis (1955-2002), in de Architect, maart 2002, p. 22.*
- *Klaske Havik, Regime van absolute puurheid. Woning te Waasmunster door Vincent Van Duysen Architects, in de Architect, april 2002, pp. 66/69.*
- *Dominique Pieters, Verlicht despotisme. Verkaveling Wilderveld in Sint-Pieters-Leeuw, in de Architect, april 2002, pp. 70/75. Met o.m. werk van Jo Crepain, Eugeen Liebaut*
- *Klaske Havik, Beperking als generator. Kinderrevalidatiecentrum Klimop van Stéphane Beel in Eeklo, in de Architect, mei 2002, pp. 58/61.*
- *Harm Tilman, Na de sprawl. Tentoonstelling van Xaveer De Geyter in deSingel, Antwerpen, in de Architect, juni 2002, p. 15.*
- *Janny Rodermond, Nieuwe vormen van expressie. Utopische esthetiek van het modernisme achterhaald, in de Architect, juli-augustus 2002, pp. 20/25. Met o.m. 51N4E (dubbelcafé voor de Vlaamse regering)*
- *Iwan Strauven, Dubieuze offerte-aanvraag voor Europese Wijk in Brussel. Hoofdstad Europa nog altijd in greep nostalgie, in de Architect, september 2002, pp. 23/24.*
- *Klaske Havik, Gebouw als marktplaats. Cultureel centrum STUK van Neutelings Riedijk in Leuven, in de Architect, oktober 2002, pp. 66/71.*
- *Marc Dubois, Een nieuwe Natie. ModeNatie in Antwerpen door Marie-José Van Hee, in de Architect, november 2002, p. 19.*
- *Peter Swinnen, Schot in de winkelhaak. Nieuwbouw designcenter van Coby Manders en Filip Pittillion, Antwerpen, in de Architect, november 2002, pp. 19/20.*
- *Dominique Pieters, Minimalisme overkill. Belgische Designbiënnale Interieur te Kortrijk, in de Architect, december 2002, pp. 16/17.*
- *Peter Swinnen, Gecamoufleerd brandpunt. Campusbibliotheek Arenberg door Rafael Moneo in Leuven, in de Architect, december 2002, pp. 46/49.*
- *Janny Rodermond, Vlaamse cultuur breed gedefinieerd, in de Architect – Interieur, nr. 7, pp. 28/29.*
- *Anneloes van der Leun, Podium voor zingeving. Heroriëntering op Magdalenakerk in Brugge door Tom Callebout en Stefaan Onraet, in de Architect – Interieur, nr.9, pp. 54/55.*
- *Harm Tilman, Vlaamse biotopen. Fotografieproject Vlaamse bouwmeester, februari 2003, p. 12.*
- *Dominique Pieters, Vitaliteit blootgelegd. Woonhuis Frankfort in Brussel door Pierre Hebbelinck, in de Architect, april 2003, pp. 64/67.*
- *Marcel Smets, Stedelijke vormen van mobiliteit. Ontleden transferia heeft positieve effecten, in de Architect, mei 2003, pp. 22/27.*
- *Dominique Pieters, Genius loci als obsessie. Projecten van B-architecten, Samyn & Partners en Vincent Van Duysen in het buitenland, in de Architect, juni 2003, pp. 38/43.*
- *Harm Tilman, "Het belangrijkste vind ik nog altijd dat goede gebouwen worden gebouwd", Interview met Katrien Vandermarliere, directeur van het Vlaams Architectuurinstituut, in de Architect, juni 2003, pp. 46/49.*
- *Ben Maandag, Zorgvuldigheid vergroot museale samenhang. Uitbreiding Boijmans Van Beuningen in Rotterdam door Robbrecht en Daem Architecten, in de Architect, juli-augustus 2003, pp. 46/51.*
- *Dominique Pieters, Onderzoekslab voor energie, Hoofdkantoor Renson in Waregem door Jo Crepain Architect nv, in de Architect, oktober 2003, pp. 30/35.*
- *Marc Dubois, Monoliet met intiem interieur. Concertgebouw in Brugge door Robbrecht en Daem Architecten, in de Architect, oktober 2003, pp. 64/69.*
- *Bruno De Meulder en Maureen Heyns, Gebroken spiegelpaleis. Stedelijke cultuur en cultureel activisme in Brussel, in de Architect, november 2003, pp. 22/29.*
- *Harm Tilman, Sluier in uitvloeiende stad. Sociale woningbouw in Schaarbeek door Mario Garzaniti, in de Architect, november 2003, pp. 30/31.*
- *Dominique Pieters, Geluidsfabriek met een hart. Renovatie omroepgebouw Flagey in Brussel door de TVA Samyn-Van Ranst-Wachtelaer, in de Architect, november 2003, pp. 32/33.*
- *Harm Tilman, "Architectuur is democratie zelf", Interview met bOb Van Reeth, Vlaams Bouwmeester, in de Architect, november 2003, pp. 38/41.*

- Dominique Pieters, *Rauwe architectuur met achtergevel. Jeugdcentrum in Eeklo door u, Architecten, in de Architect, november 2003, pp. 52/55.*
- *Bruno De Meulder, Stadspark van de 21ste eeuw. Internationale ontwerpwedstrijd voor Antwerpen Spoor Noord, in de Architect, november 2003, pp. 56/61.*
- *Marc Dubois, Meubel als architectuur. Interieur in Gent door Wim Cuyvers, in de Architect, november 2003, p. 80/81.*
- *Iwan Strauven, Opengewerkte doos. Sporthal Dracuna te Gent door CAAN architecten, in de Architect, december 2003, pp. 58/61.*
- *Dominique Pieters, Uitgepuurd zichtbeton. Kantoor Furnibo in Veurne door Buro II, in de Architect, december 2003, pp. 62/65.*
- *Harm Tilman, Tijdelijke oefenlokalen Nova, Mechelen. Verbouwing door dmvA Architecten, in de Architect – Interieur, nr. 12, pp. 22/23.*
- *Dominique Pieters, Woonhuis Frankfort, Brussel. Verbouwing door Pierre Hebbelinck, in de Architect – Interieur, nr. 12, pp. 24/25.*
- *René Erven, Extreem contrast tussen oud en nieuw. Woonhuis/optiek Tackoen in Hasselt door Lens°Ass Architecten, in de Architect – Interieur, nr. 12, pp. 56/59.*
- *Dominique Pieters, Verfijnde chaos. Verso in Antwerpen door Glenn Sestig, in de Architect – Interieur, nr. 12, pp. 64/66.*

ARCHITECTURAL REVIEW
- *Penny McGuire, Urban mosaic (Architecten: Neutelings Riedijk Architecten, STUK, Leuven), in Architectural review, vol. 213, nr. 1271, januari 2003, pp. 62/67.*
- *Musical variations (architecten: Samyn & Partners, Van Ranst en Wachtelaer), in Architectural review, vol. 214, nr. 1277, juli 2003, pp. 69/71.*
- *Catherine Slessor, Catching the wind (architecten: Samyn & Partners), in Architectural review, vol. 214, nr. 1281, november 2003, pp. 32/33.*

ARCHITECTURE D'AUJOURD'HUI
- *Sophie Trelcat, Chasse Park apartments, cinq tours de logements, Breda, Nl (architecten: Xaveer De Geyter), in Architecture d'aujourd'hui, nr. 342, september 2002, pp. 30/33.*
- *Sophie Trelcat, Centre culturel STUK (architecten : Neutelings Riedijk Architecten), in Architecture d'aujourd'hui, nr. 343, november 2002, pp. 32/34.*
- *Sophie Trelcat, Centre de rééducation Klim Op, Eeklo (architect: Stéphane Beel), in Architecture d'aujourd'hui, nr. 345, maart 2003, pp. 20/21.*
- *Roeland Dudal, François Thiry en Pieter Uyttenhove, Bruxelles-capitale de l'Europe, in Architecture d'aujourd'hui, nr. 347, juli 2003, pp. 20/24.*

ARCHITECTURA
- *Oana Bogdan, Danone blue – extension to Danone Factory, Rotselaar, Belgium (architecten: Van Broeck & Meuwissen), in Architectura, nr. 11, juni/juli 2002, pp. 20/25.*
- *Oana Bogdan, Interviu cu Hans Verplancke & Hans Croon, in Architectura, nr. 13, oktober/november 2002, pp. 22/31.*

A & D
- *Private house in Genappe (architecten: ABR), in A & D architecture and design, vol. 11, nr. 21, 2003, pp. 26/29.*
- *Industrial monument in Fontaine-L'eveque (architecten: Vincent Picart), in A & D architecture and design, vol. 11, nr. 20, 2003, pp. 20/23.*

A+U
- *Paul Wolff, The house (met o.a. Jo Coenen – villa in Lanaken), in A+U, nr. 387, december 2002, pp. 43/123.*
- *Driving through Belgium I / Houses, nr. 392, mei 2003 (met werk van o.a. Nollet & Huyghe, Dessauvage-Mohammadi Architecten, Wim Cuyvers, Stéphane Beel, Maarten Van Severen, Coussee & Goris, IDDV, Marie-José Van Hee, Koen Dekeyser, Macken & Macken, Jo Crepain, Robbrecht & Daem)*
- *Driving through Belgium II / Objects in the urban landscape, nr. 293; juni 2003 (met werk van o.a. Gino Debruyne, Wim Goes, Jo Taillieu, Pierre Hebbelinck, B-architecten, Xaveer de Geyter Architecten, Meta Architectuurbureau, Hera Van Sande & Laurent Liefooge, Office Kersten Geers David Van Severen)*

BUILDING
- *Thomas Lane, How's this for a high court? (architecten: Richard Rogers Partnership), in Building, vol. 268, nr. 8304 (41), oktober 2003, pp. 63/66.*

CASABELLA
- *Marc Dubois, Una piccola fantasia / A small fantasy: Toyo Ito pavillion Brugge 2002, in Casabella, nr. 705, november 2002, pp. 46/53.*
- *Marc Dubois, La semplice retorica della domesticità: Casa Van Middelem-Dupont (architect: Alvaro Siza), in Casabella, nr. 706 & 707, december / januari 2002-2003, pp. 36/48.*
- *Jean-Marie Martin, Biblioteca universitaria, Loviano, Belgio 2002 (architect: Rafael Moneo), in Casabella, nr. 708, februari 2003, pp. 72/85.*

DB DEUTSCHE BAUZEITUNG
- *Marc Dubois, Kontinuität statt Kontrast: Siza in Flandern, nr. 1, 2003, pp. 27/31.*

ICON
- *Kieran Long, Moneo in Belgium, in Icon, nr. 001, april 2003, pp. 72/78.*

MONITEUR D'ARCHITECTURE AMC
- *J-M Landecy, Pavillon de l'aluminium a Bruges (architecten: Toyo Ito Architect & Associates), in Moniteur d'architecture AMC, nr. 124, april 2002, p. 36.*
- *Dominique Pieters, Amenagement d'une halle médiévale, Gand (architecten: Coussee & Goris), in Moniteur d'architecture AMC, nr. 131, februari 2003, pp. 52/55.*
- *Dominique Boudet, Salle de concert, Bruges, Belgique (architecten: Robbrecht & Daem), in Moniteur d'architecture AMC, nr. 134, mei 2003, pp. 62/67.*

OASE
- *Michael Ryckewaert, De Minimale rationaliteit van woonpatronen in Nevelstad Vlaanderen, in Oase nr. 60, zomer 2002, pp. 49/61.*
- *Paul Vermeulen, Platteland in de Nevelstad, in Oase nr. 60, zomer 2002, pp. 103/109.*

ONS ERFDEEL
- *Hans Ibelings, Groeiend zelfbewustzijn in de Vlaamse architectuur, in Ons Erfdeel nr. 5, november 2002, pp. 766/768.*

RIBA JOURNAL
- *Who are Robbrecht & Daem?, in the RIBA journal, vol. 110, nr. 5, mei 2003, p. 9.*

EXHIBITIONS

Exhibitions in Belgium

06/12/2001 – 16/01/2002
Stichting Stad & Architectuur, Leuven
MIES VAN DER ROHE AWARD 2001

05/01/2002 – 03/03/2002
IHAM-galerij, Antwerpen
ARCHITECTUURFOTOGRAFIE VAN PHILIPPE VAN GELOOVEN

18/01/2002 – 14/04/2002
CIVA, Brussel
ROBERT SCHUITEN, LE FEU SACRE

07/02/2002 – 24/03/2002
deSingel Internationaal Kunstcentrum, Antwerpen
HONDERD HUIZEN VOOR HONDERD EUROPESE ARCHITECTEN

09/02/2002 – 20/05/2002
Orion Art Gallery, Oostende
PETIT CABINET D'UN AMATEUR DE RUINES (EXHIBITION OF A LOVER OF RUINS)
met foto's van Paul Casaer, Michel Couturier, Gilbert Fastenaekens, Luc Deleu, Felten-Massinger, Jan Kempenaers, Marie-Jo Lafontaine, Jacques Lennep, Hans Op De Beeck, Ria Pacquée, Boy Stappaerts, Jaymes Van Luppem, Sophie Whetnall
Curator: Johan Pas

19/02/2002 – 10/03/2002
CIVA, Brussel
ALVAR AALTO, LIRE L'ARCHITECTURE

20/02/2002 – 19/04/2002
Encore Bruxelles, Brussel
STABULATIONS LIBRES PATRICK BOUCHAIN, LUCIEN KROLL, KINYA MARUYAMA
Interventies / conversaties / projecties / lezingen / demonstraties / constructies / occupaties / enz.

20/02/2002 – 17/11/2002
Station, Brugge
Coproductie: Brugge 2002 – A Prior – Office for artistic production en Nederlands Foto Instituut
LOST LOCATIONS

29/03/2002 – 30/03/2002
Opendeur-weekend van Belgische onafhankelijke architecten
MIJN HUIS, MIJN ARCHITECT

01/05/2002 – 09/06/2002
deSingel Internationaal Kunstcentrum, Antwerpen
XAVEER DE GEYTER ARCHITECTEN AFTER SPRAWL ONDERZOEK NAAR DE HEDENDAAGSE STAD

07/05/2002 – 11/08/2002
CIVA, Brussel
DE GOEDE EN DE SLECHTE SMAAK BELGISCHE INTERIEURS VAN ART NOUVEAU TOT DE HEDENDAAGSE LOFT

01/09/2002 – 30/11/2002
CIVA, Brussel
NIEMEYER

07/09/2002 – 15/09/2002
erfgoedjongeren, Brugge
FRONTSID[T]E – BACK[-]SIDE

08/09/2002
Vliegtuighallen, Grimbergen
ALFRED HARDY 1900-1965 EENDAAGSE OVERZICHTSTENTOONSTELLING

08/09/2002 – 13/10/2002
Villa Eksternest, Rumbeke-Roeselare
HUIB HOSTE IN ZUID-WEST-VLAANDEREN

14/09/2002 – 08/12/2002
Koninklijk Museum voor Schone Kunsten, Antwerpen
HANS VREDEMAN DE VRIES 1526-1609 – TUSSEN STADSPALEIZEN EN LUCHTKASTELEN

20/09/2002 – 03/11/2002
deSingel Internationaal Kunstcentrum, Antwerpen
ARCHILAB 2002

21/09/2002 – 02/11/2002
Designcenter / De Winkelhaak, Antwerpen
'I LOVE ONTWERPEN'
Concept en vormgeving: uapS samen met Jean-Marc Ballée

01/10/2002 – 31/10/2002
Openbare Bibliotheek Tweebronnen, Leuven
VICTOR BROOS – DE KRACHT VAN HET ALLEDAAGSE

13/10/2002
Vlaams Architectuurinstituut, Brussel – Antwerpen – Gent – Brugge – Hasselt – Kortrijk – Eeklo – Vlaams-Brabant – Zuid-Oost-Vlaanderen
DAG VAN DE ARCHITECTUUR

19/10/2002-30/06/2003
Etablissement d'en face Projects, Brussel
LEGAL SPACE / PUBLIC SPACE

25/10/2002 – 23/11/2002
CIVA, Brussel
'LICHT' IN BRUSSEL

05/11/2002 – 29/11/2002
Hogeschool W&K, Departement Architectuur Sint-Lucas, Gent
NEW TRENDS OF RECENT ARCHITECTURE IN EUROPE AND JAPAN

06/11/2002 – 02/12/2002
De Warande, Turnhout
MARIE SNAUWAERT: RUIMTES
Fotografietentoonstelling over huizen die door mensen verlaten zijn

09/11/2002 – 23/02/2003
Design Museum Gent
VAN BAKELIET TOT COMPOSIET – DESIGN MET NIEUWE MATERIALEN

19/11/2002 – 13/04/2003
Musée des Archives d'Architecture Moderne, Brussel
ANTOINE COURTENS – ART DECO ONTWERPER

21/11/2002 – 12/01/2003
deSingel Internationaal Kunstcentrum, Antwerpen
PORTRET VAN VLAAMSE BIOTOPEN – DE FOTOGRAFIE-OPDRACHT VAN DE VLAAMSE BOUWMEESTER

22/11/2002 – 26/01/2003
Center for Contemporary Non-Objective Art (CCNOA), Brussel
TOPOS – ATOPOS – ANATOPOS
Christian Kieckens, Michel Desvigne (F), Olafur Eliasson (DK / D), Peter Downsborough (USA / B) Manon De Boer (NL / B), Har Hollands (NL) en Jürg Conzett (CH)

20/12/2002 – 16/03/2003
CIVA, Brussel
BRUXELLES, L'EMERGENCE DE LA VILLE CONTEMPORAINE - BRUSSEL, HEDENDAAGSE STAD RIJST UIT DE GROND

17/01/2003 – 13/04/2003
Centrum Hallepoort, Brussel
FOTO'S OVER HET LEVEN IN DE STAD

28/01/2003 – 22/02/2003
Hogeschool W&K – Departement Architectuur Sint-Lucas, Gent
HORROR VACUI – FOTOGRAFIE VAN DE LEGE STAD

20/02/2003 – 02/03/2003
Stad Antwerpen
VILLAGES AND METROPOLIS - PROJECTEN VOOR SPOOR-NOORD, ANTWERPEN

21/02/2003 – 06/04/2003
deSingel Internationaal Kunstcentrum, Antwerpen
ANNE LACATON & JEAN-PHILIPPE VASSAL

24/02/2003 – 14/03/2003
Hogeschool W&K – Departement Architectuur Sint-Lucas, Gent
'ARCHITEKTURPREIS BETON 01' – BETONARCHITECTUUR IN ZWITSERLAND

05/03/2003 – 30/03/2003
CC De Westrand, Dilbeek
PROVINCIALE PRIJS VOOR ARCHITECTUUR VLAAMS BRABANT

10/03/2003-05/04/2003
Hogeschool W&K – Departement Architectuur Sint-Lucas, Gent
ARCHITECTUURPRIJS VAN DE VEN 1928-1968

20/03/2003 – 04/05/2003
CIVA, Brussel
LES ILES FLOTTANTES

20/03/2003 – 01/06/2003
Bozar, Brussel
SOCIALE HUISVESTING NAAR HET MUSEUM?

28/03/2003 – 08/06/2003
Bozar, Brussel
REVOLUTION / RESTORATION – PART 1 PARANOÏD CRITICAL TRANSFORMATION METHOD

29/03/2003 – 30/03/2003
Opendeur-weekend van Belgische onafhankelijke architecten
MIJN HUIS, MIJN ARCHITECT

29/03/2003 – 09/06/2003
Design Museum Gent
CLAIRE BATAILLE & PAUL IBENS – PROJECTEN EN OBJECTEN 1968-2002

01/04/2003 – 27/04/2003
CIVA, Brussel
ALFRED HARDY 1900-1965 - NA-OORLOGSE PADDESTOELCONSTRUCTIES

01/04/2003 – 27/04/2003
CIVA, Brussel
DE TUINEN VAN RENÉ PECHÈRE

01/05/2003 – 15/06/2003
deSingel Internationaal Kunstcentrum,Antwerpen
KCAP / ASTOC / KEES CHRISTIAANSE (NL) – THE CITY AS LOFT

03/05/2003 – 07/06/2003
Stedelijk Museum Aalst
ACHIEL HUTSEBAUT – ARCHITECTUUR EN RECENT PLASTISCH WERK

06/05/2003 – 19/05/2003
Hogeschool W&K, Departement Architectuur Sint-Lucas, Gent
PUBLIEKE RUIMTE, EEN ANDERE AANPAK

15/05/2003 – 28/06/2003
Galerij Archetype Art+Communication, Brussel
M.D. THE METROPOLITAN DIAMOND OF EUROPE (DESIGNED BY BUNKERHOTEL)

18/05/2003 – 26/05/2003
Basisschool Van Peenestraat, Antwerpen, Art Basics for Children en SISA
MIJN SCHOOL IS EEN BLOKKENDOOS

27/05/2003 – 12/10/2003
Museum voor Architectuur – De Loge, Brussel
DE 3DE DIMENSIE – ARCHITECTUURMAQUETTES

07/06/2003 – 14/09/2003
Openluchtmuseum voor beeldhouwkunst Middelheim, Antwerpen
LUC DELEU

27/06/2003 – 29/06/2003
Hogeschool W&K, Departement Architectuur Sint-Lucas, Brussel
ARCHITECTURE IS ART, OR IT IS NOT ARCHITECTURE – EINDEJAARSTENTOONSTELLING STUDENTEN

12/09/2003 – 30/11/2003
deSingel Internationaal Kunstcentrum, Antwerpen
URBAN DRAMAS

14/09/2003 – 05/10/2003
Vlaams Architectuurinstituut, Antwerpen
DESINGEL (1958-2006): HET STENEN TESTAMENT VAN LÉON STYNEN

01/10/2003 – 17/10/2003
Stichting Stad en Architectuur, Leuven
TENTOONSTELLING ONTWERPWEDSTRIJD VOOR HET VAC IN LEUVEN

17/10/2003 – 31/01/2004
Katholieke Universiteit Leuven
INGENIEURS EN ARCHITECTEN OP DE DREMPEL VAN EEN NIEUWE TIJD (1750-1830)

31/10/2003 – 09/11/2003
CIVA, Brussel
AWARDS VAN DE BELGISCHE ARCHITECTUUR & ENERGIE-AWARDS 2003

31/10/2003 – 07/12/2003
Design Museum Gent
RETROSPECTIEVE GASTON EYSSELINCK

04/11/2003 – 21/04/2003
CIVA, Brussel
HENRY LACOSTE, ARCHITECT 1885-1986 – VAN KLASSIEKE CULTUUR NAAR AFRIKAANSE VERBEELDING

28/11/2003 – 07/01/2004
Stichting Stad & Architectuur, Leuven
MIES VAN DER ROHE AWARD 2003

30/11/2003 – 22/12/2003
Aside Architecture, Berlijn, Recyclart, Brussel
SPACES OF UNCERTAINTY

Exhibitions abroad

14/06/2002 - 01/09/2002
Norsk Arkitekturmuseum, Oslo
100 HOUSES FOR 100 EUROPEAN ARCHITECTS OF THE XXTH CENTURY
met werk van Eugeen Liebaut, Gaston Eysselinck, Marie-José Van Hee, Bob Van Reeth, Charles Vandenhove

08/09/2002-03/11/2002
Belgisch paviljoen Biënnale van Venetië – 8ste internationale architectuurtentoonstelling
LES ILES FLOTTANTES

28/09/2002 - 08/11/2002
La Galerie Blanche, Unité Le Corbusier, Briey-en-Forêt (F)
CONSTRUIT / CONSTRUIRE - CHRISTIAN KIECKENS / ARCHITECTE

06/02/2003 – 23/03/2003
Arc-en-Rêve, Bordeaux
NEW TRENDS OF ARCHITECTURE IN EUROPE AND JAPAN
met o.m. werk van EVR-architecten (Nationaal secretariaat en distributiecentrum voor Oxfam-wereldwinkels, Gent)

01/06/2003 – 30/06/2003
Hillside Terrace, Tokyo
NEW TRENDS OF ARCHITECTURE IN EUROPE AND JAPAN
met o.m. werk van EVR-architecten (Nationaal secretariaat en distributiecentrum voor Oxfam-wereldwinkels, Gent)

07/05/2003 – 07/07/2003
Nederlands Architectuurinstituut, Rotterdam
EERSTE ARCHITECTUURBIËNNALE ROTTERDAM – 'CULTURES OF AUTOMOBILITY: HOW MOBILITY SHAPES AND RESHAPES THE CITY AND ITS LANDSCAPE, NOW AND IN THE FUTURE'
Met o.a. Bunkerhotel vzw.

Awards for built projects 2002-2003

BELGIAN BUILDING AWARDS 2002

Categorie 1 - Eengezinswoningen nieuwbouw
Laureaat
- *Natalie Ries – Elena-gebouw, Brussel*

Andere genomineerden
- *Vincent Van Duysen – vrijstaande woning, Waasmunster*
- *RAUW Architecten – woning Casa H, Grimbergen*
- *Jo Crépain – woning Feyen, Sint-Pieters-Leeuw*

Categorie 2 - Eengezinswoningen renovatie
Genomineerden
- *Joël Claisse Architectures – renovatie van een woning, Brussel*
- *Egide Meertens – verbouwing van een zolder tot een studio, Riemst*
- *VOLT-architecten – creatie van een loft, Ronse*

Categorie 3 - Groepswoningbouw nieuwbouw en renovatie
Laureaat
- *Architectenbureau WIT– sociale woningen, Leuven*

Andere genomineerden
- *Frank Van Hulle en Ronny De Meyer – woningen en kantoren, Antwerpen*

Categorie 4 – Bedrijfsgebouw van het jaar
Laureaat
- *Nollet & Huyghe Architecten – Christelijke Mutualiteiten, Maldegem*

Andere genomineerden
- *Stéphane Beel Architecten – revalidatie centrum Klimop, Eeklo*
- *Jo Crépain – Poincaré-gebouw, Brussel*

Categorie 5 – Renovatie van een waardevol oud gebouw
Laureaat
- *Coussée & Goris Architecten – Hogeschool voor Wetenschap en Kunst, Brussel*

Andere genomineerden
- *Jo Crépain – Kantoor Duval Guillaume, Brussel*
- *Verdickt & Verdickt Architecten – Renovatie van een pakhuis, Antwerpen*
- *Piet en Philippe Viérin Architecten – restaurant De Karmeliet, Brugge*

BELGIAN BUILDING AWARDS 2003

Categorie 1 - Eengezinswoningen nieuwbouw
Laureaat
- *Nollet & Huyghe Architecten – rijwoning, Brugge.*

Andere genomineerden
- *VOLT-architecten – woning in agrarisch gebied, Vrasene*
- *Beulens Vanderlinden architecten – woning, Overijse*
- *Bertrand Counson – geprefabriceerde houtskeletwoning, Tailles*

Categorie 2 - Eengezinswoningen renovatie
Laureaat
- *Atelier d' Architecture Pierre Hebbelinck – verbouwing van woning, Ukkel*

Andere genomineerden
- *Popoff & Bouquelle Architecten – inrichting van een loft, Brussel*
- *Patrick David – uitbreiding woning, Vielsalm*

Categorie 3 - Groepswoningbouw nieuwbouw en renovatie
Laureaat
- *Haverhals-Heylen Architecten – stedelijk woonproject 'Pandreitje', Brugge*

Andere genomineerden
- *B-architecten – reconversie van oud diamant-bedrijf tot woonwerkcomplex, Antwerpen*
- *Alexander Dierendonck – appartementsgebouw 'Residentie Leopold', Middelkerke*
- *Poponcini & Lootens – woonproject Tolstraat, Antwerpen*
- *SCA Architecten Associatie – groepswoning met handelsgelijkvloers, Schaarbeek*

Categorie 4 - Niet-residentiële gebouwen nieuwbouw
Laureaat
- *Samyn & Partners – restaurantbrug Orival, Nijvel*

Andere genomineerden
- *Coussée & Goris Architecten – schrijnwerkersloods, Moen*
- *Bureau d'études Dethier & associés – transformatoren en elektrisch station, Luik*
- *Manders & Pitillion Architecten – designcenter de Winkelhaak te Antwerpen*
- *Architecten Bauman en Beguin – park Saint-Léonard, Luik*

Categorie 5 - Niet-residentiële gebouwen renovatie
Laureaat
- *B-architecten – BSBbis, Brussel*

Andere genomineerden
- *DMVA-architecten – omvormen van drukkerij tot 3 tijdelijke oefenzalen, Mechelen*
- *Atelier d' Architecture Pierre Hebbelinck – Museum van Hedendaagse Kunst, Grand Hornu*
- *Jan Veelaert – Verbouwing van loods tot garage-showrooms-kantoren, Antwerpen*
- *Lhoas & Lhoas – Verbouwing van een Brunfaut-gebouw, Brussel*

PRIJS VAN DE VLAAMSE GEMEENSCHAP VOOR ARCHITECTUUR 2003

Laureaat
- *Filip De Pau – stadsarchitect van de gemeente Eeklo*

Genomineerden
- *Xaveer De Geyter*
- *Marc Dubois*
- *Dirk Jaspaert*

ENERGIEAWARDS 2003

- *Damien Carnoy – Woning Simon-Stevanato, Waver*
- *Jo Crepain – kantoorgebouw voor de firma Renson, Waregem*

PROVINCIALE PRIJS VOOR ARCHITECTUUR 2002 OOST-VLAANDEREN

Laureaat
- *Wim Goes – Verbouwing, marktonderzoekbureau & Compagnie, Gent*

Vermeldingen
- *VOLT Architecten – Uitbreiding Gemeenteschool, Brakel*
- *Nollet & Huyghe Architecten – CM-kantoor, Maldegem*

PROVINCIALE PRIJS VOOR ARCHITECTUUR 2003 OOST-VLAANDEREN

Laureaat
- *Marie-José Van Hee – rijwoning, Wetteren*

Eervolle vermeldingen
- *Karel Vandenhende – sociale woningen, Gent*
- *Francisca Hautekeete – Rijwoning met winkelruimte, Deinze*

TWEEJAARLIJKE PRIJS VOOR ARCHITECTUUR VAN DE PROVINCIE WEST-VLAANDEREN VAN ANNO '02

Laureaat
- *Coussée & Goris Architecten – Fractal Building systems, Roeselare*
- *Christian Kieckens – Verbindingshal, Rambla XPO-hallen, Kortrijk*

VIERJAARLIJKSE PRIJS VOOR ARCHITECTUUR VAN DE PROVINCIE WEST-VLAANDEREN 2003

Laureaten
- *Nollet & Huyghe Architecten – rijwoning, Brugge*
- *Peter De Bruycker en Inge De Brock – Stichting Peire, Knokke*

premiewinnaars
- *Corbeel + Catteeuw + Platteau Architecten – Belgosuc, Beernem*
- *Jo Crépain – Renson, Waregem*
- *Vincent Van Duysen – Concordia Textiles, Waregem*

PROVINCIALE PRIJS VOOR ARCHITECTUUR VLAAMS-BRABANT 2002 – WONINGBOUW

Laureaat
- *51N4E Space Producers – masterplan Vierkantshoeve, Outgaarden*

Genomineerden
- *Hans Verplancke – verbouwing Verplancke-Croon*
- *Robbrecht & Daem – annex woning Galle*
- *Architectenbureau Jan Maenhout – sociale woningen Gladiolenlaan*
- *Jo Crepain – woning Feyen-Beirens / appartementen Norwest Properties*
- *Peter Kint architect – woning Jespers Vandensande*
- *Piet & Philippe Viérin Architecten – woning Van Assche*
- *Huiswerk architecten – woning Loncke-Gheeraert*
- *Architectuurstudio Luc Binst – woning De Bauw-Binst*
- *Architecten BOB361 – additie Cluytens-Putseys*
- *Els Claessens – Van der Velden-Claessens*
- *Mys & Bomans Architectuurkantoor – woning Lumbeeck-Bornauw*
- *Buelens Vanderlinden Architecten – woning Beulens-Vanderlinden*

PROVINCIALE PRIJS BEELDENDE KUNST/ARCHITECTUUR – PROVINCIE ANTWERPEN 2002

Niet uitgereikt wegens onvoldoende inzendingen

VLAAMSE RUIMTELIJKE PLANNINGSPRIJS 2002

Laureaat:
Ruimtelijk Structuurplan Gent
Genomineerd:
- *Structuurplanning (bijna 25 jaar) gemeente Bornem*

PRIJS BOUWHEER 2003

Laureaat Categorie nieuwbouw
- *Designcentrum De Winkelhaak in Antwerpen*

Laureaat Categorie herbestemming
- *de ModeNatie, Antwerpen*

Laureaat Categorie publieke ruimte
- *heraanleg van de Gras- en Korenlei in Gent*

Laureaat Categorie kunst
- *een kunstwerk van Jef Geys in het VAC Hasselt*

Laureaat Categorie landschap
- *er werd geen enkel dossier ingestuurd, bijgevolg zijn er geen nominaties.*

Laureaat Categorie infrastructuur
- *het windenergieproject in Eeklo*

Laureaat Categorie geïntegreerde opdracht
- *de Leuvense stationsomgeving*

VLAAMSE MONUMENTENPRIJS 2002

Laureaat
- *Oudenaarde - Bos 't Ename*

PRIJS BOUWINNOVATIE 2002

Categorie 'Landschapsgeïntegreerd project'
- *Inez Hermans en Tom Verheyen*

Categorie 'Stadsproject'
- *Gregory Nijs*

Categorie 'Meest beloftevolle architect'
- *Vincent Cops*

STAALBOUWWEDSTRIJD 2002

Laureaten
Categorie A - Niet-residentiële gebouwen
- *Samyn & Partners – restaurantbrug Orival, Nijvel*

Categorie B - Residentiële gebouwen
- *Bureau d'études Dethier & associés – Denis-Ortmans huis, Verviers*

Categorie C – Karakteristieke bouwdelen in staal
- *Paulissen, De Winter, Van Hunsel – Luifels Tachkemoni school, Antwerpen*

Categorie D – Burgerlijke bouwkunde en kunstwerken
- *Studio Prof. Thomas Spiegelhalter (USA) – Voetgangersbrug Maas-Scheldekanaal, Lommel*

Competitions in Belgium 2002-2003

PRIJSVRAAG CULTUREEL CENTRUM AVELGEM
- Alexander Dierendonck Architectenburo en (S)pace interieur Architectuur
- Geert De Neuter, Inez Hermans en Tom Verheyen
- Collectiv 4

PRIJSVRAAG VOOR ONTWERPEN RAMEN
Eerste laureaat
- Nollet & Huyghe Architecten

Tweede laureaat
- Stéphane Beel Architecten

Derde laureaat (ex aequo)
- Architectenbureau Dirk Coopman
- GWM Architecten

INTERNATIONALE ONTWERP WEDSTRIJD EMILE BRAUNPLEIN
Laureaat
- Paul Robbrecht, Hilde Daem & Marie-José Van Hee, Gent

Andere genomineerden
- TV Fris in het Landschap, Gent & Cnockaert, Kortrijk
- Edwin Santhagens, Den Haag (NL)
- TV Technum nv – J. Farrando – R. Berteloot, Borgerhout
- TV West 8 (NL) – Bontinck – Gedas, Antwerpen

Eervolle vermelding
- Wim Cuyvers, Gent

PRIJS 'EEN BANK IN DE STAD'
Categorie studenten
- Joni Nieuwenhuisen, VUBrussel
- Joke Laukens, Henry vande Velde Instituut, Antwerpen
- Virginie Pottiez, Hoger Instituut voor Architectuur, Bergen

Catgorie professionals
- Werner Vandermeersch, Antwerpen

PRIJS HERINRICHTING FLAGEYPLEIN VAN PLATFORM FLAGEY
- eerste prijs – Michel Billotte, Raphaël Billotte, Michel Lefèvre en Christophe Pham
- tweede prijs – Thierry Decuypere, Shin Hagiwara, Jorn Aram Bihain, Fabrizio Terranova en Graziella Vella
- Derde prijs – Raphaël Cornelis, Harold Fallon en Benoît Vandenbulcke

STUDENTENSTAALPRIJS 2001-2002
Laureaten
- Johannes Robbrecht, Wouter Willems (UGent)
- Peter Geraerts (Hogeschool W&K, Sint-Lucas, Brussel)
- Rudy Martin, Sven Van Achter (Hogeschool Sint-Lukas, Brussel)
- Michael Moradiellos del Molino (IESA Site Victor Horta, Brussel)
- Fanny Roland, Cédric Poncelet (ISA Saint-Luc de Wallonie)
- Stijn Van Schuerbeek (VUB)
- Roselyne Barez, Sonia Bessalah, Renaud Eloy, Chaimaâ Seddiki (ISA de Mons)
- Tanguy Leclercq (ULB)
- Janis Filieux (Hogeschool W&K, Sint-Lucas, Gent)
- Caroline Colignon, Nicolas Ecrepont, Sébastien Mainil (Faculté Polytechnique de Mons)
- Koen Van Looveren (Hogeschool W&K, Instituut De Nayer, Sint-Katelijne Waver)
- Xavier Mottart (ECAM, Bussel)
- Nicolas Wouters (ISA Saint-Luc de Bruxelles)

WEDSTRIJD 'LANDSCHAPSKUNST IN DE WESTHOEK' 2002
- Laureaat Stijn Claikens

ADMINISTRATIEF CENTRUM ZEDELGEM 2002
Eerste prijs
- Architectuur.be – Lannoo – Snoeck & partners, Kortrijk

Tweede prijs
- Lode Havermans, Breda

Derde prijs
- Roland Piffet, Brussel

IDEEËNWEDSTRIJD URSULINENSQUARE (RECYCLART, BRUSSEL)
Laureaten
- BFO 001 – Bjorn Gielen, Floris Steyaert

Genomineerden
- ABC 123 – André Sylvain, Cédric Callewaert, Antoine Galand, Jean-Jacques Jungers
- XXX 666 – Anthony Graci, Geoffrey Graci, Francois Hens, Christophe Pham, Baptiste Vuerich

IDEEËNWEDSTRIJD GOUDEN BEVERS 02/03: WATER IN DE STAD
Eerste laureaat
- Sébastien Sainsard (ISA – La Cambre)

Tweede laureaat
- Johan De Troeyer, Stefan Morael (Erasmushogeschool Brussel – Horteco)

Derde laureaat
- Tompy Hoedelmans, Niels Hofstra, Frank Rietveld, Erik Van der Velden (Erasmushogeschool Brussel – Horteco)

Awards 2002-2003

VLAAMSE VERENIGING VOOR RUIMTE EN PLANNING – EINDWERKPRIJS 2002
Laureaten
- Els De Vos (afgestudeerd aan de GGS-opleiding KULeuven) – Gender & Planning; ruimtelijke patronen voor diversiteit in parken
- Elisabeth Wouters (afgestudeerd aan CVO, afdeling Ruimtelijke Planning en Stedenbouw, Antwerpen) – Plaats van bestemming? Bestemmingen in relatie tot sectorale voorschriften en gebiedsaanduidingen
- Julie Loeckx (afgestudeerd aan CVO, Hogere Leergangen Sint-Lukas, Brussel) – Reconversie op de rechter Scheldeboord

PRIJS BELGISCHE STICHTING ROEPING 2003
- Bertrand Noël voor de studie 'Stedenbouwkundig streven tot opwaardering van postindustriële gebouwen en sites'

VLAAMSE VERENIGING VOOR RUIMTE EN PLANNING – EINDWERKPRIJS 2003
Laureaten
- Peter Vanden Abeele (afgestudeerd aan de GAS-opleiding, UGent) – De inzet van culturele dynamiek binnen stedelijke ontwikkelingen
- David Verhoestraete (afgestudeerd aan de GAS-opleiding, UGent) – Ruimtelijke potenties van de Westerschelde-delta, een verkennend onderzoek

THEMAPRIJS PLANDAG 2003
Laureaten
- Sofie Clusters, Hans Leinfelder en Christophe Vandevoort – Afbakening van natuur en landbouw in Vlaanderen: een nauwe trechter en een lelijke mozaïek

PRIJS VOOR DE JONGE PLANOLOOG 2003
Laueaat
- Evert Meijers – Randstad en Vlaamse Ruit: meer dan de som der delen

THUIS IN DE STAD-PRIJS 2002
Laureaat categorie 1: infrastructurele projecten
- Stad Antwerpen, herwaardering omgeving De Coninckplein

Laureaat categorie 2: niet-infrastructurele projecten
- Limite Limite, Brussel

THUIS IN DE STAD-PRIJS 2003
Laureaat categorie 1
- Mechelen – Lamot, Dijlepad en Dijlebrug

Laureaat categorie 2
- Antwerpen – De heropening van de Roma

Competitions abroad 2002-2003

EUROPAN 7 – NIEUW LEVEN IN DE SUBURB
Eerste prijs Hengelo (Nederland): O^2
- Kurt Van Belle (B)
- Patricia Medina (S)

EUROREGIONALE PRIJS VOOR ARCHITECTUUR
Laureaten
- Gerard Extra (N)
- Petra Riegler (D)
- Liesbeth vander Waeren (B)

MIES VAN DE ROHE AWARD 2003 – EUROPEAN UNION PRIZE FOR CONTEMPORARY ARCHITECTURE
Laureaat
- Zaha Hadid – Terminus Noord-Hoenheim in Straatsburg, Frankrijk

Onder de andere geselecteerden
- Xaveer de Geyter – woongebouwen in het Chassé Park, Breda
- Anne Lacaton & Jean Philippe Vassal – Palais de Tokyo, Parijs
- MVRDV – Hagen Eiland, Den Haag

DERDE LENSVELT DE ARCHITECT INTERIEURPRIJS 2003
Laureaat
- Ontwerpbureau Jurgenbey (N) – 'ontvangstkamer' in kantoor Interpolis, Tilburg

Andere genomineerden
- Atelier d'Architecture Pierre Hebbelink (B) – woning Frankfort, Brussel
- DmvA Architecten (B) – tijdelijke oefenlokalen Nova, Mechelen
- Ontwerpgroep Trude Hooykaas en Meyer en Van Schooten (N) – ING house, Amsterdam
- Strijkers interieurarchitectuur (N) – Lute restaurant, Oudekerk a/d Amstel

Lectures in Belgium 2002-2003

2002

AMARANT, GENT
Lezingenreeks over de tuinarchitectuur in de 20ste eeuw in België en daarbuiten 'Een tuin is meer dan er staat' of Paradise transformed
Case-studies Tuinarchitectuur Internationaal
- *Marc Pinte – Verenigde Staten*
- *Beatrice Krehl – Duitsland*
- *Chris Vermander – Denemarken*
- *Marc Pinte – Frankrijk*
- *Paul Achterberg - Nederland*

Kennismaking met Belgische tuinarchitecten
- *Jacques Wirtz*
- *Denis Dujardin*
- *Erik Dhont*
- *Stefaan Thiers*
- *Paul Deroose*

ARCHIPEL
Brugge 2002 - Lezingenreeks 'Bouwmeester... kunstenaars... visionairs'
- *Toyo Ito (J)*
- *West 8 (N)*
- *Jürg Conzett (CH)*
- *Souto de Moura (P)*
- *Gigon & Guyer (CH)*

CIVA, BRUSSEL
- *Vilhelm Helander – From landscapes to interiors. Periods of Alvar Aalto's architectural work*

DESINGEL INTERNATIONAAL KUNSTCENTRUM, ANTWERPEN
- *Irénée Scalbert – Jonge Architecten in Vlaanderen*
- *Xaveer De Geyter – After Sprawl*

FEDERALE DIENSTEN VOOR WETENSCHAPPELIJKE, TECHNISCHE EN CULTURELE AANGELEGENHEDEN (DWTC), BRUSSEL
Studiedag 'Problematiek van de steden in België'
- *Ruimtelijke economie van steden: analyse van de lokalisatie van economische activiteiten en gezinnen in een stedelijke regio in België*
- *Conflictbeheersing bij stadsvernieuwing: een koppeling tussen onderzoek en stadsbeheer*

KATHOLIEKE HOGESCHOOL MECHELEN – DEPARTEMENT ARCHITECTUUR [W]INTERIEURAVONDEN
- *Architectenbureau Böhtlingk (NL)*

ORPHEUSINSTITUUT, GENT
- *Stefan Drees – Muziek en architectuur*

STICHTING STAD & ARCHITECTUUR, LEUVEN
Debat
- *Marc Martens – Het RUP is een intermediair tussen visie en realisatie*
- *Marc Martens en Jan Schreurs – Omgaan met dichtheid is veel meer dan cijferwerk*

Lezingen
- *Willem-Jan Neutelings*
- *William Mann*
- *Stefan Devoldere – Onopvallend efficiënt – over alledaagse en degelijke architectuur*

Lezingenreeks 'Auditorium'
- *Caruso St John architects (UK) – knitting, weaving, wrapping, pressing*
- *SEARCH (NL) – 'urban relax'*
- *Foreign Office Architects (UK) – the Yokohama project*
- *Lacaton & Vassal (F) – travaux*

VAKGROEP ARCHITECTUUR & STEDENBOUW, UNIVERSITEIT GENT
- *Andrew Leach – Electricity, Writing, Architecture; Ponge on Electricity*
- *Randy Swanson – Errors in Inquiry and Interpretation*
- *Guy Châtel – Het project van een onaangepaste stad – Luc Deleu & TOP-office 1994-2002*
- ***Lezingenreeks 'De refter – La Belgique c'est fantastique_'***
  - *Steven Jacobs*
  - *Images/images en tekst/tekst – tijdschriften van beeld- en tekstmachien ubicumque...*
  - *Richard Venlet*
  - *Plain*
  - *Geert Goiris*
  - *Michael Borremans*
  - *Michael Vandenabeele en Arnoud Hendrickx*
  - *Paul Robbrecht – de AUE-paviljoenen op Documenta IX (1992)*

VLAAMS ARCHITECTUURINSTITUUT (VAI), ANTWERPEN I.S.M. KONINKLIJK MUSEUM VOOR SCHONE KUNSTEN, ANTWERPEN (KMSKA)
Hans Vredeman de Vries in hedendaags perspectief – actuele inzichten en betekenis voor de hedendaagse architectuur
- *S. Umberto Barbieri – De architectonische erfenis van Hans Vredeman de Vries en zijn actualiteit*
- *Lionel Devlieger – Vredeman de Vries vitruviaans? De ambigue overname van de klassieke orden in de 16de eeuwse Midden-Europese kunst*
- *Christoph Grafe – Internationalisering en de formulering van een regionaal architectonisch idioom*
- *Lara Schrijver – Nieuwe vormen van representatie en hun invloed op de productie en waarneming van de architectonische ruimte*
- *Mikel Van Gelderen – Formele experimenten met de klassieke ontwerpmiddelen van de Europese architectonische traditie: een case study*
- *Ruth Eaton – Ideale stad en utopie, van de Renaissance tot de 21ste eeuw*
- *Christopher Heuer – Bouwen, wonen, denken? Over Hans Vredeman de Vries en het Moderne*
- *Maarten Delbeke – De universele Architect*

VLAAMSE VERENIGING VOOR RUIMTE EN PLANNING, BRUSSEL
- *Gespreksavond 'Nieuwe omzendbrief woonuitbreidingsgebieden'*
- *Seminarie 01 – TW Open ruimte en landschap: Dorpskernvernieuwing Nieuwkapelle*

HOGESCHOOL W&K, DEPARTEMENT ARCHITECTUUR SINT-LUCAS, BRUSSEL
- *Corbeel + Catteeuw + Plateau architecten*
- *Karel Lowette*

2003

ARCHIPEL, BRUGGE
- *Robbrecht & Daem – eigen werk*
- *Gilbert Decouvreur – Hans Poelzig*
- *Wim Supply, Gerry Vandenabeele en Martine Valembois – 'Nueva Simplicidad'*
- *Pierre Hebbelinck – eigen werk*
- *Jo Crepain – eigen werk*
- *Alfredo Paya (E)*

BOZAR
Lezingenreeks 'De middagen van de sociale huisvesting'
- *De grote woningblokken slopen: dringt de vraag zich op?*
- *Openbare investeringen: is het glas halfvol of halfleeg?*
- *Hoe ontsnappen aan de verkrotting?*
- *De huisvestingscode: hervormen om te verbeteren*
- *Het Brussels woningfonds: eigendomsverkrijging als stimulans voor de stadsontwikkeling*
- *Geen woning, welke perspectieven? En wat met het toekomstplan voor de huisvesting?*
- *Het gemeentelijk initiatief herwaarderen*

BUNKERHOTEL VZW
Lezingenreeks 'Catchy Diamond'
- *One Architecture vs Urban Unlimited - Ruimtelijke ontwerpstrategieën in een Europese context*
- *Lucas Catherine – Stedenbouw als politiek instrument*
- *Hendrik Pinxten vs Filip De Boeck – Stedelijkheid in Vlaanderen en de rest van de wereld*
- *Creneau vs Maximal Product Vision – Ontwerpstrategieën voor een vluchtige samenleving*
- *AMO vs MUF – Ontwerpstrategieën voor een gesplinterde samenleving*

BVTL (BELGISCHE VERENIGING VOOR TUINARCHITECTEN EN LANDSCHAPSARCHITECTEN)
- *Theo De Vos – Omgevingsarchitectuurprijs 2002*
- *Marc Pinte – Landschapsarchitectuur in de Verenigde Staten*
- *Marc Pinte – Landschapsarchitectuur in Frankrijk*

DESINGEL INTERNATIONAAL KUNSTCENTRUM, ANTWERPEN
- *Anne Lacaton & Jean-Philippe Vassal – eigen werk*
- *Kees Christiaanse – The City as Loft*
- ***Lezingenreeks 'Curating the Library'***
  - *Richard Venlet – Moritz Küng*
  - *Nicolas Bourriaud*
  - *Lieven De Cauter*
  - *Tobias Rehberger – Paul Robbrecht*
  - *Aaron Betsky*
  - *Filiep Tacq*
  - *Thomas Hirschhorn – Steven Jacobs*
  - *Armand Mevis – Peter Swinnen / 51N4E*
  - *Meg Stuart – Jos De Gruyter & Harald Thys*
- ***Lezingenreeks 'Dedonderdagen'***
  - *Lieven De Boeck en Jannah Loontjens – Housing modus operandi*

GGS STEDENBOUW EN RUIMTELIJKE PLANNING / VLAAMSE LANDMAATSCHAPPIJ
Lezingenreeks 'Lectures on landscape design'
- *Thorbjörn Andersson*
- *Joerg Dettmar*
- *Christine Dalnoky*
- *Henri Bava*
- *Michel Corajoud*

HOGESCHOOL ANTWERPEN – DEPARTEMENT ONTWERPWETENSCHAPPEN
- *Juha Leiviskä – Spaces as instruments played by light*

HOGESCHOOL W&K, DEPARTEMENT ARCHITECTUUR SINT-LUCAS, GENT
- *Karel Vandenhende – eigen werk*
- *Peter Gillis – eigen werk*
- *dr. Charles Rice (University of New South Wales, Australia) – Inhabiting the bourgeois interior / historical problems & theoretical openings*
- *prof. Martin Steinmann (Ecole Polytechnique fédérale de Lausanne EPFL) – De ontwikkeling van de Zwitserse architectuur*
- *Charlotte Geldhof (FLC Extended) – Landschappen van water*
- *Kristiaan Borret – De vermenigvuldiging van het stadsontwerp*
- *Theo De Vos – Publieke ruimte, enkele tendensen*

INFORMATIECENTRUM VOOR ARCHITECTUUR, STEDENBOUW EN DESIGN (ICASD), BRUSSEL
- *Cecil Balmond (directeur ARUP Europe, Londen)*

KATHOLIEKE HOGESCHOOL MECHELEN – DEPARTEMENT ARCHITECTUUR [W]INTERIEURAVONDEN
- *51N4E – Space Producers*
- *Casimir*
- *Fabiaan Van Severen*
- *LAB (Heyndrickx-Dewachter)*

STICHTING STAD & ARCHITECTUUR, LEUVEN
Lezingenreeks 'Auditorium'
- *Sauerbruch Hutton architecten – comments on colour, amongst other things*
- *Maarten Van Severen – werk*
- *Macken & Macken – (recent) work*

- *Inside Outside (NL) – Inside outside space*
- *OMA / Office for Metropolitan Architecture*
- *Benthem Crouwel*
- *Florian Nagler*

STUDIO OPEN CITY

- *Seminar 1: Carole Schmit*
  Les Urbanistes – imagine the city like a movie
- *Seminar 2: Joachim Declerck en Dieter Delbaere*
  Field, places, urbanity: a quest for field urbanism
- *Seminar 3: Lieven De Boeck*
  Urban paradigms – Line of (desert)ion
- *Seminar 4: Alexander D'hooghe*
  Brussels as a European Myth Project

VAKGROEP ARCHITECTUUR, VRIJE UNIVERSITEIT BRUSSEL

- *Architect Niklaas Deboutte – META-architectuurbureau – De luiheid als deugd*

Lezingenreeks 'Belgische architectuur'

- *Yves Schoonjans –*
  Experimentele architectuur in België 1945-1965
- *Karel Dewilde –*
  Hoogbouw in het na-oorlogse België
- *Jonas Lindekens –*
  Hedendaagse architectuurprojecten
- *Ine Wouters –*
  Het probleem van de renovatie en reconversie

VAKGROEP ARCHITECTUUR EN STEDENBOUW, UNIVERSITEIT GENT

Lezingenreeks 'De refter – La Belgique c'est fantastique_'

- *Richard Venlet*
- *Plain*
- *Geert Goiris*
- *Michael Borremans*
- *Michael Vandenabeele en Arnoud Hendrickx*
- *Wouter Davidts – Museumarchitectuur van Centre Pompidou tot Tate Modern*

VLAAMSE VERENIGING VOOR RUIMTE EN PLANNING, BRUSSEL

- *Seminarie 16 – Stedenbouw: Beeld en concept in structuurplannen, Malle (Stramien) en Arendonk (IOK)*
- *Seminarie 02 – Open Ruimte & landschap: VEN en groene RUP's*
- *Seminarie 17 – Stedenbouw: Beeld en concept in structuurplannen, Gent (studiegroep Omgeving)*
- *Seminarie 18 – Stedenbouw: Beeld en concept in structuurplannen, Nieuwpoort (WVI) en Nazareth (Groep Planning)*

CONFERENCES / SEMINARS / SYMPOSIUMS / WORKSHOPS

2002

21/04/2002
MOMU-DIALOOG 21042002: MUSEUMARCHITECTUUR
ModeMuseum Provincie Antwerpen

30/05/2002
ONTWERPEND STUREN AAN DE STAD
Studiecyclus ontwerpend, stedenbouwkundig onderzoek, georganiseerd door de Vlaamse Vereniging voor Ruimte en Planning ism. LIN en KULeuven

03/07/2002
RED HET NOORDZEEHOTEL!
Persconferentie – panel gesprek Met dr. Leen Meganck (UGent), Norbert Poulain (voorzitter vzw Interbellum, Gent), prof. arch. Jos Vandenbreeden (departement architectuur Sint-Lucas, directeur Sint-Lukasarchief vzw, Brussel), prof. dr. Linda Van Santvoort (UGent), prof. dr. ir. Luc Verpoest (KULeuven, DOCOMOMO)

11/09/2002
JONGEREN EN ERFGOED IN VLAANDEREN
Colloquium, Brugge 2002, Frontsit[d]e-Back[-]Side, Brugge

22/09/2002 – 29/09/2002
[SHELTER]PROJECT
Onderzoek naar de relatie tussen 'design en human settlements' en hun culturele en sociale relevantie
Hogeschool W&K, Departement Architectuur Sint-Lucas, Gent

27/09/2002
STEDELIJK(E) VORMEN VAN MOBILITEIT
Studiecyclus ontwerpend, stedenbouwkundig onderzoek, georganiseerd door de Vlaamse Vereniging voor Ruimte en Planning ism. LIN en KULeuven

01/10/2002 – 02/10/2002
DE NOORD-ZUIDVERBINDING
Colloquium, Centre Interdisciplinaire de Recherche sur l'Histoire de Bruxelles (CIRHI-BRU) van de ULB en de NMBS

24/10/2002
ARCHITECTUUR IN HET (BASIS)ONDERWIJS
Symposium, een gemeenschappelijk inititiatief van CANON (cultuurcel van het departement Onderwijs), ABC (ART BASICS for CHILDREN) en het Team van de Vlaamse Bouwmeester

24/10/2002 – 25/10/2002
LICHT, RUIMTE EN ARCHITECTUUR – BRUSSEL 2002
Colloquium, georganiseerd door Internationaal Centrum voor Stad, Architectuur en Landschap CIVA, Brussel

11/11/2002 – 12/11/2002
CULTUUR WIL RUIMTE – EEN TWEEDAAGSE REFLECTIE OVER CULTUUR EN RUIMTE
Dag 1: Seminar IIII BXLEUROP
Studio Open City
Dag 2: Werelddag van de stedenbouw
Vlaamse Vereniging voor Ruimte en Planning

12/11/2002
BETON IN JAPAN
Symposium, georganiseerd door Federatie van de Belgische Cementnijverheid ism. Vakgroep Architectuur en Stedenbouw en de Vakgroep Bouwkundige Constructies (Laboratorium Magnel voor Betononderzoek) van de Universiteit Gent

30/11/2002 – 07/12/2002
BUDA-EILAND, KORTRIJK
Workshop, georganiseerd door stad Kortrijk, OSA – KULeuven, Intercommunale Leiedal

19/12/2002
ETHISCHE KWESTIES EN VRAGEN IN ONZE DAGDAGELIJKSE STEDENBOUWKUNDIGE PRAKTIJK
Rondetafelgesprek, georganiseerd door Vlaamse Vereniging voor Ruimte en Planning

2003

24/01/2003
BEDRIJVEN IN HET LANDSCHAP
Symposium over integratie en omgevingskwaliteit, georganiseerd door de West-Vlaamse Intercommunale WVI, provincie West-Vlaanderen, Streekplatform Roeselare - Tielt ism. West-Vlaamse Kamer voor Handel en Nijverheid, Vlaams Bouwmeester, Vlaams Architectuurinstituut, Vlaamse Landmaatschappij, Leiedal

27/01/2003 – 31/01/2003
ADSL-WEEK (ANTWERP DESIGN SEMINARS & LECTURES)
Met o.m. workshops met Jeremy Gould, Harrison S. Fraker jr. & Jan Thomaes, Mike Martin & Stijn Peeters, Laura, Marvin Malecha, Hugo Dworzak, Richard Duncan, Alan Bridges, Constantin Spirionidis & Maria Voyatzaki, Marijke Mollaert, Jane Burnside, Manuel Abenroth, Nur Caglar & Zeneyp Ulludag

21/02/2003
STEDEN, STEDELIJKHEID EN STEDELIJKE INTERVENTIES
Bruxel Glocal Conferentie, een productie van City Min(e)d + Bureau de Micro-Urbanism, Brussel

04-05/04/2003
CRITICAL TOOLS: THE THIRD BIENNIAL NETHCA COLLOQUIUM
Colloquium over de (on)mogelijkheid van kritische theorie, kritische praktijk, kritische geschiedenis,... CIVA, Brussel

27/05/2003
DE HARMONIE SPEELT VALS – DEBAT OVER INTEGRATIE ALS STEDENBOUWKUNDIG STRIJDPUNT
Debat georganiseerd door Stichting Stad en Architectuur

30/05/2003 – 31/05/2003
BRUSSEL – EUROPA, DE VEROVERING VAN EUROPA
Seminarie met o.a. AMO Rem Koolhaas, Renier De Graaf rond de stedenbouwkundige en architecturale manifestatie van de steeds grotere Europese Unie in Brussel, georganiseerd door Bozar, Brussel

06/06/2003
HET STATUUT VAN DE ARCHITECT
Colloquium 4 n.a.v. de 40ste verjaardag van de wet d.d. 26/06.19963 tot instelling van de Orde van Architecten

20/06/2003
DE ARCHITECT TUSSEN OPDRACHTGEVER EN OVERHEID
Colloquium 5 n.a.v. de 40ste verjaardag van de wet d.d. 26/06.19963 tot instelling van de Orde van Architecten

08/07/2003 – 12/07/2003
ACSP-AESOP THIRD JOINT CONGRESS: THE NETWORK SOCIETY: THE NEW CONTEXT FOR PLANNING
georganiseerd door KULeuven, Leuven

23/09/2003 – 24/09/2003
INTERNATIONALE BOUWMEESTERCONFERENTIE
Met de rijksbouwmeester van Nederland, de Nederlandse spoorwegbouwmeester, de stadsarchitect van Den Haag, de stadsbouwmeester van Antwerpen, het kwaliteitsteam van de stad Gent en de stadsarchitect van Eeklo

25/09/2003 – 30/09/2003
WORSHOP ARCHITECTUURKRITIEK
Met Johan Lagae, Marieke Van Giersbergen, Koen Van Synghel, Paul Vermeulen georganiseerd door Vlaams Architectuurinstituut

06/11/2003 – 08/11/2003
DE BIJDRAGE VAN HET ITALIAANSE GEDACHTEGOED TOT DE EUROPESE CULTUUR
Colloquium voorgezeten door Umberto Eco, georganiseerd in het kader van Europalia georganiseerd door Bozar, Brussel

07/11/2003 – 10/11/2003
COLLOQUIUM 30 JAAR BRAL, DE BRUSSELSE RAAD VOOR LEEFMILIEU
Europawijk, Lower Manhattan, Maritiemwijk & Palmera bewonersmobilisatie en participatie bij stedelijke projecten (conceptie, uitvoering, beheer en opvolging), en stadsprojecten en publiek-private samenwerking die plaats biedt aan bewoners

10/11/2003
WERELDDAG VAN DE STEDENBOUW
Reflecties rond de inhoud en de betekenis van een duurzame ontwikkeling van onze leefomgeving georganiseerd door de Vlaamse Vereniging voor Ruimte en Planning

19/11/2003
CONGRES STEDENBELEID
Debat naar aanleiding van de voorstelling van het witboek Stedenbeleid, georganiseerd door Ministerie van de Vlaamse Gemeenschap

08/12/2003
FORUM SOCIALE WONINGBOUW IN BELGIË
Georganiseerd door het Informatiecentrum voor Architectuur, Stedenbouw en Design (ICASD)

18/12/2003
LESSONS IN MODERN LIVING. POST-WAR MODEL HOMES
Studiedag omtrent naoorlogse modelwoningen en de wijze waarop ze worden ingezet om het 'moderne' leven te promoten. Met o.a. Mil De Kooning, Johan Lagae, Fredie Floré , Tim Putman (GB) en Penny Sparke (GB). Georganiseerd door de Vakgroep Architectuur en Stedenbouw van de Universiteit Gent

Interdisciplinary events

2002

25/05/2002 – 26/05/2002
HET GEHEUGEN VAN DE STAD / THE CITY OF MEMORY
Octopus – experiment for a contemporary artistic structure in Bruges, coproductie van Brugge 2002 & A Prior – Office for artistic production Interdisciplinaire workshop met o.m. Stefano Boeri, Paul Robbrecht & Hilde Daem

21/09/2002 – 24/11/2002
RICHARD VENLET – PARAMOUNT BASICS (EXTENDED)
Museum voor Hedendaagse Kunst Antwerpen (MUHKA), Antwerpen

22/09/2002 – 29/09/2002
[SHELTER]PROJECT
Hogeschool W&K, Departement Architectuur Sint-Lucas, Gent

28/09/2002 – 06/10/2002
FESTIVAL RECYCLART
De Noord-Zuidverbinding

09/12/2002 – 22/12/2002
POSTKARTE: BERLIN
Stedelijke curiositeiten en confrontaties Recyclart, Brussel

Films / Documentaries

BUILDING, 2003
DVD van Anouk de Clercq,
Joris Cool en Anton Aeki
Hommage aan het werk van Robbrecht en Daem, geïnspireerd op het Concertgebouw in Brugge
Montevideo/Time Based Arts

L'OCCUPATION DES SOLS
Film van Marie-Françoise Plissart
Coproductie van MDW productions, Arte Belgique, RTBF Bruxelles, CBA, mmv. Centre du cinéma et de l'audiovisuel de la Communauté française de Belgique et des télédistributeurs wallons

PETIT PALAIS, 2002
DVD van Anouk de Clercq,
Joris Cool en Anton Aeki
Werk gemaakt voor een presentatie in het Petit Palais in Parijs, Frankrijk

Television programs

21/03/2003
NACHTWACHT
BOUWEN MOET VERBODEN WORDEN
met Vlaams Bouwmeester bOb Van Reeth en architect Luc Deleu

Radio programs

KLARA – ALINEA
VRT, PRODUCER/PRESENTATOR: CHANTAL PATTYN

21/02/2002
– Paul Robbrecht: Concertgebouw, Brugge
28/03/2002
– Lucas Cathérine: "Bouwen met zwart geld" over de urbaniseringspolitiek van Leopold II
24/05/2002
– Joep Van Lieshout – AVL: Franchise Unit & Pioneer, Middelheim, Antwerpen
03/05/2002
– Wim Cuyvers: Monografie ism. Marc De Blieck
09/05/2002
– Xaveer de Geyter: tentoonstelling 'After Sprawl' in deSingel
13/09/2002
– Piet Lombaerde: Hans Vredeman de Vries - 2 tentoonstellingen in Antwerpen (KMSKA en Rubenshuis)
20/09/2002
– Linda Loppa: Opening van het ModeMUseum
01/10/2002
– Piet Van Wayenberghe: Opening Flagey, Elsene
21/10/2002
– Lieven De Cauter en Hilde Heynen: publicatie *'Dat is Architectuur', n.a.v. De Dag van de Architectuur, VAi*
27/12/2002
– Paul Robbrecht (bis): opening Concertgebouw, Brugge
26/03/2003
– Claire Bataille en Paul Ibens
10/06/2003
– Luc Deleu: Tentoonstelling Openluchtmuseum Middelheim, Antwerpen
26/06/2003
– Paul Robbrechts: verbouwing van het Museum Boymans van Beuningen in Rotterdam
11/09/2003
– Moritz Küng: tentoonstelling Urban Dramas in deSingel

THE EDITORS AND THE AUTHORS

Tom Avermaete
Studied architecture at the Henry van de Velde Institute in Antwerp and the Royal Danish Academy in Copenhagen. He did a supplementary course in Architectural Studies at the University of Leuven. In early 2004 he obtained his PhD at the same university with a thesis on the French architects Candilis-Josic-Woods and their contribution to the architectural culture of the nineteen-fifties and sixties. Since 1996 he has been a visiting lecturer in Architectural History at the University of Copenhagen and from 1997 to 2003 worked for the OSA research group at the University of Leuven. Since November 2003 he has been the coordinator of the Centre for Flemish Architectural Archives (CVAa), attached to the Flemish Architecture Institute. He has published in *Agora, Archis, A+, OASE, Planologisch Nieuws, Kunststatus* and *Verb* as well as in several books. He is also a member of the organising committee of the NeTHCA, the Network for Theory, History and Criticism of Architecture, and a member of the editorial staff of *OASE, Architectuurtijdschrift / Architectural Journal*.

Adam Caruso
Studied architecture at the McGill University in Montreal. He worked for Florian Biegel and Arup Associates before starting his own practice with Peter St John in 1990. In 1995 the firm won the international design competition for the New Art Gallery with public square in Walsall in England. This project was opened to the public in February 2000. The firm also completed the Gagosian Gallery in London and a signposting system for the Bankside area in London.In 1999 the firm was in the finals of a competition for the new centre for contemporary art in Rome, and in 2000 won first prize in the competition for restructuring the baroque Stortorget in Kalmar in Sweden. This project, as well as the first phase of the master-plan for the Museum of Childhood in London, was completed in spring 2003. Adam Caruso has for ten years lectured at the University of North London and was a visiting professor at the architectural academy at Mendrisio in Switzerland from 1999 to 2001. He is currently Professor of Architecture in the Department of Architecture and Civil Engineering at the University of Bath.

Lieven De Boeck
Is an architect. After his traineeship under Luc Deleu, he has since 1997 worked for Xaveer De Geyter Architects, where he was engaged on, among other things, *After-Sprawl*, a study of the contemporary city. In 2002 and 2003 he was a researcher in the Visual Arts at the Jan Van Eyck Academy in Maastricht, where he completed his publication entitled *Wonen*. He has given several guest lectures at, among other places, the Berlage Institute, the College of Science and Art in Brussels and in the Studio Open City programme. He is currently a visiting professor on the PhD course in the School of Humanities at the University of Greenwich.

Caroline Goossens
Graduated from St Luke's Higher Architectural Institute in Ghent as an interior architect in 1994. Since 1999 she has written regular articles on design, interiors and architecture for *De Standaard, A+, Frame* and *Items*. She is part of the network centring on *FLC-extended*, a loose association of freelance designers. She has since 2001 also been a practical lecturer in the Interior Design Department at St Luke's College in Brussels.

William Mann
Is an architect. He studied at Cambridge (UK) and Harvard (USA). He is business manager of Witherford Watson Mann Architects in London: current projects include new offices and service facilities for Amnesty International UK in London. The firm recently acquired the brief for 12 social housing units, a new public space and the restoration of a 17th-century inn in Gistel near Ostend in the framework of the Flemish Government Architect's 'Open Call' for designs. He has published on British and Flemish architecture in *Archis, A+U* and *a+t*.

Ákos Moravánszky
Teaches architectural theory at the GTA Institute, part of the Swiss Federal Institute of Technology in Zurich. He obtained his PhD at the Institute for Art History and Preservation at the Technical University of Vienna in 1980. From 1978 to 1980 he completed his MA in Architecture in Budapest and from 1983 worked as editor of the *Magyar Épitömüvészet* architectural magazine. His posts included those of guest researcher at the Zentralinstitut für Kunstgeschichte in Munich, was invited to the Getty Center in Santa Monica in California as a Research Associate in Art History and Humanities from 1989 to 1991 and was visiting professor at the Massachusetts Institute of Technology from 1991 to 1996. He was recently appointed Szent-Györgyi Fellow at the Hungarian University of Crafts and Design in Budapest.
His main areas of interest are architectural theory and architectural history in Central Europe in the 19th and 20th centuries. Here are a few of his recent publications: *Competing Visions: Aesthetic Invention and Social Imagination in Central European Architecture* (Cambridge, Mass.: The MIT Press, 1998); *Spacepieces: Valentin Bearth & Anrea Deplazes* (Luzern: Quart, 2000), *Architekturtheorie im 20. Jahrhundert: Eine kritische Anthologie* (Vienna, New York: Springer, 2003). He edited the book *Das entfernte Dorf: Moderne Kunst und ethnischer Artefakt* (Vienna, Cologne, Weimar: Böhlau, 2002).

Bruno Notteboom
Is an engineer-architect and urban planner. Since 2004 he has been an assistant at Labo S (Urban Planning Laboratory) in the Faculty of Architecture & Urban Planning at the University of Ghent, where he supervises research projects and is working on his PhD on the image of the landscape in Belgium. He previously worked as a freelance urban planning designer and researcher for urban planning firms in Belgium and the Netherlands, as well as the OSA (Urbanism and Architecture Research Group, University of Leuven) and Labo S, and was a project assistant at the Flemish Architecture Institute. He has published in *OASE, A+* and *Ruimte en Planning* and is on the editorial staff of *Achtergrond 01. Bedrijfsgebouwen. Architectuur, landschap, economie en beleid* (Flemish Architecture Institute, 2003).

Raf Snoeckx
Is an architect and planner (GAS spatial planning, University of Ghent). In 1999 he was selected for the Flemish Government Architect's first *Meesterproef*. He is the cofounder of the architect's collective *De Gouden Liniaal* in Hasselt, which collaborates with a changing team of young graduates on small and medium-sized projects.

Sven Sterken
Is an engineer-architect. He studied at the Universities of Ghent, Paris and Pretoria and has been a visiting scholar at several institutions including the Getty Center for the Arts and Humanities in Los Angeles, the Architectural Association school in London and Chandigarh College of Architecture. He is currently concluding his PhD thesis in Architectural history on the architect and composer Jannis Xenaksis. He currently works as a freelance lecturer and critic and as a researcher at the Faculty of Architecture of the University of Ghent and the Jan Van Eyck Academy in Maastricht.

Pieter T'Jonck
Is an engineer-architect (Leuven, 1983) who works in Leuven. He was a trainee at Paul Van De Poel's firm in Antwerp and with Stéphane Beel in Bruges. He won the WIG, '92 architectural competition and the competition for the extension of the academy in Leuven. In addition, he was a studio supervisor at the University of Ghent from 1996 to 2002. At present he lectures in the History of Stage Design at the academy in Antwerp (evening classes). He is one of the founders of the ASK! Postgraduate arts course and has for years been an active member of Studio Open City. He publishes regularly in various periodicals and books, at home and abroad, on theatre, dance, architecture and art.

Katrien Vandermarliere
Is an art historian and from 1991 to 2002 was responsible for the architecture programme at deSingel International Arts Centre in Antwerp. She curated around 50 exhibitions of Belgian and international architects. In connection with this she compiled a series of publications on architecture and related disciplines for deSingel. From 1999 to 2000 she was a member of the editorial staff of the Flanders Architectural Yearbook. In her capacity as director of the Flanders Architectural Institute (since May 2002) she is the editor-in-chief of the 2002-2003 edition. She has been a member of the jury for several architecture competitions in Belgium, a member of the Committee for Architecture and Design (until May 2002) and since 2003 has been a member of the HGIS culture subsidy subcommittee of the Dutch Fund for the Stimulation of Architecture.

Hera Van Sande
Obtained her degree as architect at the University of Ghent in 1991. She taught there from 1993 to 2001. In 1996 and 1997 she was a researcher at the Shibaura Institute of Technology in Tokyo on a Japan Foundation Fellowship. In 1994 and 2000 she also obtained Europalia Nippon Kinen Fellowships in Japan. She worked as a project architect on the construction of Toyo Ito's pavilion as part of Bruges 2002. In 2003 and 2004 she worked with Toyo Ito on the competition for the Music Forum in Ghent. She is the author of the monograph *Toyo Ito: Bruges 2002 Pavilion* and was a co-author and member of the editorial staff of the book *Japan Concrete*. Since 1993 she has had her own architectural practice. She is currently on the editorial staff of the architectural magazine *a+u* and teaches at the Universities of Ghent and Brussels.

Koen Van Synghel
Is an architect and writer. He reviews contemporary architecture and art for the VRT's Klara radio channel. He writes regularly on contemporary architecture for periodicals at home and abroad and contributes the two-weekly column 'A Taste of Architecture' in *De Standaard* newspaper. He published *Young Architects in Flanders* in association with deSingel International Arts Centre in Antwerp and *City-Branding, Image-Building and Buildings' Images* (NAI-uitgevers). He has taught Architectural Design in St Luke's Department of Architecture at Hogeschool WenK in Ghent and Brussels since 1994. Together with Filip de Boeck he is the curator of 'Kinshasa, the imaginary city', an exhibition in the Belgian Pavilion at the 2004 Venice Architecture Biennial. Since 2004 he has been the Bozar Architecture programme compiler at the Centre for Fine Arts in Brussels.

Els Vervloesem
Obtained her diploma as architect at the Henry van de Velde Institute in Antwerp in 2001. In 2001 and 2002 she was a trainee at T. O. P. Office under Luc Deleu, where she worked on *De Onaangepaste Stad* project (The Unadapted City). Since 2002 she has been on the 'Human Settlements' postgraduate course at the University of Leuven.

Edith Wouters
Is an engineer-architect (University of Leuven) and a Master of Building Management (Hogeschool De Naeyer, Mechelen). She has also studied at the Istituto Universitario di Venezia under the Erasmus system, at the Henry van de Velde Institute in Antwerp (postgraduate course in Conservation of Monuments and Landscapes) and at St Luke's College in Brussels (postgraduate in Urban Planning). Together with Paul Vandenbussche she has since 1977 headed TEEMA Architects. Among other things this firm recently won the brief for building 10 social homes in Rijkevorsel in response to the Flemish Government Architect's 'Open Call' for designs. She coordinated the Flanders Architectural Yearbook 2000-2001 for deSingel International Arts Centre, where she has also worked on several exhibitions and publications. Since early 2003 she has been a part-time project leader at the Flemish Architecture Institute.